COPING WITH CATASTROPHE

Disasters strike with sudden violence, tearing bodies, lives and families apart. *Coping with Catastrophe* is a practical handbook for people who provide psychosocial aftercare for victims of disasters. Peter E. Hodgkinson and Michael Stewart are leading experts in the field of disaster aftercare, and this book is based on their unique and extensive experience, which includes the Bradford fire, the Zeebrugge disaster, the Lockerbie plane crash and the Hillsborough disaster.

Trauma has become the subject of much research since the first edition of this book; both its nature and treatment are now better understood. This is reflected in the second edition, which includes the latest findings on the nature and effects of trauma, the psychological debriefing process and the effects of emergency work, as well as the latest treatment models for post-traumatic stress and abnormal grief.

Using the survivors' own words, the authors provide a vivid and moving account of the experiences of survival and bereavement under different types of conditions. They summarise the most up-to-date thinking about the psychological effects of disaster, and describe the therapeutic strategies available for treating victims with persistent problems, emphasising the welfare needs of staff involved in rescue and support. They also discuss in detail the practical aspects of co-ordinating disaster relief, such as the organisation and planning of specific services like outreach facilities and crisis helplines after the event.

Eminently practical and easy to read, *Coping with Catastrophe* provides readers with information and skills to respond effectively and confidently to the needs of disaster survivors. It will be of immense value to a wide variety of helping professionals and carers, including social workers, psychologists, doctors, voluntary counsellors, and all those whose work brings them into contact with disaster victims.

Peter E. Hodgkinson and **Michael Stewart** are Joint Directors of the Centre for Crisis Psychology in Yorkshire and leading experts in the field of disaster aftercare.

COPING WITH CATASTROPHE

A Handbook of Post-Disaster
Psychosocial Aftercare

Second Edition

*Peter E. Hodgkinson and
Michael Stewart*

London and New York

First published 1991
by Routledge
11 New Fetter Lane, London EC4P 4EE

Simultaneously published in the USA and Canada
by Routledge
29 West 35th Street, New York, NY 10001

This revised and updated edition published 1998 by Routledge

Typeset in Times by Routledge
Printed and bound in Great Britain by MPG Books Ltd,
Bodmin.

British Library Cataloguing in Publication Data
A catalogue record for this book is available from the British Library

Library of Congress Cataloguing in Publication Data
Hodgkinson, Peter E., 1953–
Coping with catastrophe: a handbook of post-disaster psychosocial
aftercare / Peter E. Hodgkinson and Michael Stewart. – 2nd ed.
Includes bibliographical references and index.
1. Disaster relief–Management–Handbooks, manuals, etc.
I. Stewart, Michael, 1952 Feb. 4– II. Title.
HV553.H64 1998
363.34' 8' 068–dc21
97–26570
CIP

ISBN 0–415–16939–9 (hbk)
ISBN 0–415–16853–8 (pbk)

If there is a devil, his fist came up out of the earth that day.

Bradford fire survivor

THIS BOOK IS DEDICATED
TO OUR FATHERS,
ALLAN HODGKINSON
AND MATT STEWART

CONTENTS

ILLUSTRATIONS

TABLES

FIGURES

PREFACE TO THE
FIRST EDITION

This book is a practical guide to disaster management for the helping professional. Its aims are to provide the reader with information and skills to respond effectively and confidently to the needs of disaster survivors. The chapters are intended to be read in sequence, but each stands in its own right, and readers may choose to read some in less depth than others. It begins with an examination of the experiences of survival and bereavement by disaster. Knowledge of these feelings, thoughts and behaviours provides the helper with the map of the territory about to be explored. It continues with a review of the present state of knowledge about the effects of man-made disaster. It then discusses the way services for the survivors of disaster need to be organised if they are to be effective, and the initial processes of working with those affected. Other methods of intervention are discussed: consulting to traumatised groups, psychological debriefing and specific psychological treatments for post-traumatic stress reactions and pathological grief. Lastly the experiences and needs of the second group of potential disaster victims, the rescuers and helpers, are explored.

Coping with catastrophe requires courage and humility as well as knowledge and skill. Readers may conclude that these are the qualities any helper should have. They are. Our hope is that this book will help them mobilise these resources in tragic and catastrophic times.

Peter E. Hodgkinson and
Michael Stewart
March 1990

PREFACE TO THE
SECOND EDITION

In the seven years that have passed since this book was first written, trauma has become the subject of much research. Both its nature and treatment are now better understood. The second edition of this book reflects this.

Many more clinicians are now interested in trauma, and the subject has a higher public profile. Inevitably, this has led to a backlash, partly media led, and in part a reaction by some professionals to the messianic fervour of others. As with all criticism, there is a kernel of truth in this. Media images of troupes of counsellors arriving at the sites of disasters, however distorted, remind us that this increase in attention has led in some helpers to an over-hasty, ill-considered rush to 'be there'. This is based on the needs of the helper, not those of the survivor. The second edition of this book hopes again to present a balanced view of those needs and what the helper has to offer. For many survivors of catastrophe, this will inevitably be limited. The helper must have the humility to remember this.

Peter E. Hodgkinson and
Michael Stewart
June 1997

ACKNOWLEDGEMENTS

Many people have contributed to the material presented in this book. First and foremost are the survivors themselves, notably Duncan Firth, a man of generosity, courage and humanity. Secondly are the many professionals we have met and trained in the aftermath of catastrophe. Thirdly, and by no means least, are our wives, Dawn Hodgkinson and Karen Stewart, and our families who have enabled us to do the work itself and write this book.

Peter E. Hodgkinson and
Michael Stewart
March 1990

1

SURVIVAL AND
BEREAVEMENT

Disasters strike with sudden violence, tearing bodies, lives and families apart. Yet, sitting at home in the UK, witnessing natural cataclysms such as earthquakes through the eye of the television camera, there may be little sense of reality – such things simply do not happen to *us*. A tragedy nearer to home, such as an air crash, happens so rarely that potential disaster can still be dismissed as a threat with little substance.

Catastrophes such as the crash of the Pan Am jet onto the Scottish town of Lockerbie in 1988 concentrate the minds of those who think, 'It won't happen to us, it always happens to someone else'. Who could have been less vulnerable to being literally wiped off the face of the earth than someone lying in bed, or watching television in the comfort of their sitting room? Technological disasters, experienced with increasing frequency, seem to have a particular ferocity of suddenness and violence, and kindle powerful emotions of anger and blame. After one catastrophe a newspaper cartoon depicted a tombstone inscribed with the legend, 'This will never happen again', reminding us that technological disasters will always occur, because we are human and we make mistakes.

Disaster survivors are ordinary people – the only thing that distinguishes them from the reader of this book is that *they* happened to be in the wrong place at the wrong time. Their very ordinariness presents helpers with new challenges in terms of the organisation of services, and with an old problem, perhaps the central problem of existence – loss.

Psychological reactions to disaster, complex as they are, can be understood essentially as the reactions of normal human beings to sudden, unexpected and terrifying events in their lives. In disasters, people lose loved ones, relatives and property. Above all, in psychological terms, they lose faith – not religious faith, but faith in the fact that life has a certain consistency and meaning. The fabric of everyday existence is torn away to reveal danger and risk. For the survivor, the encounter inevitably involves a corruption of innocence. Once something of this nature has happened to a person, it is very difficult for them to believe that life can ever be the same again; that they can let their children walk across the street; or that they can safely go to bed at night. It is also difficult for them to avoid thinking not only that something else terrible may happen, but that in some way they have been singled out, or even that 'if such a terrible thing can have happened to me then I must have done something to deserve it'.

What is survival? Survival is not just the difference between living and dying – survival is to do with quality of life. Survival involves progressing from the event and its aftermath, and transforming the experience. The difficulty of 'moving on' is described best by the words of survivors themselves. One young woman who survived the 1987 Zeebrugge disaster wrote the following some ten months after the tragedy:

> I have had what can only be described as a weird year. Firstly, I became engaged, then John and I were survivors of the 'Herald'. Soon afterwards, John's job took him away and I was left to recover from my injuries and to come to terms with what I had been convinced was my death as I happened to be under water and would still be there if John had not come back for me. I tried to get back to work, but it was impossible, and I failed. Soon after the wedding John was away again, but I was so busy I had no time to even take breath – at Christmas we never seemed to be in. Now it's all over there are no plans to be made, only time to reflect. I am not complaining – we have been so very lucky and are very happy. But now it's beginning to hit home. I seem to be spending more time thinking about what happened and crying about it a lot more than I have done. I am not unhappy or depressed, just still trying to sort out what happened and why we have been so lucky.

A bereaved relative who was not on board that night described her reactions during the first year:

> I just feel that nobody can help me. I have been suffering from panic attacks and I hardly go shopping any more – I am frightened to drive and cannot even get in the bath without anybody in the house. I and my brother had a terrible fear of boats when we were very young, and I was thinking of him and his wife all day. The news-flash that night will live with me for the rest of my life. I feel so guilty for being like I am – hurt, miserable, angry and bitter, for they are the ones who suffered that night. They were so loving, so caring – everything a brother and sister-in-law should be – I couldn't have wished for better. They were my life, always there when I needed them, and now I feel so lost.

In this first chapter we will recount the many aspects of the emotions, thoughts and behaviours of those who survive disaster and are bereaved.

Knowledge of this provides the map of the territory that the survivor and helper will have to explore.

SURVIVAL

Trauma is not an invention of the twentieth century. Homer's *Iliad* contains much that is instructive about combat stress (283). Samuel Pepys' diary gives descriptions of post-traumatic stress in survivors of the 1666 Fire of London (59). The First World War saw the phenomenon of 'shell shock'. The concept of post-traumatic stress appears, disappears and reappears in various guises over the centuries.

Detailed exploration of the experience of survival developed following the terrible episodes of the Second World War such as the dropping of the atom bomb and the Holocaust. An American psychiatrist, Robert Jay Lifton, arrived in Hiroshima in 1962. His observations on survival, even though they are descriptive rather than explanatory, hold good today (188). Five central experiences borne by survivors are described.

The death imprint

The 'death imprint' consists of indelible imagery of the encounter with death, intruding whilst awake, or during sleep in the form of nightmares. It comprises a condensation of the experience – images of the impact such as the sight of bodies dismembered or crushed, the sounds of screaming, or the smell of burning flesh. No details are spared the survivor who may appear to have a 'spellbound fascination' with the events.

The way in which everyday experiences can trigger these images or flash-backs is described in those who experienced Nazi concentration camps.

> Associations . . . can occur in any connection whatsoever, from seeing
> a person stretching his arms and associating this with fellow prisoners
> hung up by their arms under torture, to seeing an avenue of trees and
> visualising long rows of gallows with swinging corpses. Children
> playing peacefully may suddenly, without any apparent cause, call to
> mind other children, emaciated, tortured, murdered (78).

A survivor of the 1988 Piper Alpha Oil Platform explosion (247) wrote the following vivid account of how a television programme was the trigger for a flashback experience:

> I was idly watching television. Suddenly, with a vivid jolt, I was
> back on Piper, experiencing the intensity of those first moments
> after the initial explosion. The television programme I was watching

3

dealt with the Korean War and a cameraman had captured the moments immediately after the explosion of a terrorist bomb. Debris was still falling from the surrounding buildings. People were rushing around, preoccupied and intense. Many were injured. Blood streamed down their shocked, bemused faces . . . .

There was no terror. People moved around me on the 64-foot level, actively if anxiously. An injured man was being carried down the metal stairs. I rushed to the compressor and tried to find a way of switching it off. Davey Elliot came to help me, blood still oozing down his face.

Yet around me, sitting there at home, were the noises of everyday life – Suzie playing happily with her toys on the carpet, cars speeding past the window, cups rattling in the kitchen, the cat purring on my lap.

Survivor guilt

Survivor guilt, where the person questions why they survived when others did not, can be of two sorts. Firstly, there is what might be called 'existential guilt'. Here the person dwells in a very general way on their survival – 'Why me?', or 'Why did God choose me?'; or perhaps, 'Why me when I am old and so many children died?' Secondly, guilt may be focused on actions or their absence – 'Did I do enough, could I have saved more people?' Guilt may be especially intense when parents survive their children, or where there is competition for survival.

One survivor of the Zeebrugge disaster was a lorry driver who was on the ferry's vehicle deck when the ship capsized. His lorry ended up in the middle of a stack of articulated vehicles balanced on their sides. Frozen with fear, he heard his vehicle groaning under the weight of two lorries above, and knew that he would die. He then remembered that his trailer was a refrigerated container and hence was strengthened – he had a little time before he was crushed. He smashed his suitcase through the window, climbed over the bonnet of his truck and into the water, which now flooded half of the hold. He swam towards the exit, but as he did, he heard the screams of trapped lorry drivers – 'God help us, Christ help us, God help us'. He swam on, climbed out onto the side of the ship, and was one of the first to smash portholes, let down hawsers into the ship and begin the rescue. Several hours later he was removed to a tug, frozen with cold, his hands lacerated. He could have humanly done no more than he did, yet he did not remember these actions – only the unanswered screams of the trapped men in the hold from which he escaped. 'They were drivers, like me, and I did nothing to help them'. Three years later he committed suicide. Crew members of the *Herald of Free Enterprise* who swapped shifts with colleagues, putting them in their place on the night in question, felt an intense sense of guilt, even though shift swaps were a normal part of their work routine.

Guilt presupposes the presence of choice and the power to exercise it, which in reality during the impact may not have been possible. The experience of guilt may be an unconscious attempt to deny or undo this sense of helplessness (60). Guilt may also be based on a revised view of oneself. Thus many parents believe that if the choice was between their child's life or their own, then they would sacrifice themselves. In the impact of disaster, however, parents may forget that they have children. One mother fled the burning spectators' stand at Bradford without thinking that her son had been with her. She never disclosed this in counselling, choosing rather to make a public breast of it on national television three years later.

'Animating guilt' and 'static guilt' represent two different entities (188). Animating guilt is a spur to self-examination which can allow guilt to move 'towards the anxiety of responsibility'. Static guilt keeps the victim bound to the experience, unable to move on. The task of the helper may be to assist the survivor to progress from static to animating guilt 'and then from guilt to responsibility and some behaviour which alleviates the guilt'.

In survivors of the Nazi concentration camps, it has been suggested (69) that the chronicity of survivor guilt may have a symbolic function, 'a kind of testimonial. By continuing to suffer himself, the survivor seems to be trying to provide an enduring memorial to his slaughtered friends and relatives.' It is therefore a mechanism of expressing loyalty. Recovering from the effects of persecution would mean betraying the dead and perhaps forgiving the persecutors. There may also be an aspect of atonement – survivors may have to face the recognition that they come from the same population, the human race, as those who have committed atrocities against them.

This last point is important for those who approach the experience of survival from the standpoint of psychodynamic thinking, taking into account unconscious and repressed feelings. Individuals have aggressive, even destructive and murderous, feelings, which are repressed rather than acknowledged. Following disaster, the guilt experienced may be partly connected to a deep awareness of these feelings, and in particular to a sense that one's own past aggressive feelings, either to loved ones or to others, were in some way implicated in their destruction.

In considering the allied concept of self-blame, two distinct types can be identified (151). 'Behavioural self-blame' involves blaming one's own behaviour, and is adaptive, whereas 'characterological self-blame' involves reflections about one's personality characteristics and is maladaptive, associated with depression.

> Thus, the rape victim who believes she should not have hitch-hiked or should not have walked alone is engaging in behavioural self-blame, whereas the rape victim who believes she is

a bad person or a poor judge of character is engaging in characterological self-blame.

Behaviours are potentially modifiable, 'personality characteristics' may not be. If a behaviour is changeable, then the catastrophe may be avoided in the future, and hence behavioural self-blame raises the possibility of hope. A study of combat veterans (173) demonstrated a type of characterological self-blame, 'I should have known better' guilt, reflecting the cognitive distortion of hindsight bias ('I *should* have known better' leading to the false premise of 'I *could* have known better'). Again, this should be amenable to cognitive therapy.

In survivors of terrorist attacks, survivor guilt was present in 7 per cent of those with post-traumatic stress disorder and in just over 1 per cent of those without (193). Of the survivors of a building collapse, 44 per cent experienced guilt; 15 per cent gave no reason, 33 per cent 'wanted to have done more to relieve pain and suffering or death' including several individuals pinned under rubble who had tried to console those who were near them and more frightened or hurt more seriously: 'They had been upset when fellow victims, some of whom they never saw, fell silent; they assumed they were dead'. Fifteen per cent felt guilty because they had not stayed to help and 27 cent experienced guilt because they felt fortunate in being alive (340).

In a group of survivors of the 1987 Zeebrugge disaster (157), assessed at thirty months post disaster, survivor guilt was present in 60 per cent. Guilt about things not done was twice as common as guilt about things done, and it was more common to experience guilt or shame about letting others down than letting oneself down. Feelings of guilt were associated with greater general psychological distress. Guilt about things one failed to do was associated with mental intrusion rather than avoidance, whereas guilt about things one did was related to avoidance but not intrusion. The two types of guilt may reflect different attributional patterns, or may be directly related to the type of symptom. For example, guilt about things done may be more distressing, and therefore avoidance is used in an attempt to filter it out. There is evidence (29) that people who blame themselves are more likely to withdraw socially and less likely to use coping strategies involving other people. Whilst self-blame predicts poor outcome, external blame does not (293).

Another allied experience is that of shame. Survivors may feel ashamed about remaining alive, or about the way they handle their feelings. The blocking of feelings (the psychic numbing described below) may play a role in the development of feelings of shame (183). The survivor may become ashamed of what may have seemed to be callousness in the eyes of others.

Communities may compound the sense of shame by shunning survivors. Some survivors of the Bradford fire described how people who knew them would cross the street rather than have to speak to them. Parents bereaved of young children often experience this shunning as meaning that they carry a threat to other parents. The loss of status and ability contributes further to the sense of shame. Survivors of the atomic bombings in Japan, the *hibakusha* ('explosion-affected persons'), received little or no official recognition of their suffering for many years, becoming a 'stigmatised and forsaken group' (312). They were discriminated against in marriage and employment, even by other survivors who bore no visible evidence in the shape of scars to indicate that they too had passed through the same experience. In a study of Vietnam war veterans (348), those with PTSD scored highest on a measure of shame, as well as two subfactors of shame, alienation and inferiority. Shame was strongly linked to depression.

Psychic numbing

Numbing is a defensive manoeuvre, preventing survivors from experiencing the reality of the catastrophic destruction and death about them, and the massive personal threat implied. It blocks the experience of too much unbearable pain at any one time, and its first manifestations are present in the so-called 'disaster syndrome', where immediately following the impact, survivors may be stunned and dazed. Observers may think the survivors are behaving remarkably calmly. They may seem to be in control and coping bravely – in fact, they have not yet begun to react. They are behaving as though they are calm observers of someone else's experience (138).

Defences of repression, denial and isolation are natural and necessary in the short term. For some they may be retained to allow certain painful tasks to proceed. Thus after the Zeebrugge disaster, senior seamen performed such tasks as working in the mortuary identifying dead colleagues. Whilst doing this they remained distanced from their feelings, drinking heavily and joking. It was at least six months before they could talk about these experiences.

One victim of several armed robberies remarked, 'It's like I'm on drugs – I feel disconnected, as if there is a veil between me and everyone else'. For many survivors, these defences give way to a more open expression of feelings, but for some they may persist, leaving the survivor emotionally 'living dead', as with the so-called *Musselmänner* of Auschwitz. Such a state does not equate with survival.

Nurturance conflicts

This conflict refers to the suspicion of offers of help from outsiders and in particular to the experience of distrust, the fear that such offers may be false. Survivors may become 'touchy and sensitive to the responses of others' and develop 'a form of severe victim-consciousness' (258) which sometimes reaches the level of paranoia. One survivor of the Bradford fire appeared to cope well in the first weeks following his discharge from hospital. He socialised in his local club and was regularly seen out walking and shopping. All of a sudden, this stopped. He refused to leave his own home and his partner sought help. He had, he said, grown tired of being asked to recount the story of his escape from the inferno. At first, people were naturally inquisitive. Then it seemed to him they were accusing him of some impropriety in the manner of his escape.

Survivors may become very precious about their experience, discounting those who 'can never really understand'. This may stem (184) from a feeling of weakness and a sense of being demeaned, or from being made to feel less than human in a cruel world. They may set up groups from which 'those who cannot understand' are excluded. This can have the effect of generating a powerful sense of survivor identity which provides a vehicle for anger and action, restoring a sense of control. It gives vent to feelings of having been let down by the very exclusion of authority and officialdom. At the same time, however, it may freeze the survivors in time, with the sole identity of 'victims'.

Quite simply, however, disaster survivors are a random selection of ordinary people, who may know nothing of emotional help or the professionals who offer it. They may never have experienced such intense emotions in their lives before, or may be ashamed of their feelings, fearing that they are going mad. They may have no notion of what their feelings represent, or that they are a signal that they may need assistance, and have no idea of what help entails. The notion of talking about painful inner experiences to a stranger may be unfamiliar, frightening and shameful. One survivor of the Bradford fire, an elderly woman who was recovering in hospital from her burns, was approached by a social worker who introduced himself and asked how she was. 'Oh no . . . the welfare,' she exclaimed, 'that it should come to this!'

Survivors of the 1987 Zeebrugge disaster were asked (343) to rate four statements which it was hoped would tap negative attitudes to emotional expression. These were: (i) I think you should always keep your feelings under control; (ii) I think you should not burden other people with your problems; (iii) I think getting emotional is a sign of weakness; and (iv) I think other people don't understand your feelings. The more survivors disagreed with these notions, the lower were their levels of psychological symptoms and the higher their received social support. The 'stiff upper lip' therefore appears to interfere with the successful psychological processing of traumatic experiences.

Quest for meaning

It has been said that 'you cannot understand disasters of any kind without considering the need to give meaning and inner form to the experience, and to life thereafter' (188). The survivor needs to make a 'formulation' of their experience in the attempt to explain and gain mastery over it. Formulation is a key element of psychological processing, and hence of much psychological treatment of trauma.

The survivor's search to understand the experience of the disaster exists on a number of levels, which might be termed a 'hierarchy of formulation'. In terms of the development of understanding over time, a chronological sequence might be:

1   Why did it happen?
2   How did I escape?
3   Why did I escape?
4   Why do I feel like this?
5   What does the way I feel now mean about me as a person?
6   What does all that I have been through mean about the way I understand life?

Firstly, there is the need to understand *why* the incident happened, and this may be enhanced in technological disaster. Many survivors of the Zeebrugge disaster became fascinated by any reference to the accident and its cause. They scanned the papers, cutting out references to the tragedy, and avidly watched any relevant item of news on the television. (This was not universal as many could not bear to see or read any such references.) The verdict of the public inquiry was particularly important, not so much in justifying their blame or anger, but in the public establishment of clear responsibility. Some survivors describe that the experience is almost like needing a public declaration that they themselves did not cause the disaster. The Zeebrugge inquiry conclusions alone enabled some survivors to put to rest their quest for meaning.

Secondly, it may be crucial to understand the means of survival. Zeebrugge disaster counsellors took diagrams of the ferry with them on visits to survivors, enabling many to make sense for the first time of their route of escape. Knowledge may bring sadness, as one girl realised during this exercise that she was separated from her mother, who perished, only by a row of seats. Knowledge, however, is almost invariably better than wondering. Some who did not find this sufficient found it necessary to return to identical ships, or even the wreck itself, to really understand how they escaped. It also became necessary for many to trace those who had helped them, to build on their stories of survival, or simply to thank them. *Heraldlink* and *City Link*, newsletters which were jointly edited by survivors and professional helpers after the Zeebrugge and Bradford disasters, were used to satisfy this need to turn over every stone in order to accomplish a thorough understanding of all that had happened.

Why the person escaped is a question that may be difficult ever to answer, and as we have noted is one of the roots of survivor guilt. Survivors also have to face the question as to why they feel as they do. They are taken unaware by the strength of their feelings, and self-concepts such as 'I am strong', or 'Men don't cry', may be damaged, leading to a possibly valuable, but often negative, personal re-evaluation.

The survivor's life is, however, irrevocably changed – there is no going back. The true meaning of survival involves finding a place for the experience in a new view of the world, its institutions and authorities, the value of life and family relationships, and risk and hazard.

POST-TRAUMATIC STRESS DISORDER

It must not be assumed that all response to trauma is inevitably negative. After a tornado in Xenia, Ohio, in 1974 (308), despite a 'significant rise in symptoms of psychological stress', 84 per cent of people claimed that their experiences had shown them that they could handle crises better than they thought, and 69 per cent felt that they had met a great challenge and were better off for it. Twenty-seven per cent claimed relationships with close friends and family had improved, and 28 per cent reported their marriages to be more satisfying. Whilst technological disaster may result in higher distress levels than natural disaster (259), those involved in technological tragedies may experience similar positive views. Thus of a group of rescue workers involved in the aftermath of a major rail disaster (290), 35 per cent felt more positive about their own lives as a result of their involvement. Quite simply, the confrontation with death can reveal the importance of many aspects of life.

The effects of experiencing major trauma can be summarised as the following (106):

- A proportion of survivors, perhaps up to 25 per cent, may have no particular reaction at all.
- Twenty-five per cent may experience transient psychological symptoms, dissipating over six weeks (101, 95).
- Fifty per cent will experience more significant, persisting symptoms with which they need assistance.
- Twenty-five per cent will go on to develop post-traumatic stress disorder (PTSD) (105).
- Half of the cases of PTSD will remit within the first year (351).
- Half of the cases of PTSD may be chronic, continuing over decades if not treated.
- Up to a third of survivors may develop more chronic symptoms, including PTSD, anxiety and depression.

However, clinicians must take care not to overestimate the prevalence of

PTSD, and not overdiagnose it. They should not forget that survivors will experience more well-observed conditions such as anxiety, whether general or phobic; depression; or indeed, no formal condition at all (353).

The concept of PTSD was first described in 1980 in the 3rd edition of the *Diagnostic and Statistical Manual of Mental Disorders* of the American Psychiatric Association (DSM-III). This was revised in 1987 and again in DSM-IV which was published in 1994 (7). In 1992, the World Health Organisation included the concept of PTSD in ICD-10, the tenth revision of the International Classification of Disease system (350).

PTSD as defined by DSM-IV has three main groups of symptoms: re-experience phenomena, avoidance or numbing reactions, and symptoms of increased arousal.

Qualifying criteria

Firstly, the nature of the trauma is defined. The person must have 'experienced, witnessed, or was confronted with an event or events that involved actual or threatened death or serious injury, or a threat to the physical integrity of self or others'. (It is interesting to note that it has been estimated (105) that three-quarters of the general population of the United States has been exposed to some event in their lives which meets this sort of criterion.) Secondly, the degree of the trauma is defined. The person's response must have 'involved intense fear, helplessness or horror'; or in the case of children, involved 'disorganised or agitated behaviour'. If both of these criteria are met, then the person must have a requisite number of symptoms from the three areas of symptomatology.

Re-experience phenomena

These involve the traumatic event being persistently re-experienced in one (or more) of the following ways:

- Recurrent and intrusive distressing recollections of the event including images, thoughts or perceptions (in young children, repetitive play in which themes or aspects of the trauma are expressed).
- Recurrent distressing dreams of the event (in children there may be frightening dreams without recognisable content).
- Acting or feeling as if the traumatic event were recurring (includes a sense of reliving the experience, illusions, hallucinations, and dissociative flashback episodes, even those that occur upon awakening or when intoxicated). In young children, trauma specific re-enactment may occur.
- Intense psychological distress at exposure to internal or external cues that symbolise or resemble an aspect of the traumatic event.

11

- Physical reactivity upon exposure to internal or external cues that symbolise or resemble an aspect of the traumatic event.

Intrusive recollection and nightmares will be familiar from descriptions of the death imprint. Intrusive imagery occupies a broad spectrum (40), from 'dim impressions to vivid, detailed memories that again and again abruptly enter consciousness and are difficult to dispel (intrusive-repetitive images) to pseudo-hallucinations, hallucinations, or hypnogogic phenomena (imagery which comes on the border between sleep and wakefulness)'. It is not the same as post-traumatic rumination, which lacks the visual element, but which is extremely common. Some evidence suggests that those who have a more highly developed visual imagery ability may be more prone to flash-backs and nightmares (38).

Traumatic nightmares in people suffering PTSD tend to occur early in the sleep cycle and are accompanied by considerable body movements – in some cases bed partners may be physically attacked. They often have elaborate content, tending to be exact replicas of actual events (329). Other types of post-traumatic dreams include those of similar events (e.g. car crashes in general rather than the specific one in which the person was involved) or merely dreams which are simply described as threatening. It is possible that there is an association between intrusive images and dreams as not only is their content similar, but in some cases dream disturbances precede the onset of flashbacks (67).

What is the role of intrusive imagery? Its presence may suggest failure to adapt mentally to the traumatic event. Alternatively it may be positive evidence of processing of information about the trauma, where post-traumatic anxiety is perpetuated through imagery, and a resolution achieved (142). The negative element is that 'trauma linked imagery, thoughts, or perceptions lead to painful affect, which leads to a defensive or coping reac-tion' (28), perhaps involving avoidance or denial. There is thus a cycle of re-experience followed by avoidance and denial.

'As if' phenomena describe the feeling 'as if the event was recurring'. One woman who had been involved in a car accident, in which the vehicle had rolled over several times, was a passenger in a car several years later when an oncoming vehicle began to skid towards them. She described how 'As I looked at it I was suddenly back in that car, going over and over, hearing the sound of smashing glass'. Intensification of feelings by reminder or re-exposure is a different phenomenon, which is more common. For survivors of the Zeebrugge disaster images of the impact and general distress could be triggered by merely hearing the sound of running water in a bath or shower. Similarly, a traumatised bank clerk who was the victim of an armed raid experienced a raised voice or sudden movement in the banking hall as the signal of another hold-up, leading to the re-experience of many of the feel-ings related to the original event. Here, the re-experiencing is related to hypervigilance. The bank clerk is alert to the possibility that any person coming through the door is a potential raider.

The occurrence of physiological reactions to re-exposure to an actual or symbolic reminder of the trauma is common. These reactions which are familiar anxiety symptom manifestations of the autonomic nervous system (palpitations, sweating, etc.) have been measured closely in a few individuals. Thus in a study of a concentration camp survivor and a partisan (68), blood pressure rose specifically when discussing the trauma, as distinct from other life stresses. 'Emotional support and empathic listening to an account of nightmares coincided with an impressive fall in blood pressure' in one of the subjects.

Avoidance or numbing phenomena

These include persistent avoidance of things associated with the trauma and numbing of general responsiveness (not present before the trauma), as indicated by three (or more) of the following:

- Efforts to avoid thoughts, feelings or conversations associated with the trauma.
- Efforts to avoid activities, places or people that arouse recollections of the trauma.
- Inability to recall an important aspect of the trauma.
- Markedly diminished interest or participation in significant activities.
- Feelings of detachment or estrangement from others.
- Restricted range of affect, for example unable to have loving feelings.
- Sense of foreshortened future, for example does not expect to have a career, marriage, children, or a long life.

Many of these phenomena are familiar from Lifton's description of psychic numbing. Survivors use many different mechanisms to ward off thoughts about the trauma including attitude switching (64 per cent), narrowing of attention (52 per cent), inflexible or constricted thought (48 per cent), altered meanings (41 per cent), disavowal (25 per cent), and warding off reality by the use of fantasy (15 per cent) (183). Memory failure is also sometimes apparent.

Avoidance of real situations associated with the trauma is frequent; thus the victims of a building collapse were observed to avoid passing under bridges. Many survivors of the Zeebrugge disaster not only shunned the prospect of ferry travel again, but could not even bear to see the sea, and in the immediate aftermath of the disaster could not face taking a bath or shower. Not being able to avoid such situations, and having to re-enter them, can lead to an increase in anxiety. This has been observed in those who return to sea after maritime disaster (181). After the 1989 M1 air crash in the UK, injured passengers were airlifted from the motorway to hospital, and many expressed obvious concern at the prospect of further air travel so soon after the trauma (6). A man subject to six occurrences of armed crime began to avoid anyone who looked 'suspect'. Driving along he became aware he would have to pull up at traffic lights outside a pub where a group of youths were drinking. He drove down a back road to avoid the junction.

Diminished interest in normal activities is an extremely common symptom in those with PTSD. Feelings of detachment and estrangement are more variable, as is restricted ability to feel. However, their presence and intensity is indicative of a more severe reaction. A sense of foreshortened future has been described by many survivors of trauma. Even for children involved in the Chowchilla school bus kidnap, twenty-three out of twenty-five suffered from the sense that their futures would be greatly limited. 'They expected an unusually short life span or a future disaster, or they were unable to envision marriage, children or career' (310). One 12-year-old remarked: 'I worry I'm going to die when I'm young. I don't think I want a wife. If I do, I would always have to take care of her.' In a similar vein, an 11-year-old girl stated: 'I think I'm going to die young. I'm sure of this. Maybe twelve years old. Someone will come along and shoot me.' Adults often share the same bleak perspective on the future, thinking they will never get married, have children, or live to be old.

Of a group of general traumatic stress patients, 75 per cent felt hopeless about the future (143), and this raises the important question as to whether some of these features reflect depression rather than the specific entity of PTSD. Clearly, there is overlap between the symptoms of depression and PTSD both in respect of emotional numbing and increased arousal. Also, there is often a co-morbidity of depression and PTSD: 34 per cent of the survivors of terrorist attacks with PTSD (193) also qualified for a diagnosis of depression, and it was the most common overlapping diagnosis in a group of in-patients with PTSD (108). That there is a common pathway is indicated by the finding that the development of depression (and PTSD) was mediated by the amount of intrusions experienced at four months (207).

Symptoms of increased arousal

These involve persistent symptoms (not present before the trauma), as indicated by at least two of the following:

- difficulty in falling or staying asleep;
- irritability or outbursts of anger;
- difficulty in concentrating;
- hypervigilance;
- exaggerated startle response.

14

PTSD is accompanied by a number of physical changes, both neurophysio-logical and biochemical (119). In short, 'people with PTSD suffer from generalised hyperarousal and from emergency reactions to specific reminders' (328). These include:

- increased arousal of the sympathetic nervous system;
- hypofunction of the hypothalamic–pituitary–adrenocortical axis;
- dysregulation of the endogenous opioid system (decreasing pain threshold).

Sleep disturbances are commonly found in survivors as difficulties in drop-ping off (initial insomnia), frequent waking or early waking. Sleep disturbances in PTSD are more characterised by anxiety than general insomnia (149). Increased irritability is also frequently reported. Those affected find themselves easily angered by inconsequential events, such as a family member leaving a cup on the floor. There is also a relationship of PTSD with more serious violence (52).

Duration and effect

Lastly, the duration of these symptoms must be more than one month, and the disturbance must cause 'clinically significant distress or impairment in social, occupational, or other important areas of functioning'. If the symp-toms are of less than three months' duration, the PTSD is described as 'acute', and if the duration of symptoms is more than three months, the PTSD is described as 'chronic'.

The effect of PTSD on interpersonal relationships demonstrates how the symptoms act together to cause this 'impairment of social functioning'. This account of the wife of a Zeebrugge survivor sums up the possible problems succinctly:

> Since that fateful day it is hard to describe just how much our lives have changed. We thought he was so lucky to have survived, not knowing he would never be able to return to the sea. We moved away hoping that by putting some distance between us and the Channel it might help – it hasn't. The patience he once had is gone, he snaps at the children, some days I cannot do anything right. He gets depressed and isolates himself, sometimes he just sits and cries and all I can do is be there for him when he needs me. Sometimes we shout and argue over silly things that would have normally passed unnoticed and at other times there are long silences where once we would have talked things out.

This brief description demonstrates avoidance, irritability, detachment and depression. Where one partner is a survivor of an event the other did not experience, the survivor often feels that the partner cannot understand because they were not there, and comfort may only be found in the company of other survivors. He or she may never share all that happened, leaving the partner feeling excluded or resentful. The partner in turn may compound things by remarking 'I can't understand what all the fuss is, you weren't hurt or anything, were you?'

One couple involved in the Zeebrugge disaster felt that it was certain that they would die. They said their 'goodbyes' to each other, thanking each other for the reasonably happy life they had spent together. Both were saved. As the months wore on, they found that having said 'goodbye', it was very difficult to say 'hello' again, and found themselves distant and irritable with each other, arguing over petty things.

The previous delicate balance of a relationship may be badly disturbed by the new self-image that survivors acquire as a result of their actions. One man, previously dominated by the wife he rescued, found that his acts of heroism changed his view of himself as passive and helpless. He began to distance himself from her, whilst she reversed their previous roles, becoming house bound. For some survivors the experience does in time contribute to personal growth, despite confusion in others around them.

A study of survivors of terrorist attacks in Northern Ireland (193) was the first to identify a specific relationship between the presence of PTSD and marital difficulties. Taking into account only those difficulties that had arisen since the incident, disharmony was found in 46 per cent of those with PTSD and 23 per cent of those without. There was no difference in the levels of disharmony whether the victim had been male or female. The quality of the relationship prior to the trauma was, however, not known, and it is possible that an unsupportive relationship itself could cause a particularly severe or prolonged reaction (304).

OTHER FORMAL POST-TRAUMATIC CONDITIONS

PTSD – ICD-10

The ICD-10 diagnosis of PTSD is simpler, focusing mainly on re-experience phenomena. Under these criteria, PTSD

> arises as a delayed and/or protracted response to a stressful event or situation (either short or long lasting) of an exceptionally threatening or catastrophic nature, which is likely to cause pervasive distress in almost anyone (e.g. natural or technological disaster,

combat, serious accident, witnessing the violent death of others or being the victim of torture, terrorism, rape, or other crime).

PTSD must arise within six months of the traumatic event. Emotional numbing and increased arousal symptoms are not essential to the diagnosis, but 'there must be a repetitive, intrusive recollection or re-enactment of the event in memories, daytime imagery, or dreams'.

Acute stress disorders

DSM-IV introduced the concept of acute stress disorder. This shares the same initial qualifying criteria as PTSD. In terms of symptomatology, the person must have experienced a range of dissociative symptoms during or after the event, suffered persistent re-experience phenomena, avoided stimuli that arouse recollections, and suffered symptoms of anxiety or increased arousal. This disturbance must last for a minimum of two days and a maximum of four weeks.

ICD-10 also describes an acute stress reaction, lasting for about three days, showing 'a mixed and usually changing picture; in addition to the initial state of daze, depression, anxiety, anger, despair, over activity and withdrawal may all be seen, but no one type of symptom predominates for long'.

Adjustment disorders

DSM-IV describes adjustment disorder, a response to a stressor developing within three months of its onset. Depressive, anxiety or behavioural symptoms may appear, and should not be present for more than six months.

ICD-10 also describes adjustment disorder. This may arise as a result of a 'significant life event e.g. the possibility of serious physical illness'. Symptoms may include 'depressed mood, anxiety, worry, a feeling of inability to cope . . . or conduct disorders'. The change should not last for more than six months, and should not be of 'sufficient severity or prominence in its own right to justify a more specific diagnosis'.

Disorders of extreme stress

ICD-10 introduced the concept of 'enduring personality changes' to describe longer term changes in personality following massive trauma, where the person becomes avoidant, hostile, distrustful and hopeless. This acknowledges that PTSD does not adequately describe all the more severe post-traumatic reactions.

Notions such as 'complex PTSD' (118) or 'disorders of extreme stress' (330) have been proposed. The latter contains five areas of symptomatology:

1   Impairment of regulation of affective arousal, including difficulty in controlling anger, suicidal impulse, risk-taking behaviour or sexual feelings.
2   Dissociation and amnesia.
3   Somatisation, the experience of a range of bodily symptoms.
4   Alterations in the perception of self and others such as chronic guilt and effects on relationships including inability to trust and the victimisation of others.
5   Alterations in systems of meaning, including loss of previous beliefs.

Diagnostic frameworks – a mixed blessing?

When first proposed, the concept of PTSD described nothing new, but it represented an attempt to provide standard criteria, and to define when a 'normal' reaction to trauma becomes 'abnormal'. It allowed comparison in research between groups of people experiencing different stressors. For survivors themselves, the concept was a validation. It indicated that their suffering was a recognised entity, and hence legitimated their experiences, both internally for themselves and externally in the eyes of others.

The cutoffs for diagnosis, both in terms of time and number of symptoms required to be present, are arbitrary, and represent, of course, no absolute truth. However, most clinicians experienced in the area of PTSD accept that the concept has face validity even if it is overused.

The recognition that post-traumatic reactions which are not classifiable as PTSD can also be disturbing has led in the sixteen years since DSM-III to a minor proliferation in trauma-related diagnostic categories. Whether this scramble to classify everything was the sort of recognition that was needed is open to question. There are clear dangers in the overmedicalisation of approaches to survivors of trauma. These are explored in depth in this book, but they relate practically to the difficulty that victims have in coming forward for help. The fear of psychiatric stigmatisation may delay this. Survivors also find the act of diagnosis confusing. They may be told for therapeutic purposes that their experiences are normal reactions to abnormal events, but for the purposes of medico-legal examination a 'disorder' has to be not only identified, but emphasised.

POST-TRAUMATIC STRESS IN CHILDREN

Do the post-traumatic reactions of children differ from those of adults? Whilst the way certain symptoms are demonstrated differs, there is much greater concordance than dissimilarity.

Children had been described as not experiencing intrusive imagery of the flashback type (309), but with children involved in the capsize of the *Herald of Free Enterprise*, 'most experienced intrusive thoughts, and some experienced full-blown flashbacks' (355). Similar findings emerged in a group of children experiencing a sniper attack on their school playground (249). They often suffered intense nightmares about the events, which some believed were predictive about the future. Unique to children is post-traumatic play, encountered in eighteen of twenty-five children involved in the Chowchilla school bus kidnap (310). One 13-year-old described the following:

> Me, Mary, and Brian, my little cousin [not one of the kidnapped children], play we kidnap each other. But that don't remind me. We play it almost every day when we go over [to Brian's]. We take turns. We tie him up. We hide him from the other one. Then they break loose or stuff. We've scared each other badly with that game. We've played it in the dark. Sometimes we pretend we're leaving the person. When I'm 'kidnapper' I leave them there waiting for me.

Children and adolescents also demonstrate avoidance. Thus, 'many young people do not want to talk about their feelings with their parents so as not to upset them' (355). (At the same time the parent may avoid talking to the child about the trauma for exactly the same reason.) Similarly, they may not want to talk to their peers, often for fear of mockery.

Anxiety may be particularly prominent in children. After trauma children may regress to fears typical earlier in development. They may be frightened to go upstairs on their own to use the toilet or go to bed. They may insist on sleeping with the light on, or having a sibling in their room, or even their bed. They may be particularly prone to intrusive thoughts at night. Their sleep may be badly disturbed, with screaming in the night, either in response to dreams, or 'night terrors'. This may lead to them insisting on coming into the parental bed. Nocturnal enuresis may occur after the child has been dry for many years.

Children may show marked avoidance and heightened awareness of danger. After the 1965 Aberfan disaster (175) surviving children were 'unwilling to go to school or out to play', and would be particularly upset during periods of bad weather like that which had preceded the slide of the tip onto their school. Children may be particularly frightened for the safety of parents. They may show clinginess rather than the symptoms of emotional numbing. Yet, traumatised children are sometimes described by parents as shutting themselves off in the house in their rooms, withdrawing from family and avoiding friends. In some, frank depression may develop, although this may be difficult to distinguish from the normal fluctuations of mood of adolescence. Guilt is often observable in teenagers. Children may demonstrate increased irritability, squabbling with parents, destroying possessions or fighting with siblings or school friends. Concentration is often affected, and this may have a deleterious effect on school performance.

However, although the resilience of children should not be overempha-sised, disturbances are generally short lived, and whilst a wide range of symptoms may be reported by children, long term effects are generally minimal (15). Unfortunately the same cannot be said for 'multiple-blow' trauma, such as repeated abuse.

INFLUENCES ON COPING WITH TRAUMA

What determines the way in which a person responds emotionally in the aftermath of a traumatic event? Coping and recovery depend on successful processing. Emotional processing is the 'process whereby emotional distur-bances are absorbed, and decline to the extent that other experiences and behaviour can proceed without disruption' (251). The persistence of symp-toms of post-traumatic stress may represent the failure of processing. Satisfactory emotional processing can be said to have taken place when:

1 Probes such as reminders no longer elicit disturbance.
2 The internal feeling of distress declines.
3 Disturbed behaviour declines.
4 'Routine' behaviour, such as good concentration, returns.

Three areas will influence the quality of a person's emotional processing and their recovery from trauma: dimensions of the person, dimensions of the trauma, and dimensions of the recovery environment.

Dimensions of the person

What makes people resilient to trauma? What contributes to the ability to tolerate suffering? Sadly, these are questions to which we have few answers. Indeed, the answers are likely to be complex. There is, for instance, no rela-tionship between courage and PTSD – in the First World War, men who developed shell shock were as likely to be decorated as other soldiers (221). We do, however, have some knowledge of what constitutes vulnerability. This includes demographic factors, such as age and sex; individual and familial risk factors; and the characteristics known as 'personality'.

1 *Gender*. It has been suggested (100) that 'gender might best be regarded as a factor that relates to the specific expression of symptoms rather than one which defines risk per se'. However, whilst males are at greater risk for exposure to traumatic events, once exposed, females appear more often to develop PTSD, and there is greater risk of it becoming chronic (226).

20

2   *Age*. Younger children (5–10) are more vulnerable than older children (11+) to the same traumatic events. Risk increases with middle age and beyond owing to the 'burden of additional age-related stressors' (105).

3   *Individual and familial risk factors*. These include:

   (a) previous severe adverse life events (306);
   (b) prior victimisation (e.g. childhood sexual/physical abuse) (27);
   (c) pre-existing mental health problems such as anxiety or depression (337);
   (d) family psychiatric history (62).

4   *Personality*. Before the event, the survivor was a person with characteristic ways of feeling, thinking and behaving. Important in recovery will be the person's beliefs and attitudes, which are a major influence on coping strategies. Styles of personal responding which are known to influence emotional processing are neuroticism and introversion (251), being inner oriented (155), and the need to suppress expression of feelings (96). Following a Norwegian factory fire (337), personality factors which were found to influence the development of psychological difficulties included high basic levels of anxiety and dependent, insecure, highly sensitive, introverted and neurotic traits, with a tendency to withdrawal and regression.

Studies of the course of emotional reactions in volunteer fire-fighters involved in the 1983 Australian Ash Wednesday bush fires (203, 205, 206) have raised interesting questions about the importance of previous personality in the development of PTSD. In these studies, the relative importance of the disaster, post-disaster experiences and personality factors were examined four, eleven and twenty-nine months after the fires. Whilst severity of exposure to the disaster and the losses sustained played a significant role in the levels of immediate distress, they made no detectable contribution at twenty-nine months. Other life events following the disaster appeared equally as important as the disaster itself in determining distress, even at four months, leading to the suggestion that 'life events have a more important role in perpetuating post-traumatic morbidity than in contributing to its onset'. (However, these subsequent life events may of course be related to the original event.)

At all stages, pre-existing personality factors constituting 'vulnerability' had a more important role in determining distress, this importance increasing as time went on, indicating that personality factors were a more important cause of long term disorder than acute disorder. Neuroticism (as measured by the Eysenck Personality Inventory) was the major factor, but a past history of treated psychiatric disorder was also a predictor of PTSD. Cognitive and emotional preoccupation with the fire played an important role in the onset of disturbance in the months immediately after the disaster, but the extent of this initial preoccupation did not determine the outcome at twenty-nine months. Thus a number of survivors were preoccupied with distressing imagery without developing a long term disorder. A link also appeared between such imagery and neuroticism, suggesting that whilst cognitive and emotional preoccupation with the trauma may be an important factor in the development of PTSD, it may also be an indication of a pre-existing emotional style.

These results indicate that different factors have disproportionate influences on recovery at different times after the disaster. However, at no time was the effect of disaster-related factors greater than the pre-existing personality factors. Whatever criticisms may be levelled at the study (namely that the 'personality' measures are *post hoc*, and may themselves be influenced by the traumatic event), its findings demand attention.

Perhaps a more useful way of framing 'personality' in this context is to focus on psychological resources, or coping style. It may be easier to present survivors with clear reasons for adopting particular coping strategies than to approach imponderables such as 'personality'. People differ, for instance, in the extent to which they use approach or avoidance as a coping strategy. 'Approach facilitates action, while avoidance interferes' (100), yet on the other hand, avoidance can temporarily reduce stress allowing other coping strategies to be used. Active coping styles are assumed to be more effective than palliative. After the Buffalo Creek damburst, cleaning and repairing one's home, and being able to give personal help to others, was the best predictor of extent of later psychopathology (103).

Disaster, as has been suggested, can break down an individual's belief in a predictable and controllable world. Therefore, the extent to which a person retains a belief that they can control outcomes (internal control), rather than seeing outcomes as generated by factors outside their control (external control), might be expected to have a positive effect on outcome. External locus of control has been found to be associated with greater symptoms of PTSD (100).

In a study of survivors' ways of coping (46), it was found that the most commonly reported were the 'emotion-focused' coping strategies of avoidance, emotional suppression and wishful thinking. These, however, were temporary expedients rather than consistent ways of coping. 'Problem-focused' coping was used more extensively in those with an internal locus of control.

Dimensions of the trauma

Although it is possible that the longer PTSD lasts, the less important is the role of traumatic exposure, it is generally accepted that 'premorbid risk factors become less important as the intensity of the stressor experience increases' (218). The most catastrophic events may be expected to affect most people, irrespective of history. A 'dose response' relationship exists: the more intense and threatening the experience, the more the risk of PTSD.

Thus, difficulties will arise if the stressor is intense or severe (139) and involves heat and noise (30) or darkness; is sudden, unanticipated and uncontrollable (145), irregular, occurs in large chunks, and involves loss such as bereavement (137), threat to life, personal injury, or exposure to death. Other important elements include the duration of the trauma, whether it was experienced alone or with others, whether the threats involved in the event were single or multiple, and whether there is a possibility that they may reoccur (344). The threatening nature of the situation may be objective, for example the frequency of violence in combat stress, or the number of people who die. However, the experience of threat is also subjective: believing one is about to die, even though the threat is not objectively there, or is uncertain, is common in accidents, and is difficult to erase.

Obviously, dimensions of the person and the situation will interact with each other to govern how the person feels, thinks and reacts in the situation itself, and in the course of recovery.

Dimensions of the recovery environment

Key elements in the recovery environment will include isolation and levels of social support (256), coupled with perceptions of the helpfulness of such support (290), ongoing stressors, cultural rituals for recovery, community, society and media attitudes towards the event, and opportunities for alternative ways of coping and behaving (295).

The role of social support as a potential mitigator of stress has received considerable interest. However, 'although there exists some evidence that social support can buffer the impacts of life changes, it must be interpreted with extreme caution' (311). In a follow-up of survivors of the 1988 *Jupiter* cruise ship disaster, the support received from family and friends decreased significantly over an eighteen-month period. However, higher crisis support in the immediate aftermath was found to predict less post-traumatic symptomatology at a later date. In a follow-up of survivors of the Zeebrugge disaster (133), those who reported family conflict in the first year showed higher symptom levels, as might be expected. In the study of negative attitudes to emotional expression referred to earlier (343), these were related to lower levels of received social support, indicating that a number of different factors influence the presence/absence of social support.

A MODEL OF TRAUMA AND POST-TRAUMATIC STRESS REACTIONS

PTSD and other formally defined conditions are only a partial description

23

of human response to catastrophe. They describe certain symptom outcomes, yet do not describe the process behind the symptoms. This process we might properly call 'trauma', the symptoms of PTSD being the visible sign of this internal process.

Cognitive processes are a key to understanding 'trauma'. As we have observed, the experience of threat is subjective. It is not just the objective features of the traumatic event that govern the extent of response, but the meaning that it has for the person. Individuals strive to attach meaning to events, to make the world comprehensible (335). Indeed, the 'constructive perspective' would hold that 'the human mind is a product of the personal meanings that individuals create' (218).

As we have already suggested, the meaning in question may vary from that of the event itself, to the implications that the event has for the rest of existence. A family may escape uninjured from a car crash, yet the parents may be plagued by 'What if' or 'If only' thoughts. 'What if' thoughts may create a scenario for them which did not happen, in which the children may have been injured or killed, and 'If only' thoughts may create a perspective in which they were culpable for the accident for deciding to go out, and deciding to take that route at that time. The accident is no longer a random event. The world may suddenly be full of danger, and they may be incompetent parents for failing to deal with it.

The person who experiences a traumatic event is a person with a history, and we have examined above some of the features of this which make people more vulnerable to psychological distress. But people are more than the sum of their 'risk factors' – they have a basic account of who they are, based upon their personal history. They have a view of why they are like they are, of what has influenced them to react as they do. Just as they have a picture of themselves, so they have a picture of the people around them, how and why they behave as they do, and the way the world generally works. The experience of a traumatic event, or how it comes to be seen, causes 'a rupture in the person's personal, family and community identity' (60). It may seem as if a severing has occurred between the present and what has gone before. The individual may now report being a 'different person', whose reactions seem alien. The pre-existing individual may seem a stranger. People around them may also seem now to be strangers, and the world a foreign place. If unprocessed, the rupture continues, severing the meaning of all that happened in the past from the present and the future. Part of emotional processing is the re-establishment of continuity between past and present, and the integration of the traumatic experience. Literally, the present and the future need to be made sense of in light of the past.

Thus, one of the major goals of emotional processing after trauma may be to achieve 'cognitive completion' (140), to integrate the stressful experience with enduring models of the world and one's relation to it. The various steps in the process of formulation described earlier in this chapter are part of this process. In war veterans, a process of 'sealing over' has been described. The veteran makes use of grand rationales ('I did it for King, Country and Freedom') to put their behaviour and reactions in some sort of context. It 'allows for a gentler management of the whole experience as unique and consistent with itself, although separate from other experience' (291). Survivors of technological disaster rarely, however, have the opportunity of such rationales. Yet 'integration' or 'completion' must be achieved. 'This more arduous process involves not permeating an experience with an overall meaning, but rather, weaving each strand of the experience into the overall fabric of their lives' (291).

Sadly, many people remain preoccupied with the rupture. Some may find their previous life so distant that they cannot retrieve any positive memories about the past. Others may be bound up with 'unfavourable comparisons between life *as it is*, as compared with what it *might have been* had the traumatic event not occurred' (218) Others may idealise life beforehand, comparing life before with life as it is now, grieving for what has been lost.

The core of the rupture is that individual assumptions about oneself and the world, which are generally held without the awareness that they actually exist, are violated by trauma. These are the 'cognitive structures', or schemata, the 'implicit beliefs, schemes and readiness sets that provide the "if . . . then" rules by which one functions . . . the core organising principles' (218). Key assumptions include (151):

1	'I am invulnerable – it can't happen to me.'	v	'I am vulnerable – anything can happen to me.'

In order to function in an inherently dangerous world, to drive fast on a motorway, for instance, one must have a sense of invulnerability. Or at least, one must think 'If I take reasonable care, nothing untoward will happen'. Disaster survivors learn that they were taking good care, but catastrophe still overtook them. They are now ultimately vulnerable, and anxiety may predominate. PTSD has been described as a 'fear structure', a programme to escape danger, containing information about the feared situation, and verbal, physical and behavioural responses to it. Of course, many fear structures exist in everyday life, but 'what distinguishes PTSD from other anxiety disorders is that the traumatic event was of monumental significance and violated formerly held basic concepts of safety' (86).

2	'The world is safe, orderly, predictable.'	v	'The world is dangerous, chaotic, unpredictable.'

One of the major experiences of victimisation is the feeling of having lost control over things. Normally, daily life has a certain comforting predictable monotony. Even for those whose lives are chaotic, the chaos is predictable.

25

Disaster survivors, however, learn that the world is suddenly completely unpredictable. For those who have been cautious, careful people, the world may lose its meaning.

3 'I am a good person.'   v   'I am a bad person.'

The notion that one is good, decent and worthy, a concept crucial in maintaining self-esteem, may be seriously questioned by survivors, who may 'see themselves as weak, helpless, needy, frightened and out of control' (151). Moreover, there is a basic assumption that 'good things happen to good people – bad things happen to bad people'. The frightening possible transition here is to: 'something bad happened to me, therefore I must be bad'. Many survivors feel the curious sense that their presence at the disaster had in some vague way 'something to do' with it happening.

In conjunction with these 'primitive, global, positive assumptions' (342), which may be shattered by catastrophe, there will exist a layer of attitudes towards expressing disturbed and disturbing feelings. As we have described earlier, many of these attitudes are negative. Such feelings may be viewed as socially unacceptable, distressing to others, a sign of weakness, or a signal of madness or loss of control. If the world is now seen as chaotic and unpredictable, action to deal with negative feelings may be useless, and those to whom one might turn for help unworthy of trust.

It has been suggested (55) that a 'traumatic memory network' is formed, containing 'event cognitions' (159), or intrusive imagery. Traumatic images are then subject to further appraisals, giving rise to thoughts about the imagery. It is here that the recognition (in either a more automatic or a more conscious way) that previous assumptions have been violated takes place. As 'crisis theory' predicts (44), 'coping' now takes place. For some, coping involves facing the intrusive imagery and ruminations, and effective processing will occur. Indeed, in one study, higher initial levels of intrusion were associated with lower levels of symptoms later on (55), confirming a positive link between intrusion and processing. Imagery thus may lead to 'revising the automatic processing of such information, to revising the relevant schemas . . . and to completing the processing of the stressful information' (141).

Early on, therefore, features of the traumatic event itself (stimulus features) are of primary importance. Traumatic memories stimulate a process of resolution. However, it is as if there is a transitional point at which previous personality including traditional ways of coping assume prominence. Thus, for some, coping will involve avoidance of traumatic images, or their triggers. Whilst some successful avoidance is a part of coping, too much may lead to emotional numbing (55). At this point the survivor is trapped in the pit of rumination, worrying about what to do, and reflecting on how they and life have changed. Not only may they be trapped in their particular 'fear structure', but given the shared pathway between emotional numbing and depression (29), depressed mood may well be stimulated by the helplessness generated by this process of rumination and review. The 'breaking point' of crisis theory has been reached, and psychological disturbance predominates. The sense of rupture with the past is complete. Figure 1.1 shows a diagrammatic model of the relationship between these various factors (after 54).

BEREAVEMENT

Although bereavement may be caused by a traumatic event, trauma and grief are different entities, their effects operating separately, yet overlapping and interacting.

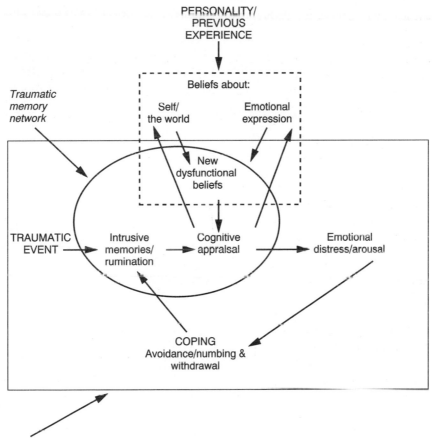

Figure 1.1 A model of post-traumatic stress reactions

Bereavement reactions

Just as human beings form attachments, so they lose them. Loss may be the single most difficult aspect of existence to come to terms with. The reaction to loss through death, bereavement, has a core of emotional reactions, known collectively as grief. Grief is often spoken of as having 'stages', yet those who work with the bereaved soon realise that this is not really the case. The notion of 'stages' implies an orderly progression, whereas the bereaved oscillate between a variety of experiences, which blend with each other, and are not successive. Secondly, it is not at all clear that all the elements of the process of 'working through' must be experienced and the intensity and duration of the elements for different individuals differ widely. Thirdly, there is no empirical evidence to suggest that stages do, in fact, exist.

A more useful approach may be to see grief as having a number of components (254): thoughts, feelings and behaviours which are interlinked, some of which tend to come earlier in the process of working through, and some later. These components wax and wane continually, blending dynamically. Alternatively, grief may be seen as comprising a series of tasks, which must be completed for successful resolution (349). These tasks include accepting the reality of the loss, experiencing the pain of grief, adjusting to an environment in which the loved one is no longer present, and withdrawing from the deceased and reinvesting emotional energy in new activities and relationships (220).

The main components of grief are presented below, in a rough chronological order. Each will rise and fall in intensity, the intensity lessening over time.

Shock

Shock is a universal, initial response to bereavement, whether expected or not. It may be momentary or prolonged, and experienced as disbelief and numbness, or as pain, calm, apathy or feelings that one is not real (depersonalisation) or that the world around one is not real (derealisation). It is as if feelings have been 'turned off'.

Disorganisation

Disorganisation is variable. The bereaved may collapse instantly, or may appear superefficient, becoming more disorganised over time. The experience is one of confusion.

Denial

Denial is a defence, the repression of an item of reality from conscious awareness. It serves to protect the bereaved person from experiencing too much pain at any one time. It may be momentary or prolonged, and occurs throughout the process of working through; breaking down and returning in a way that may be both mystifying and alarming to those around the bereaved person. The facts of the loss may be denied, with the person behaving as if the loved one was still present, setting a place at the table or keeping the dead person's room just as it was the day they died. Alternatively, the meaning of the loss may be denied, the bereaved explaining 'it was a release' or 'she was never a good wife'. The fact that death is irreversible may also be denied, as demonstrated by a sudden interest in spiritualism. Auditory and visual experiences of the dead person's presence are normal experiences of momentary denial. Sometimes these are experienced as comforting; for others they are anxiety provoking, summoning fears of madness. The behaviour of searching also reflects denial. Here, the bereaved may find themselves actively looking for the dead person in places associated with them.

Depression

Depression is too broad and vague a term to be meaningful, but all its usual physical manifestations may be present. Two elements may often be seen. The first is 'desolate pining'. This is an active feeling, deep and empty, mixed with waves of psychic pain and an intense sense of unfillable yearning and longing. Secondly there is 'despair', a passive feeling of blackness, helplessness and hopelessness.

Guilt

Guilt is traditionally associated with depression. It may be real or imagined, and both seem equally troublesome. Similarly, guilt may be for a thought ('Why don't you drop dead?'), or an action such as causing a car accident in which the loved one dies. It may be particularly problematic in the setting of a previously ambivalent relationship.

Guilt may be from a feeling of release, an absence of sadness, or from angry feelings towards the deceased. As with 'survivor guilt' already discussed, it may derive from sins of omission, or from sins of commission.

Anxiety

All the physical feelings of anxiety may be experienced, as well as specific fears or a nameless sense of dread. The bereaved may fear being overwhelmed by the strength of their feelings, or may be frightened for the future in terms of survival in view of increased responsibility, financial changes or life style changes. There may also be a heightened awareness of one's own vulnerability and mortality.

Aggression

Aggression is one of the most difficult aspects of grief. It is uncertain whether it is experienced by all bereaved or needs to be expressed at all. It is experienced on a continuum, from irritability towards friends and family (who 'can't understand'), to resentment and envy (towards those who still have husbands or sons), to anger against those who could have done more to prevent the death, to posturing against God for His unfairness, and finally to a deep anger towards the deceased for dying and leaving, the element which may be so difficult to express.

Resolution and acceptance

When the feelings decrease in intensity, there are longer gaps between their occurrence, and denial is absent, there can then occur a taking leave of the dead person and an acceptance that life must go on.

Reintegration

Reintegration involves taking up a new life in which the dead have no part. It is a long and painful process of setbacks and progress, with returns to grief at certain times such as anniversaries of the death, wedding anniversaries, birthdays, and family occasions such as Christmas.

Bereavement in children

The grief reactions of children differ in a number of ways from those of adults (248).

Concept of death

Children need to be able to 'understand the physical reality of death in order to grieve'. The notion of the irreversibility of death strengthens from the age of 5 onwards. However, differences in concept of death have no correlation with the development of symptoms (162). Believing that 'they won't understand', parents often prevent children going to funerals, yet there is now evidence that there is potential value in this, even for young children (339).

Sustaining sadness

The ability to sustain sadness is one which comes with maturity. However, absence of sadness may be the result of attempts to disbelieve what has happened. Children who express the least sadness in parental bereavement may be the most behaviourally disturbed (163).

Recognising loss

Children are often prevented from registering empty situations – thus because they may eat earlier than the adults of an evening, they may not have the opportunity to sit at the dinner table at which the adult is absent. Alternatively they may anticipate missing a person at a specific special point in the future, such as a birthday. Children may actively search for the dead person, co-opting others to help. They may have very active reunion wishes, perhaps emerging in dreams, which can be frightening. Bereavement themes may dominate their play.

Memories

The memory of the last time they saw the dead person, or the last 'emotionally charged interaction', may become particularly important. The sense of 'unfinished business' may be keen.

Children will often reminisce about the dead person, recalling things adults thought they were too young to remember. As children develop, they may continually renegotiate the relationship with the image of the dead person in their mind, where the deceased may be present at all sorts of important life events.

Emotion

Children may show marked anxiety, becoming demanding and clingy, frightened of separation. They may fear that others will die, and need to restore the sense of safety and security. They may also be angry, disturbingly so with the person who has died and left them. There may also be guilt.

These problems may show themselves at school, where the child may have concentration difficulties and their work suffers. Peers may be cruel, and behavioural difficulties may appear.

SUDDEN VIOLENT DEATH

Bereavement is universal, yet there may be many problems in working it through. It has been estimated that one-third of the bereaved have a poor outcome in terms of resolution (197), and that a third of major bereavements may result in a need for counselling to help resolve the loss (258).

Four main areas contribute to the progress of recovery, the type of death, the characteristics of the relationship between the deceased and the survivor, the characteristics of the survivor, and their social circumstances. The major findings in these areas are summarised in Table 1.1. It will be seen that sudden, unexpected or untimely deaths and those that are painful or horrifying represent risk factors for poor outcome.

It is helpful to distinguish three kinds of untimely deaths (338): premature deaths, unexpected deaths and calamitous deaths. Premature deaths, epitomised by the deaths of children, damage our 'social and emotional reality, including our belief in a future in which potentials become fulfilled'. Unexpected deaths are those which are sudden and unpredicted, and the stress may be measured by 'how drastically the death violates our inner timetable of expectation'. Calamitous deaths are not only unpredicted, but 'violent, destructive, demeaning and even degrading'. Bereavement by disaster may comprise all three of these elements.

Table 1.1 Risk factors in bereavement (after 83) (Factors ranked in approximate order of importance within each section)

Type of death	Cause for blame on survivor (214, 215, 231)
	Sudden/unexpected/untimely death (195, 240)
	Painful/horrifying/mismanaged death (214, 215, 231, 255)
Characteristics of the relationship	Symbiotic/dependent relationship (240)
	Ambivalent relationship (240)
	Spouse death (98, 237)
	Child under 20 dies (236, 273)
	Parent (especially mother) dies leaving child(ren) aged between 0 and 5 or 10 and 15 (236, 273)
	Parent dies leaving older, unmarried adult offspring (236)
Characteristics of the survivor	Grief-prone personality (intense clinging/pining) (240)
	Insecure/overanxious/low self-esteem (237)
	Previous psychiatric history (237)
	Excessive anger (240)
	Excessive self-reproach (240)
	Physically ill/disabled (244)
	Previous unresolved losses (72)
	Inability to express feelings (17, 57)
Social circumstances	Family absent/seen as unsupportive (49, 73, 211)
	Detached from cultural/religious support system (104)
	Unemployed (244)
	Dependent children at home (36)
	Low socio-economic status (2, 194)
	Other losses (164)

Shock

The sense of shock is enhanced following death in disaster. The suddenness and unexpectedness inherent in such situations may be compounded by the feeling of disbelief and bizarre reversal – people are involved in normally safe activities, such as returning from work, or are engaged in enjoyment, such as going on holiday or attending a football match, and then suddenly perish in horrifying circumstances. The disbelief of one Zeebrugge widow is evident in these words: 'I simply cannot think that he might be dead – he was so big, so strong – if anyone was going to survive it would surely have been him'. This 'cognitive dissonance' may continue for months or years (262).

Guilt

Guilt may occur in the absence of an ambivalent relationship. One survivor of the Zeebrugge disaster had organised the trip (an annual event to celebrate her husband's birthday) for that particular day against his wishes. He wanted to go on his birthday, but she asked him to go two days later to accommodate two friends from work, a mother and daughter. She was the only one who returned. She was hospitalised within two months in a psychiatric unit, with a diagnosis of depression. She spoke of her memories of hearing her two friends shouting for help, and seeing her husband disappear into a mêlée of bodies and then being submerged. 'I am a murderer', she said. She was unable to go and see the man who was both husband and father to her two dead friends. 'How can I see him?' she asked, 'I killed them.' Grief is known to be complicated when there is a cause for blame on the survivor (215).

Guilt frequently arises in the presence of ambivalence. Another Zeebrugge widow had a row with her husband the night before the disaster. He slept downstairs and came to her the next morning to tell her he was leaving. She retorted, 'Fuck off, I don't care if you never come back'. He died, and she found it necessary to attend many days of the three weeks of inquest, almost in an act of atonement. Again, ambivalence and excessive self-reproach complicate resolution (240).

In bereavement by disaster, as in all sudden death, the sense of 'unfinished business' with the deceased may be intense, and things left unsaid may be problematic in terms of guilt.

Anger

Although anger is a normal part of many bereavement reactions, excessive anger complicates recovery (240). In technological disaster there is often a very clear and justifiable focus for the anger of the bereaved. The issue of preventability may come to preoccupy the bereaved intensifying anger and the duration and severity of grief (252).

Intense anger is natural in deaths where there is an identifiable perpetrator, such as murder. The bereaved may experience murderous retaliatory impulses, of which they may be very ashamed. Lifton suggests that this intensity of anger is connected to the 'internal struggle to assert vitality by attacking the other rather than the self in order to prevent a sense of inner deadness' (184).

When many die together, as in disaster, the possibility exists of a communal uniting of anger. Following the Zeebrugge disaster, parents who had lost adult children, for whom no compensation was indicated in British law, banded together to form the Herald Families Association. They were enraged that they were symbolically denied recognition that they had been bereaved. Their avowed aim was to see the prosecution of the ferry operator for negligence, and the institution of safer ferry standards. It remains to be seen whether such channelling of anger is an aid or a block to recovery.

Intervention of authority

The intervention of authority can enhance confusion and uncertainty. People may be informed that loved ones have survived when they have in fact died. The demand for statements which are necessary to aid later identification can feel like a persecution, or if guilt exists, may reinforce it. Later, bodies may be delayed from burial by seemingly unnecessary bureaucracy.

Helplessness

The sense of helplessness may be intense. This may relate to powerlessness to prevent the death, especially if the bereaved was also the survivor of the impact. One Zeebrugge widow was able to climb onto a ledge where there was, however, no room for her husband. She held him by the hair to keep him from the freezing water until she had no further strength, whereupon she had to let him go to his death. A bereaved father went to see his son's body, to find, to his horror, that one of his son's legs was missing. 'Where was his leg?', he moaned desperately to his counsellor (having been unable to tell any of the family). Just as the counsellor was helpless to answer his question, so he had been helpless to protect his son.

Aspects of the death

Aspects of the death of the loved one may be particularly important. Firstly, in some bereavements by disaster, no body is recovered. Normally following a death, the disbelief is gradually eroded by the reality of the absence of the deceased, and undeniable is the presence of a dead body. The transformation of the loved one's body – the pallid colour, coldness, unyielding texture, fixed limbs and immobility – provide incontrovertible evidence of death. A mental transformation also has to take place whereby the loved one is recognised as no longer existing in the external world, their physical representation remaining only as an image in the internal world.

Although a majority of people (73 per cent) choose not to view the corpse of the loved one (208), there is generally an acceptance that someone, such as a relative, has actually done so, and as further evidence, physical deterioration, heralding death, may have been evident from hospital visits. In sudden violent death, this last element is rarely present. One widow of the Zeebrugge disaster who did not see her husband's corpse described the conceptual problem this created for her thus: 'I cannot accept that he is dead – he left home vital, strong . . . not seeing him again I just cannot imagine him dead, his body without life'. She could not believe that the ashes in the casket, which she slept with in her bed each night, were related to the body she loved. It was as if some transitional image of him was missing in the process of acceptance of the fact of his death.

Viewing the body of the deceased, which was in the first part of this century a common custom, is an important part of accepting the 'certainty of death', especially in sudden unexpected loss. In the absence of a body, this certainty, which is necessary for effective grieving to begin, may never be established. If the body is recovered, but not seen, this may in certain circumstances lead to a failure to establish this certainty, and in others, to a delay. For some, the sight of the body transformed by death is an important but transitory image which allows an effective internalisation of the concept that the familiar, palpably alive physical presence of the loved one no longer exists in the external world and that memories of this are all that remain.

Following the Zeebrugge disaster, many people (three times as many as were actually on board) were reported as missing, possibly on the capsized ferry. Many of these had been missing for years. Those who had long term 'missing bodies' therefore seemed to need to create an end for their loved ones. Many bodies were not recovered until five weeks had passed, and during this period many bereaved were plagued by thoughts and dreams that the loved one had never been aboard, or had swum ashore and was wandering in an amnesic state. (After the Bradford fire, relatives thought that the loved one had in some strange way gone away to 'think'.) One mother was convinced that her 2-year-old had floated ashore and was being looked after by a family on the Dutch or Belgian coast – she begged for a picture to be placed in local newspapers so that he might be recognised. Relief only came when his body was recovered and buried. Such a fantasy was still present in the grandparents of a 7-week-old baby whose body was not recovered at the time of the first anniversary. In another family, whose adult son was never found, the parents still at one year spoke of his 'coming home', as if despite their intellectual acknowledgement that he was dead, and that it was his corpse they spoke of, at a deeper level they still expected him to walk through the door. They felt that the task of being parents was not complete until they had buried him. The counsellor who worked with these families described the problem thus: 'it was as if they did not know whether they could grieve or not; they knew what the task was, but they did not have the means to complete it'.

Naturally, the need of the relatives that every effort be made to recover lost bodies is overwhelming. When the oil rig *Alexander L. Keilland* was wrecked in the North Sea in 1980, thirty-six of the 123 deceased were not recovered. An initial attempt to right the rig failed, and only after three and a half years of uncertainty and campaigning on the part of the bereaved was the rig successfully righted. Only six bodies were found, and the rig was hastily sunk at sea.

For Norwegians (112) 'it has been an unbreakable rule for families and relatives to search for people lost in accidents'. This is based on the tradition that those who are drowned and not buried in a churchyard are unable to rest in peace, and return to haunt the living, drifting restlessly and vengefully across the ocean or along the shores. The characteristics of these ghosts include the following:

- they cry dreadfully;
- they search restlessly;
- they cling to and press people down; and
- they strike with sickness.

These can be seen as projections of the feelings and experiences of the bereaved for whom the 'certainty of death' of the loved one has not been established.

The seven bodies not recovered from the mud torrent that destroyed Buffalo Creek in 1972 left the remaining residents with an unspeakable horror, collectively held – 'people up and down the hollow live in fear that those remains will suddenly reappear one day' (81). One man found it diffi-cult to look at the creek 'because he half expects to see a decomposed hand reaching out of it'. A devoted gardener gave up her hobby because her first attempt at planting a rosebush after the flood unearthed a bone she thought might be human. A 9-year-old dug up a set of false teeth and suffered from nightmares thereafter.

Another problem stems from the fact that the badly damaged body may bear no resemblance to humanity, much less the physical appearance of the loved one. The Bradford fire left welded bones in pools of melted human fat. The relatives did not see these sights. For one family identifying effects, the following scene was enacted:

A constable carefully placed the contents of a plastic bag on the table. There was an assortment of charred, blackened articles; a watch strap, a small piece of string vest, a corner of shrivelled cardigan, a silver ring, indistinguishable from any other. In slow motion the relatives fingered the remains. When they got to the end, they started again. There was some nodding and shaking of heads, some whispers, sighs, staring. There were no tears – it was silent. Twenty minutes later they agreed he was dead. 'He did wear a cardigan ... he had a watch ... he always wore a string vest'. We left in silence (300).

With scanty evidence, the family had attempted to create certainty, a certainty which proved to be frail, for many such were left wondering 'Who was in that coffin?', or 'Was there anything in that box?' This is more than denial, this is doubt. Whereas denial gainsays the facts, doubt has a logical edge. The computer-aided precision of scientific detective work in identification is not emotionally satisfying. Some bereaved develop a 'questioning syndrome' (130), where doubt about the identification, or even the death, runs rife, and may block progress to resolution.

After the Zeebrugge disaster, bodies recovered immediately were mostly identified visually by relatives. Two patterns were apparent – one small group of relatives made premature identifications of bodies that were in fact not those of their loved ones. Others had to make repeated visits, even when the physical damage to the corpse was not extensive, allowing subtle changes in the body to block acceptance of reality. Thus some relatives need immediate certainty of the death, at the cost of the truth, whilst some prefer to postpone this certainty to allow room for hope.

The anguish associated with viewing the mutilated remains of a loved one is reflected in the words of a bereaved parent on Buffalo Creek:

My son was crushed up so bad, I went about four times trying to identify him. His head was just smashed to jelly. He had just a little bit of sideburn left, where you could tell it was him. All the bodies had swelled up so bad, you had to just keep looking and looking (81).

In many circumstances relatives may be prevented by well-meaning officials from seeing such sights. Following the Granville train disaster (290), thirty-six of the forty-four bereaved interviewed had not seen the body. The majority of those who had were widowers, and of eight, only one regretted this. Overall, those who saw the body had a more satisfactory outcome in terms of resolution of grief than those who did not. Twenty-two of the thirty-six who did not view regretted this, countering the argument of 'remember him how he was' with the assertion that 'nothing could be as bad as my fantasies of how he looked'.

In the first year after the Zeebrugge disaster (133) 19 per cent of a group of bereaved relatives said that they had viewed the bodies of the deceased. Interviewed between three and twelve months after the disaster, this group was significantly worse off on measures of general distress and anxiety. This of course conflicts with the picture of those bereaved by the train disaster. However, the two sets of interviews were carried out at different times – in the first year (Zeebrugge) and the second year (Granville) – and the difference possibly lay in this factor.

Indeed, a different picture appeared for the Zeebrugge bereaved at thirty months (134). The bodies recovered immediately, on the first night, were largely unchanged in appearance, but others, who spent six weeks under water before recovery, were changed. However, the reactions of those whose loved ones were recovered immediately, and those whose loved ones were recovered later, proved similar. Those who viewed bodies which were more damaged were not psychologically worse off. Whilst there were no real differences in overall psychological symptoms or measures of grief between those who viewed and those who did not (in contrast with the first year figures), significant differences were found on measures of trauma. Intrusive symptomatology (unpleasant, intrusive images and thoughts) was significantly lower in those who had viewed, as were symptoms of mental avoidance.

It would appear therefore that the one thing that might be feared, that is an increase in intrusive imagery or thoughts about the loved one and the events in which they met their death, did not occur in those who viewed. The notion that trauma and grief are separate entities is supported by these findings. Viewing had a positive effect on the psychological impact of trauma, but not on grief. When contrasted with the picture for Zeebrugge bereaved in the first year, it seems possible that those who view may be more distressed in the short term, but less distressed in the long term.

Following the Granville disaster, less than 10 per cent said they regretted viewing, and nearly two-thirds regretted not viewing. Thirty months after the Zeebrugge disaster, 11 per cent regretted viewing on the first night as against none at six weeks; 40 per cent regretted not viewing on the first night and 52 per cent at six weeks. It seems therefore a consistent picture that the decision to view is rarely regretted (particularly when thought through, as were decisions to view bodies recovered at six weeks), whilst the decision not to view is regretted by roughly half. Thirty-three per cent of the bereaved felt prevented from viewing.

People view bodies primarily not to identify them to the authorities, but to reassure themselves that it is indeed their loved one, and more simply for the sake of saying 'goodbye'. These reasons, and the process of viewing, would be familiar to those who work in casualty departments, or in maternity wards where babies may be stillborn, sometimes malformed (275).

It cannot be assumed that it is the process of viewing which leads to the lower levels of psychological symptoms. It may be that those who are more 'hardy' request to view and would have fewer symptoms anyway. However, for practical purposes, those who choose to view can do so with little psychological risk in the majority of circumstances. One important qualifier is that currently we know little of the effects of viewing bodies which are so badly damaged that they bear little resemblance to human beings at all. Perhaps this is an individual matter, in that a relative might be just as happy to view a relatively undamaged arm whilst the remainder of the severely damaged body remains covered. Good practice in relation to the viewing of bodies is reviewed in Chapter 5.

The potential consequences of these dilemmas is reflected in the story of one mother, who lost her son in the Zeebrugge disaster, and who began to wonder whether it was indeed her son's body in the grave. She had been advised not to view him. Attendance at the inquests failed to reassure her that it was her son who had been identified. She was invited to see photographs of his body after death. The first she viewed was one taken after the morticians had worked on him. She turned the photo round as if she could not work out which way was up. 'That is his forehead', she said, with some doubt in her voice. She was asked if she wished to see a photo of him as he was recovered, and was given a full length photo of him lying prone after his body had been hosed of mud. 'That's my boy – he could just be asleep in the garden now', she said, kissing her finger, putting it to the face in the photo, and handing it back.

The search for understanding

As with survivors, the bereaved need to develop understanding of the meaning of the tragic events, and may begin with the reasons for the death and the events surrounding it. 'The mourner obsessively reconstructs events in an effort both to comprehend the death and to prepare for it in retrospect' (252).

Information culled from death certificates is an initial clue to answering questions about the cause and nature of death, such as whether the loved one might have died painfully or not. Similarly, attendance at the inquest may bring answers to many questions, from information from post-mortems, or witness statements. One family who lost a son in the Zeebrugge disaster were able from this information to retrace his last steps and stand at the point where he met his death on an identical ship. Similarly there is a need to find out from other survivors what the loved one was doing when they died, such as whether they were involved in rescuing people, which may give more meaning to the senselessness of the loss.

Multiple loss

The father of five children who died together in a house fire wrote the following (233). 'It was a disaster, it was untidy, it was illogical, horrible and shocking, just as it was an affront to life. Reactions? Horror, shock, anger, utter disgust at life's cruelty.' It was nine years before he and his wife discussed in detail the events of that terrible day.

Those who are multiply bereaved are most depleted. They are coping with both the cumulative effects of several losses and the virtual eradication of social support networks, not only in terms of physical absence, but in terms of other relatives unavailable owing to their own grief. The bereaved person is thrown into a state of overload. 'Mourning for a given loved one is compromised by the concurrent crisis of the ongoing stalled, or delayed mourning for the other loved ones' (252). A cycle of incomplete grieving for each individual is set up, the unfinished business from grieving one preventing the completion of grieving for another. The bereaved person is faced with a variety of dilemmas. How can these loved ones be prioritised in grieving? How can they be differentiated?

PATHOLOGICAL GRIEF

In the follow-up of bereaved from the Granville train disaster (290), a hierarchy of risk was established. Most at risk in terms of poor resolution of grief were mothers losing children (aged up to their early twenties) and next were fathers in the same position. Intermediate were widows, with widowers faring best. Having a supportive social network, seeing the body, and receiving an intervention from an experienced counsellor tended to mitigate distress, but impressions gained from speaking to many of the families fifteen months after the event, particularly those who had lost young family members, indicated that 'many had not got over the loss, nor ever would, and, from what some of them said about their reaction at the time, it was clear that no amount of intervention at the time would have made any difference. There were people who could not or would not let go of the lost person and did not want to be assisted to do this.' In another study of bereavement by disaster (53), the personal meaning of the event proved to be of great importance. When the relationship was perceived as central, and the death as preventable, an intense and prolonged grieving process was observed.

The strong reactions of parents to the deaths of young adults give a good example of the violation of meaning that the bereaved experience. A young adult will have gone through the separations and struggles of adolescence, to become a person in their own right. The parent, perhaps approaching middle life, comes to see the child as their 'immortality', a representation of themselves which will survive their own death. With the young person gone, their immortality is gone. They may feel that their life has now had no meaning, or one which was only temporary. Nor, being at the age they are, is it often possible for such parents to have another child. One father in his fifties, who lost his only son in the Zeebrugge disaster, had supported him through university (he was in his last year when he died), their plan being that as soon as he qualified he would join his father's business. With the years, he would take over, and his father would retire. Now the business would not survive his own death, the father felt that there was no point in continuing it at all. The fact that he had a surviving daughter did not alter this feeling.

Other studies of those experiencing unexpected bereavement reinforce this picture. Those whose loved ones die suddenly and unexpectedly show a higher level of physical and psychiatric illness than those bereaved by expected deaths (198): 44 per cent of such a group (199) experienced intense grief with a high level of anxiety, and a lesser level of depression. Guilt was problematic for a number, with widows concerned about what they could have done to prevent the death of their husbands, and parents wondering if they had been good parents and if they had done enough for their children. Failure to view the body led to a longer initial period of denial. The loved one's grave became of great importance: 22 per cent visited the grave daily at first, and three-quarters of this group continued to do so at the two-year point. Those who had visited the grave once a week in the beginning did so once monthly at this stage. These visits were consciously motivated by a need to honour the memory of the deceased, to come as close as possible to them in order to mitigate the sense of abandonment, to try to understand what had happened, and to satisfy a need for activity. Unconsciously, these visits may well represent a search for the deceased, and hence represent denial.

At the start of this section it was suggested that trauma and grief overlap and interact. Trauma may clearly impede grieving. This is probably for four main reasons:

1   Re-experience phenomena, such as traumatic imagery concerning the death, may be triggered by memories of the deceased. Indeed, 'traumatic re-experiencing may replace grief-associated thoughts of the deceased' (227). The ways in which memories of the dead person are transformed by the process of normal grieving may therefore be blocked.
2   Post-traumatic rumination about the circumstances of the death, its cause, or real or imagined responsibility for it may preoccupy the bereaved, blocking normal grief-work.
3   Post-traumatic avoidance will prevent exposure to stimuli which normally trigger grieving and the extinction of grief.

4   Post-traumatic emotional numbing, leading to detachment, will prevent
     opportunities for supportive interactions with others which, amongst
     other things, allow for discussion which facilitates emotional processing
     of grief.

Bereavement is 'excluded from significant diagnoses' under DSM-IV (288).
'Even if a patient meets all the criteria for depression, DSM discourages us
from making that diagnosis if the person has been bereaved.' Given that the
diagnosis of PTSD is based upon etiology, the occurrence of a causative
event, it seems positively neglectful that such a well-recognised stressor as
bereavement should not be acknowledged as being causative of a cluster of
symptoms which can be sufficiently disturbing to emotions, thoughts and
behaviours to warrant formal recognition as a significant disorder in its own
right. ICD-10 'does not mention bereavement as an exclusionary factor in
diagnosing depression, or PTSD, and almost totally ignores grief'. It cate-
gorises grief-related problems under the heading of adjustment disorder, and
under that of prolonged depressive reaction if lasting longer than six
months. This, however, is only a 'mild depressive state'. DSM-IV suggests
that

> Bereavement is generally diagnosed instead of Adjustment Disorder
> when the reaction is an expectable response to the death of a loved
> one. The diagnosis of Adjustment Disorder may be appropriate
> when the reaction is in excess of, or more prolonged than what
> would be expected.

Only after two months is bereavement allowed to be considered as a major
depressive episode, if it persists in sufficient intensity. Although it is
acknowledged that there are features which differentiate grief from depression, no appropriate alternative is provided. As it has been succinctly put
(288), 'people may grieve, or be depressed, or both'. The major diagnostic
systems fail to address this properly.
   Outside of the major diagnostic systems, two sorts of attempts to classify
pathological grief can be observed: one based loosely on causation, and one
based loosely on its characteristics. On the basis of a longitudinal study
(240), three common patterns, or syndromes have been described:

1   The unexpected grief syndrome. Following the sorts of unexpected and
     untimely deaths typical in disaster, the intense experience of shock and
     disbelief delays the full emotional reaction and blocks moderate to high
     levels of anxiety. 'Typically, the grieving process is complicated by a
     persisting sense of the presence of the dead person, feelings of self
     reproach, and feelings of continued obligation to the dead which make
     it hard for the bereaved to make a fresh start' (86).

2   The ambivalent grief syndrome. Following a death in a relationship where there has been considerable ambivalence, the initial reaction may be one of relief, there is little felt need to grieve, and anxiety levels may not be high. As time passes, intense pining and despair emerges, reactions becoming more prolonged and self punitive in nature. 'The bereaved may feel compelled to make restitution for their failure, but see no satisfactory way to complete the process of grieving. These two types of reaction seem to account for most of the delayed griefs which are seen in psychiatric settings' (240).

3   Chronic grief. Following relationships characterised by dependence or clinging, the grief, expressed in full from the outset, endures for an abnormal length of time. 'Surprisingly, it is not always the survivor who was the more dependent member' (238).

These three grief syndromes may occur in any combination.

Other attempts to describe morbid grief have focused on the observable behaviour of the bereaved (182). Again, three patterns have been described:

1   Avoidance. Phobic avoidance of persons, places or things related to the deceased, combined with extreme guilt and anger about the deceased and the nature of their death often results in delayed grieving. A study of those bereaved by the Zeebrugge disaster (135) confirmed the notion that avoidance and denial are central to prolonged grief reactions as well as to post-traumatic reactions. Avoidance was strongly associated with all factors of a measure of grieving, whereas intrusion was only related to a reduced range of factors.

2   Idealisation. Here, grief and guilt are absent, but anger about the deceased and their death is usually present. This anger is directed at other people, places or things, and not at the deceased, who is idealised.

3   Prolonged grief/physical illness. The third pattern is of prolonged grief coupled with physical illness and recurrent nightmares in which the deceased is seen as alive. The illnesses are generally those which are seen as stress related, or exacerbated by stress, such as hypertension, diabetes, duodenal ulcer and asthma, and a diagnosis is often made of reactive depression.

2

TECHNOLOGICAL DISASTER

Technological disaster is an increasing phenomenon, occurring as the result of human error, or the malfunction of some structure or system. The creation of progressively complex systems enhances the potential for catastrophic mishap. Whilst such disasters often involve a fatal combination of the forces of nature and human error, there appear to be certain differences between natural and technological disasters (12).

Natural and technological disasters are both sudden and powerful. Whilst there is sometimes an element of warning in natural disaster (even though it may be ignored), there is generally none in technological catastrophe. There may only be seconds from the realisation that something is wrong to the impact, or lack of warning may make avoidance difficult. There may be awareness that a particular structure is inadequate for its purpose, or inadequate under certain extremes, such as the Buffalo Creek dam, which burst in 1972 with tragic consequences to the Appalachian communities in its wake, yet the population at risk is kept in ignorance. Alternatively, a system may be known to have failed, yet no remedial action is taken, and those at risk remain unaware of the danger. Thus prior to the Zeebrugge disaster, ferries had been reported as sailing with their bow doors open.

Both types of disaster can cause visible damage to a familiar environment, but some technological disasters do not have this effect. The invisible threat of environmental poisoning, such as nuclear pollution from an accident like that at Chernobyl, may be catastrophic yet cause no visible damage. This may make acceptance of the reality more difficult. Transport disasters often occur in a location unfamiliar to the survivors and inaccessible to the bereaved or even the rescuers.

Whilst natural disaster, such as volcano eruption or flooding, is often predictable to some degree, technological disaster is not. Technological catastrophes are never supposed to happen, and hence predictability is not an issue. The Zeebrugge disaster could not have been predicted as ferries are not supposed to sink, and the King's Cross underground fire could not have been foreseen as escalators are not supposed to erupt into flame.

Both types of disaster may have a clear low point, generally the impact stage, but some technological disasters do not. Thus the effects of toxic pollution may manifest themselves at different times for different people who have been exposed, sometimes unknowingly, simultaneously. The importance of the low point is that it provides a focus from which things may be expected to recover – in 'disasters without a footprint' (19), uncertainty about the process of recovery may be increased. People are left 'suspended in a stage of anticipation' there is no immediate closure to the situation, increasing the likelihood that individuals may use denial in an attempt to create their own closure.

Natural disaster is not seen as controllable, as indeed, nature is not controllable. As humans are supposed to be the masters of the technology they have created, catastrophe signifies a dramatic loss of control. This may be of particular importance owing to the possible relationship between the sense of loss of control and helplessness, and the known relationship between helplessness and depression (280).

The extent of effects of natural disaster tends to be limited to the immediate survivors, such as those made homeless in a particular location, whereas the effects of technological disaster may not. Thus the Chernobyl accident increased the fears of many people about the safety of nuclear power. A major air disaster may result in those who have anxieties about flying seeking alternative forms of travel. Lastly, the persistence of effects of natural and technological disaster may differ. A review of disaster follow-up studies (259) shows similar levels of psychological disturbance in the survivors of both after one year, but with a greater persistence of difficulties after this time for survivors of technological disaster.

Survivors of technological disaster differ from the survivors of natural catastrophes, therefore, in terms of (i) the emotions they pass through, (ii) the psychological symptoms they suffer, and (iii) the social processes they encounter (93).

In this chapter we will enhance the understanding of survival established by Chapter 1, by considering the experience and after-effects of a range of technological disasters, and also at 'personal disasters' which are 'human made', such as crime.

DISASTERS OF TRAVEL

Travel by road, rail, air and sea is a key feature of the modern world. People want to travel anywhere in the world as quickly and as cheaply as possible, and this has been the occasion for a multiplicity of tragedies.

45

Maritime disaster

The immediate experience of disaster at sea is vividly described by a survivor of the capsize of the *Herald of Free Enterprise* off Zeebrugge in 1987.

> The very next instant glasses and plates started to slide from the table on to the floor. I grabbed the table to steady myself, but I lost my grip and fell smashing into a table on the other side of the room. Looking up I saw to my horror people plummeting through the air and smashing through the glass partitions. The noise was indescribable, a cacophony of smashing glass, vehicles crashing down in the cargo hold and worst of all the screaming of my fellow passengers. The lights then failed, leaving the ship in total darkness. A new sound then came up through the ship, the sound of sea water rushing through the broken windows and doors. When I was a child I was rescued from drowning, and this memory of choking to death in water came rushing back and I could feel the terrible panic rising in me.

Shipwreck may involve a protracted struggle for survival. In 1973, a small cargo vessel, the *Southern Star*, with a crew of ten men capsized and sank off Tasmania. The men drifted for nine days on a raft, enduring cold and rough seas with little water and food, during which time one man died. On reaching land, three men sought help, which they found four days later, by which time two more of their fellows had died. Later, they described the ways in which they had coped (116).

The most common means of coping was through attachment ideation. The men thought for long periods about those they were closely attached to – wives, mothers, children and girlfriends. 'I just kept thinking about my wife and family – that was all I had to live for', remarked one. Another thought about his children – ' . . . when I paddled, I used to recite their names . . . it gave me determination'. Another method of coping used by all of the survivors was the drive to survive, the will to live. One man said 'this was my only thought . . . to get out of it . . . I never felt like giving up'. When the fear was voiced that there was no hope, one man described his response – 'I said we're going to get out of it . . . don't be so bloody stupid . . . we're this far . . . we're going to make it now'.

Modelling was another strategy used by all. It focused on the Chief Officer who became a 'model of competence, rationality and hope'. The emergence of leaders is a feature of the post-impact stage of many disasters. On the *Herald of Free Enterprise*, which contained a large number of military, many soldiers became group leaders. However, those with no leadership experience may find the resources to lead fellow passengers to safety. Unfortunately, leaders may have to take difficult decisions. Whilst passengers were escaping from the *Herald* up a hawser, one man froze and could not climb further, and cajoling and threats proved useless in getting him to move. One soldier climbed up the rope – 'I hit him and knocked him off into the water . . . I never saw him again and I think he drowned, but there was nothing else I could do'.

The other strategies used by the *Southern Star* survivors were prayer and hope. Although none of the men were previously religious, nearly all prayed. For some this took the form of bargaining – 'If You get me out of this lot, I'll play ball'. Out loud, the men often spoke of their hopes. This kept their spirits higher, and became more powerful through the force of suggestion by being spoken aloud. The power of these sorts of strategies may be reflected in the fact that the men who died did not use them.

In September 1994 the car ferry *Estonia* sank in the Baltic Sea with the loss of some 900 lives. Thirty-two survivors were taken to hospital where observations were made over four days (302). Immediately after rescue, the majority of survivors were calm and showed little emotion. This changed within a matter of hours. Denial was a prominent feature, typically a refusal to believe a relative was dead. Dissociative amnesia was present in four survivors who had lost relatives. They remembered 'everything except the final hours before being rescued', but their memories returned within two days. Two survivors showed euphoria in association with their denial. Anxiety was also prominent. Most survivors developed symptoms of increased arousal, which were generally worse in the night (when the disaster had happened). Six survivors showed phobic anxiety for darkness and enclosed places. Four survivors developed depressive reactions, with guilt evident, while three showed aggression, often alternating with strong feelings of guilt.

In 1975, in the Mediterranean, the aircraft carrier *USS Kennedy* collided with the guided missile cruiser *USS Belknap* which was extensively damaged. The crew participated in the fire-fighting and rescue for several hours, with no lighting, largely inoperative equipment, and with the ship rolling uncontrollably. Of the 336 on board, seven died and forty-six suffered injuries. When contrasted with the crew of a similar ship three years later (136), the following longer term psychological effects were seen: 11 per cent of the crew during this period had attended hospital for psychiatric reasons, the majority of these being anxiety-related problems. The highest percentage of difficulties was reported in a group who had been flown home, and hence separated from their crewmates. Thirteen crewmen were investigated more closely (202). All had symptoms associated with PTSD, and phobic anxiety was particularly strong, as most wanted to avoid sea duty and several wanted to be discharged from the navy. Similarly, nine months after the Zeebrugge disaster, of all forty-two crew survivors only three were on sea duty, seventeen having ended their seafaring careers.

The long term psychological effects of maritime disaster are reflected in the fate of the seven *Southern Star* survivors. Five out of seven were still suffering two years later from problems including depression, guilt, insomnia, poor concentration, nightmares and anxiety (116). Similar long term effects were found in the survivors of the explosion which destroyed the tanker *Mission San Francisco* following its collision with a freighter in the Delaware river in 1957. Thirty-five out of forty-five crew survived and were followed over a period of three and a half to four and a half years (181). Out of thirty-four survivors interviewed, twenty-six had received psychiatric help, and twelve had received this help as hospital in-patients. The main sorts of problems experienced were depression and anxiety, and a wide range of physical disorders, notably gastro-intestinal symptoms. Sleep was disturbed in many cases. Only a third were at sea with reasonable regularity, and well over a third had given it up. Nearly five years on, 71 per cent had appreciable psychological difficulties.

For these seamen, their problems had got worse with time rather than better. This was particularly true of the group who returned to sea on the basis that it was their livelihood, and who were regularly re-exposing themselves to a situation which had been the source of sudden massive anxiety – 'the knowledge that "it had happened" generated and perpetuated the fear that "it will happen"'. They were continually resensitising themselves, and their anxiety consequently never dissipated.

Survivors of the Zeebrugge disaster who were assessed for compensation purposes during the first year following the disaster showed high levels of distress. All were found to be suffering from recognisable psychological distress, with 53 per cent assessed as moderately to severely depressed, and 90 per cent as suffering from PTSD (110). The survivors and bereaved of this disaster have been followed over five years. Interviewed during the first year, seven factors appeared in standardised assessments made of symptom levels (133). These were severe depression (by far the most important factor), anxiety, re-experiencing, reactive depression, anger, avoidance and constricted affect. Post-traumatic symptoms played a smaller (although clear) role in the picture of distress than had been expected. Predictably, the bereaved suffered more depressive symptoms whilst the survivors had significantly more symptoms of post-traumatic stress. The multiply bereaved had higher anxiety scores, but were not significantly more depressed than the singly bereaved. It was severe depression that showed the most improvement during the first year.

Those who reported social supports as being helpful did not appear to benefit from any protection, not differing in the extent of symptoms from those who perceived the quality of support as mixed. However, when survivors were asked whether family conflict was present in the early days following the disaster, those who reported such conflict (33 per cent) were more troubled by severe depression and re-experience phenomena.

Counselling had a beneficial effect, but only in terms of lower levels of anxiety, constricted affect and avoidance.

Whether survivors were injured or not had no effect on extent of symptoms. Their perception of how they coped during the disaster showed a complicated pattern of trends in terms of effect on later distress. Those who managed as well as they expected tended to have the lowest scores on re-experience phenomena, whilst those who did much more than they expected and those who felt they let themselves or others down had lower anger scores. Those who felt that they were going to die (78 per cent) had a trend towards less depression.

At thirty months (156, 158), crisis support from family and friends and life events were the two best predictors of measures of general psychological distress. Thus other factors above and beyond exposure to the traumatic event are important in determining the severity and chronicity of symptoms. The perception of helplessness during the disaster and bereavement were the two best predictors of intrusive phenomena. At five years (160) levels of distress were still raised, albeit decreased. Intrusion and avoidant symptoms were predictive of depression and anxiety; thus 'the longer the time elapsed since the trauma, the more likely will intrusive thoughts predict poor outcome'.

Air disaster

The aeroplane is the safest means of transport yet it is the most common travel-related phobia. Factors which may cause psychological complications for those involved in the aftermath of air disaster include the absence of any community focus for survivors and bereaved (passengers having come from many different places); the possibility that the crash site is far away or isolated and inaccessible (although 85 per cent of air crashes occur at airports); and the likelihood that a great deal of physical damage will have been done to the corpses, creating problems for the process of identification, and making acceptance on the part of the bereaved difficult. Thus, after the 1985 Gander air disaster, in which all 248 American soldiers returning from a peacekeeping mission in Sinai died, in many cases it was over six weeks before a positive identification was made, and two and a half months before the last 'body' was identified (327).

A survivor of the 1989 Kegworth M1 air disaster gave the following account (229) of the impact.

> There was a severe bang and we heard the captain say on the intercom 'Prepare for a crash landing'. The lady next to me put her head down and waited for the worst ... I tried to do everything I could to take her mind off what was happening. She squeezed my hand. ... When we hit the ground there was just a massive crash

like a multiple car accident . . . I could see a tree outside and knew we had hit the ground and must get out as quickly as possible.

The profound post-impact shock which results is reflected in the responses of those who escaped from the 1985 Manchester aircraft fire: 'dazed passengers were wandering in front of the blazing aircraft. They were like lambs, they needed directions' (261).

When disaster response plans at airports represent the best of organisation and emergency technology, it is striking that little account has been taken of the human needs of those who are involved. Five major categories of persons who may need psychological care include the cockpit crew, the cabin crew, the passengers, the families of victims, and the crisis workers and personnel (341). Given that aeroplanes may crash on communities, they too may be added to this list.

A 1974 Boston air disaster killed all eighty-nine passengers aboard and a joint social work and nursing team from Boston City Hospital offered a support service, meeting relatives as they arrived at the mortuary, and conducting a supportive yet fact-finding interview offering an opportunity to express feelings (172). Grief at the death and anxiety about the future were coupled with apprehension about viewing and identifying the deceased, concern with funeral arrangements, and hostility towards the airline, especially as the identification procedure became more complicated and demanding. This hostility and bitterness often involves issues of blame and accusations of negligence, and crystallises into a lengthy battle for financial compensation. Conversely, the pilot, crew and company may feel an intense guilt, even if this is not rationally based.

> Families who lose their fliers . . . are exposed, with little warning, to a long-dreaded and long-feared actuality which mandates a total change in their lives. . . . In addition to [their] mourning, [they] may feel anger at the dead flier for abandoning [them] or for continuing a career that they all knew was so dangerous. This anger may be complicated by the guilt that [they] feel over the anger, by the depression at [their] loss, and by . . . fears for the future. Furthermore, the family of crew may be subjected through speculative newscasts and gossip to . . . subtle belittling of the dead [crew's] flying ability, reasons why [they] should not have been flying that day, rehashing of the events so that everyone understands what the right thing to do would have been. . . . When the cause of the mishap is directly attributable to 'pilot error', the effects of guilt, anger, and blame on the crew's family may be especially intense (154).

Designers, service personnel, air-traffic controllers, flight instructors and other pilots may feel anxiety or responsibility.

Grief is felt intensely throughout a company after a crash and even across companies because of the camaraderie within the industry, such that, for example, flight attendants will send large funeral flower sprays to the offices of another company's flight attendants as an expression of condolence after a crash (341).

Grief within a company can be complicated by pre-existing poor morale that may intensify common reactions of guilt or anger.

A follow-up of eight of the sixty-four survivors from the world's worst air disaster, the 1977 Tenerife jumbo jet collision, in which 580 passengers died, reflects the devastating psychological after-effects. Each victim suffered from all or 75 per cent of the symptoms of a traumatic neurosis, uncontrollable emotions (especially anxiety and rage), sleep disturbances and mental repetitions of the trauma in nightmares or daydreams (243).

One of the survivors of this disaster suffered considerable guilt and self-blame because he had been unable to save his wife:

[Martin] sat stunned and motionless for some twenty-five seconds after the [other plane] hit. He saw nothing but fire and smoke in the aisles, but he roused himself and led his wife to a jagged hole above and behind his seat. Martin climbed out onto the wing and reached down and took hold of his wife's hand, but 'an explosion from within literally blew her out of my hands and pushed me back and down onto the wing'. He reached the runway, turned to go back after her, but the plane blew up seconds later. . . . [Five months later] Martin was depressed and bored, had 'wild dreams', a short temper and became easily confused and irritated. 'What I saw there will terrify me for ever', he says. He . . . avoided television and movies, because he couldn't know when a frightening scene would appear (243).

The reactions of a 44-year-old woman who lost her son, daughter-in-law and two grandchildren in an air disaster indicate the profound nature of the reactions:

Having heard of the crash, she was full of dread but was unable to confirm whether they had been on the plane or not. It was a week before their deaths were confirmed. She could not see their bodies or go to the site of the crash. She dreamed constantly of it and of them. She was despairing and filled with anger that they had been cheated of life by the accident, when all had seemed to be going so well for them. She felt that she was 'old', had lived her life and that somehow she should have died in their place (258).

Aircraft may crash on the communities beneath them. The 1988 crash of a

Pan Am jumbo jet onto Lockerbie resulted in the deaths of all passengers and crew and eleven people on the ground. Sixty-six residents of the town were interviewed ten to fourteen months after the disaster for the purposes of compensation claims (35). The main diagnoses were PTSD (forty-eight survivors) and depression (nineteen survivors), followed by other anxiety disorders. Eighteen did not suffer from any recognised disorder. There were few predictors of diagnosis, but symptomatology as measured by questionnaire was influenced by age, death of friends and exposure to unpleasant sights. At thirty-six months the same pattern of diagnoses persisted. Those who had recovered were individuals whose suffering had been relatively mild when seen previously. There was thus a core of chronic reactions, totalling 56 per cent of those interviewed.

In 1987, two aircraft belonging to a famous British aerobatic team, the Red Arrows, collided and crashed onto a small Lincolnshire village. Nobody was killed, but one home was demolished and two badly damaged by one plane, whilst the other crashed in a nearby field. Six months later, villagers were interviewed about their feelings since the event (178). Only 14 per cent remembered feeling worried about their own safety since the crash, mainly those who had seen some of the events, or who had interpreted the explosions as coming towards them; 20 per cent felt angry that the crash had occurred, but 15 per cent felt nothing at all, these largely being men with military experience. Just under half those interviewed felt personally affected by the incident, especially younger people with dependent children. Thirty-two per cent had symptoms commonly associated with trauma, but only half felt these were directly related to the crash. Unsurprisingly, those who lived nearest to the site of the accident were those who had more symptoms characteristic of PTSD. Just over half were worried about the incident and a possible recurrence, a fear perhaps made worse by continued low flying and the fact of three further crashes in the vicinity by the same team. The community, it appeared, was sensitised and resensitised.

Rail disaster

At 8.00 a.m. on 18 January 1977 the 6.09 from Mt Victoria, near Sydney, Australia, passed under the Bold Street bridge at Granville, and its engine was derailed. The stanchion of the bridge was knocked down, and its concrete span fell to crush two carriages. Those nearby described an 'awful silence' before survivors began to emerge. It was two days before the slab was finally drilled into smaller pieces and lifted. Flattened bodies were found intact in the carriages – as one rescue worker described: 'It was like a pizza – all crushed they were'.

The reaction of most survivors after their escape was one of 'numbness, unreality and of almost detached calm' (24). One survivor, a bank manager, looked back along his carriage and saw many severely injured people. The thought in his mind, however, was that he would not be able to appear at work with his clothes torn and dirty. Other passengers from the rear of the train walked calmly past the crushed carriages showing little, if any, emotional response. Panic was virtually absent, and survivors lay or sat quietly and passively, following evacuation instructions with 'almost child-like obedience'. For the survivors, the onlookers, and even those trapped alive in the wreckage, it was as if they were experiencing a dream-like state of unreality.

Changes in emotional responses occurred within a matter of hours. Survivors often cried uncontrollably, and felt extremely fearful, as the horror began to dawn on them. Often it was being reunited with family members that caused this change, as if seeing loved ones brought home the realisation of what might have been lost. This reaction lasted several days during which many survivors felt an urgent need to talk about their experiences and to get as much detail as possible about the disaster.

Over the following days uninjured survivors made a 'superficial return to normality'. Returning to work they became increasingly unwilling to discuss their experiences and often actively avoided media coverage. Symptoms of anxiety, irritability, insomnia, nightmares and depression persisted and often worsened. In particular, an almost universal fear of train travel developed, and

> those who went back to commuting often misinterpreted the normal sound of the carriages passing over points and bridges as the commencement of another derailment. For many weeks after the accident, the train leaving at the same time as the fatal one was almost deserted.

Many survivors began to experience guilt for failing to save fellow passengers, and a sense of anger at those held responsible for the crash. Alternatively, those who would normally have been in the crushed carriages 'were elated, yet felt guilty as though they had condemned the occupants of the seats to death'.

The reactions of the bereaved were initially those of shock and disbelief (258). One widow recalled that first day:

> They announced it in a news flash. It hit me like some terrible blow. At first I couldn't believe it. We watched the television. It was something like a nightmare. It didn't feel real. I couldn't convince myself he was there. I kept thinking he must be at work, although I really knew he wasn't.

A bereaved father described his experiences:

> My daughter . . . used to sit in the first carriage and when I heard about the crash, I thanked God because I thought she'd be all right. Then I rang her work just to check and they said she wasn't in yet. I felt my heart start to thump and a feeling of panic was rising inside me.

After an agonising day attempting to obtain information, he was asked to go to the morgue.

> It was her all right – I knew from her dress, although it was all torn and bloodstained, and part of her face was crushed, and she was sort of swollen all over. I just broke down. I felt my heart was breaking. There she was dead.

Eighty-three people were killed, and a similar number were injured. A counselling service was set up immediately in the city morgue (257) and the bereaved were followed up over a period of eighteen months. Three groups of bereaved were identified: widows, widowers, and parents losing an adult child. At approximately one and a half years after the disaster many of the bereaved were still suffering greatly: 25 per cent had adjusted well, 45 per cent were doing badly, and 30 per cent fell in the intermediate category. Mothers who had lost young adult children fared worst, followed by widows and fathers, with widowers faring best (290).

Those who were faring badly were divided equally between those whose physical health had deteriorated and those whose psychological health had suffered, except for the mothers, most of whom experienced chronic depression. A fifth of all those followed up had had contact with the psychiatric services, and two mothers had been hospitalised. Those who had supportive social networks tended to do better, as did those who had received bereavement counselling, particularly if it had been provided with skill and had been perceived as helpful.

Many painful feelings had to be endured by the bereaved. Anger was prominent. One bereaved father commented: 'I hated the world and the railways and everyone. Our lives seemed to have no point anymore – there was nothing to go on for. I gave up all interest in life and still feel that way now.' A bereaved mother was more specific in her anger:

> I was so angry about my son's death. It should never have happened. The railways had been in a shocking state for years – everyone knew that. Then they said it was no one's fault. It had to be. He should never have died. I felt like smashing them all, punishing them. I would sue them for everything I could. There was no other way to get back at them for what they had done.

Guilt was another very difficult feeling. One parent described how:

I nearly went mad. My son never caught that train as a rule. . . . But that morning we had an argument, and he asked me to drive him to the train, and I wouldn't. I said, 'you can walk. You can find out how tough life's meant to be.' So he did, and he missed his train and caught that one instead. I've killed him just as surely as if I'd put the gun to his head and fired the bullet.

As another parent described, particular reminders could be devastating:

I thought I could manage things . . . until the children started playing trains. They had this big train. They used to play with their father before he was killed. But now they played a game called the bridge smash. They'd smash the train into everything. . . . It was quite violent really. I couldn't bear it. It was like my nightmares, and it brought them all back.

In the long term, the emptiness of life had to be faced. This is summed up in the words of one bereaved person: 'I've been visiting the grave each day for months now. I feel all right while I'm there – as though I'm with her. But the rest of the time, my life is empty. I can't believe she'll never come back.'

Summary – common features of transport disasters

The following features of transportation mass disaster (TMD) have implications for the emotional adjustment of those involved (125).

1 TMD almost always occurs without warning, very suddenly. This increases the sense of shock for survivors, which is reflected in the high reported incidence of 'disaster syndrome' immediately post-impact.
2 TMD may take place in locations inaccessible immediately to rescuers, increasing the number of fatalities through the deaths of injured survivors, and subjecting others to a protracted struggle for survival.
3 TMD often occurs in an environment unfamiliar to survivors, increasing their sense of disorientation. This also creates problems for relatives of survivors and the bereaved, in terms of increased delay in the arrival of news and other communication problems including language barriers.
4 Particular types of TMD may be totally catastrophic with nearly 100 per cent fatalities, as in air disaster.
5 TMD may involve impact at speed which results in severe damage to bodies, a factor which increases the stresses on recovery teams, causes additional difficulties in identification and creates particular emotional difficulties for the bereaved, especially if they do not see the corpse.
6 In some instances of TMD, bodies may be buried hastily, perhaps unidentified, at impact sites. Similarly, bodies may never be recovered at

all, as often occurs in maritime disaster, this being potentially extremely problematic for the bereaved.

7 In TMD, of all forms of technological disaster, there may be particularly high levels of long term psychological disturbance in victims.

8 Re-entering the situation in which the trauma occurred may be necessary for all sorts of reasons, and this may have a resensitising effect, causing high levels of long-lasting emotional distress. One of the particular features of TMD PTSDs is phobic avoidance.

9 The sense of loss of control and helplessness is high in the aftermath of TMD, which may influence levels of depressive difficulties.

10 Anger is prominent, often directed at the operator.

11 Guilt is a prominent emotion for survivors, and may be particularly so for the crew involved, whether this is rationally based or not.

12 The importance of post-disaster cohesion amongst survivors is important, particularly where a group of crew are concerned.

13 The survivors and bereaved of TMD will be scattered over a wide geographical area, and there is rarely a community focus. This may lead to an intense sense of isolation, and present considerable difficulties to attempts at organised psychological support.

14 There may be widespread, if temporary, loss of confidence in a particular type of transportation, especially in certain locations associated with the disaster.

DISASTERS OF FIRE

The spread of fire is quick. It is difficult for those who have never experienced a fire to comprehend this. One woman who left her house to ring for the fire brigade, returned within sixty seconds to find that fire had engulfed the stairs, dooming her family to death. 'I had seen bonfires . . . ', she said, 'they looked so contained.'

Many of the initial reactions of those escaping from the 1985 Bradford fire were of calm acceptance. Those who suffered burns did not actually experience being burnt. Rather, they experienced two sensations, one physical and one psychological. On a physical level, survivors experienced heat, from which they fled. Once on the pitch, having escaped, many went home without inspecting themselves. They felt nothing except a sense of physical and mental numbness. Some drove home to have their relatives point out that they had no shoes on – they had been burnt off. In some cases, trousers and socks had melted, unnoticed, into flesh. One man received a cursory inspection at hospital of his face and hands. On the bus home someone pointed out that his trousers were full of blood and pus. He returned to hospital, experiencing pain for the first time.

On the psychological level, the experience was of terror, leading to the single-minded attempt to escape. Panic is assumed to occur often in fire, yet if the criterion of lack of goal-directed action is applied, it might be said that few involved at Bradford panicked. Most actions were indeed goal directed towards escape. Unfortunately, the single-minded way in which this was carried out often led to anti-social behaviour, which was the cause of strong feelings of shame and guilt.

It was a disaster of fire, Boston's 1942 Coconut Grove nightclub fire, which proved the spur for major progress in the understanding of bereavement reactions (185). A celebration of a football victory turned to tragedy when a young man lit a match whilst trying to change a light bulb and set fire to a decorative palm tree. The sudden spread of fire resulted in the deaths of nearly 500 people.

On the 'disaster ward' of a local hospital, of thirty-nine patients admitted, seven died within sixty-two hours. Of the survivors, 'at least fourteen presented neuropsychiatric problems' (50). One such was a woman who had severe burns to hands and face. She remembered the fire pursuing her upstairs, and:

> By the time she got up there she already found herself stumbling over many bodies and was afraid that she would not reach the door. She felt suddenly that the fire was God's punishment because she had fallen below her standards. She prayed aloud and other people fell in with her prayer. While she was praying she somehow was shoved over a pile of dead bodies and finally her hand reached out into fresh air.

In hospital she had frequent flashbacks, and had an intense fear of being left alone without ready access to others. She was bitter and resentful.

A young man of 32 received only minor burns, but his wife died after five days. Initially he seemed relieved of his worry about her fate and returned home, but within weeks he was returned to hospital by his family. He was agitated, preoccupied and frightened, unable to concentrate on anything. 'Nobody can help me. What is going to happen? I am doomed, am I not?', he would remark. He complained of his extreme tension, inability to breathe, weakness and frantic fear that something terrible was going to happen. 'I'm destined to live in insanity or I must die. I know that it is God's will. I have this awful feeling of guilt', he said, constantly reviewing the events, where he had fainted trying to pull his wife out, and had been shoved out by the crowd. 'I should have saved her or I should have died too', he said. He felt full of 'an incredible violence' and did not know what to do about it. On the sixth day of his hospital stay he jumped through a window to his death.

The experience and consequences of fire in packed buildings are also captured in the 1977 Beverly Hills Supper Club fire. At 9.30 p.m. fire broke out at the club near Cincinnati, Ohio. More than 2,500 people were present, mostly in the central cabaret room, listening to the orchestra. When the fire became apparent, evacuation began, but as the smoke became dense, two exits from the cabaret room became jammed with those trying to escape. One hundred and sixty-five died. The accounts of survivors speak for themselves (191)

> As smoke billowed into the room, Mr K lost contact with his wife. He quickly assessed his distance from the exit and concluded he could not make it out and would face almost certain death unless something miraculous were to happen. He then suddenly found himself walking across the tops of booths bypassing the blocked passage way. As a result, he was amongst the last patrons to leave the fire safely. But once outside, he realised that he had saved his own life without tending to his wife's safety. He anticipated intense shame when his children would ask why mother was not out safely with him. Three hours later, he learned his wife had been carried to safety through a separate exit, and an emotional reunion followed.

Mr L was a member of the orchestra:

> When the fire began, he remembered remaining behind to assist the conductor in collecting copies of an original score from the musicians' stands. As dense smoke entered, he signalled the danger to the conductor and left, thinking the conductor was directly behind him. After he passed through the exit, it 'exploded with fire'. The conductor was still inside, and he suspected he had died. Mr L assisted others in going through the stack of bodies outside the supper club, trying to identify the conductor and other members of the orchestra. At one point he saw his best friend, Michael, outside the club, but later learned that Michael had collapsed and died.

Some six months later, the Fire Aftermath Center was opened, and attempted to mount an outreach service to the survivors, bereaved and rescue workers. Few survivors formally engaged with the centre (190). A number of victims were followed up at the one-year mark (107). One group were survivors of the event, (the 'At Fire' group), the other (the 'Not at Fire') group largely comprised the bereaved. One year on, the latter group had higher levels of general symptoms, with anxiety and hostility predominant. There was a significant decrease in all measures in the second year for the 'Not at Fire' group, but not for the 'At Fire' group, for whom levels of hostility actually increased.

In 1978, a fire broke out at the City Hotel, Boras, in Sweden, where many young people were celebrating their graduation from school. Of about 175 young people, twenty died and forty-nine were injured to some extent. Three months after the disaster (196) everyone, injured and uninjured, appeared in the acute stage to be suffering psychological distress to much the same extent. After six months, 25 per cent of the injured and nearly 50 per cent of the uninjured had no symptoms at all. Eight months later a smaller group were interviewed. At this point, over half had symptoms of anxiety, and rage was prominent for 25 per cent. About a third felt they had 'got over' the experience, and these tended to be people who did not report traumatic events involving loss in their childhood. The judgements of the professional interviewers, however, were at variance with survivors' views on their own state of recovery – none of those who were judged to have had a good resolution felt that they themselves had got over the experience, and none of those who felt that they had recovered were observed to have achieved this.

After the 1987 King's Cross underground station fire, fifty individuals contacting a helpline service were assessed during the first year (326): 66 per cent scored on tests in the range likely to indicate psychiatric 'caseness'. Both amount of traumatic exposure and personality (e.g. neuroticism) were implicated in the high levels of intrusion, avoidance and general distress. Spontaneous debriefing, talking about one's experiences to family and friends soon after, appeared to lead to lower symptom scores. Although this finding was not robust, those who did talk reported it as helpful.

Fire, possibly of all traumas, brings the most vivid intrusive imagery. For one Bradford survivor, the cue was the flashing blue lights of police cars from the station next door. The blue sheen coming over the top of the curtains playing across her ceiling would make her break into a cold sweat, palpitate and hyperventilate. The experience of fire also generates fear and hypervigilance. Another Bradford survivor sleeps with his keys by the side of his bed, the longest pointing towards the door, so he knows which direction to go in smoke. There would be a constant fear of matches, electrical appliances and sparks from open fires.

In Chapter 1 we examined three areas of violated assumptions (151): the increased sense of vulnerability; the loss of the sense of predictability; and the loss of sense of basic goodness. These fit with the two main experiences of surviving fires: the experience of being in fire, and the experience of being burnt (131). The experience of being in fire, with its consequent imagery, hypervigilance and fear, is clearly related to the increased sense of vulnerability and the loss of the sense of predictability.

The experience of being burnt generates different problems. Embarrassment and shame were common in respect of burn scars. One woman whose hair had been burnt off at Bradford remarked: 'When I go to bed with my husband at night, he knows and I know'. The process of healing was long and tedious. One man's daughter had to remove his body stocking daily, get him into a tepid bath, and wash him so that a nurse could examine his wounds. This became her sole task in relation to her father, and she came to feel taken for granted. Her father in turn felt humiliated. These sorts of experiences attacked the survivors' sense of competence, eroding their sense of basic goodness.

DISASTERS OF BUILDING COLLAPSE

Ever since places to live and work in have been built, they have fallen down, either because of unsound construction, or because forces of nature have proved too powerful. The UK's 1966 Aberfan disaster, where 116 children and twenty-eight adults died when a coal tip slipped to engulf a school, is a painful example of the interaction of lack of foresight, the power of nature, and the vulnerability of human structures.

The Hyatt Regency Hotel in Kansas City was the setting for an appalling building collapse disaster in 1981. A large number of individuals were enjoying a Friday night tea-dance. Others were dining in an open mezzanine restaurant that overlooked the dancers on the lobby floor, and some were in an enclosed restaurant on the same level. An unknown number of observers were watching from the vantage point of the sky walks, which spanned the west side of the lobby. In all, there were probably 1,500 to 2,000 people in the vicinity of the sky walks when two of them collapsed suddenly onto the dance floor below, killing 114 and injuring more than 200.

Some spoke of a 'snap or cracking sound, others a rumble or a roar' (340). To some it appeared 'like a slow motion movie . . . women's dresses billowing out as they fell . . . then the whole mass settled'. On the dance floor there was 'a huge pile of steel, concrete dust, and people . . . then water flowing down from broken pipes on the fourth floor . . . the blood, the dust, and the water made a strange, penetrating odour that seemed to last forever'. The frailty of the human body was pitifully exposed, as 'Bodies had literally exploded under the tremendous impact; limbs had been amputated; a foot, a leg, an arm independent of a body was not an infrequent sight'. One person was

> compressed into the shape of a letter Z. The stomach of one man protruded through his mouth. Another man was cut neatly in half just below the thorax . . . other bodies were split open and some were crushed beyond recognition. A few persons, still conscious, were partially pinned, while in other instances several were trapped together and often tried to console each other.

Under the supervision of stunned staff, guests formed orderly lines and left quietly, most being subdued, polite and helpful. Some began to help remove rubble from easily accessible victims, and within ten minutes the emergency services had arrived. Hospitals that night found themselves dealing with the mildly injured and disturbed relatives in addition to the severely injured. Within three days the city's seven community mental health centres were maintaining long opening hours offering counselling, and for three to four weeks special groups were well attended.

Survivors, rescuers and observers (but not the bereaved) were interviewed in the succeeding five months: 85 per cent suffered repeated recall of the event, and in 20 per cent this was severe enough to interfere with everyday functioning. Sadness was almost as frequent a complaint, and 55 per cent of a group who suffered recurrent feelings of anxiety and/or depression found this experience frightening; 74 per cent had sleep disturbances and half had dreams, 24 per cent experiencing nightmares, although not always of the disaster. Guilt was present in 44 per cent, either from being fortunate to be alive or from not having done enough to relieve pain and suffering or save life. Anger was experienced by 55 per cent, although for nearly half of this group it was non-specific in nature, and for 22 per cent this anger was directed at the builder. Those who were over 40 tended to experience a higher frequency of symptoms, particularly in terms of recurrent anxiety and depression. The presence of emotional problems prior to the disaster did not, however, predict a worse outcome.

In terms of strategies which helped with these difficulties, 37 per cent found talking about the event to be the best means of coping, whilst 18 per cent found getting back into the routine of work most helpful; 80 per cent found the support of their families helpful. Nearly a third of the sample had attended group counselling sessions and all but one person found this helpful; 20 per cent stated that they did nothing. Not all victims viewed their experiences negatively. Some stated that they were more tolerant of people, did not get so angry, enjoyed life more, could not ignore suffering, felt closer to their loved ones or had reaffirmed their faith in God.

DISASTERS OF ENVIRONMENTAL POISONING

Hiroshima, Seveso, Three Mile Island, Bhopal and Chernobyl are names that reflect the uniquely twentieth-century phenomena of human beings' capacity to poison catastrophically themselves and their natural environment. In addition to loss of human life, people may be condemned to crippling illnesses, future lives in the form of unborn babies may be destroyed, powerful anxieties about such possibilities as genetic damage may be raised, the animal world may be dramatically affected, and the earth, air and water may be irrevocably polluted. This pollution may have occurred suddenly, with dramatic initial symptoms such as choking and blindness, as at Bhopal, where nearly 3,500 died and 55,000 have needed hospital treatment. The threat may be palpable in the form of a cloud of toxic waste, or may be invisible as with radiation, its effects insidious, with cancers appearing after many years.

The 1981 toxic oil catastrophe in Spain resulted in over 20,000 people being affected, including 349 deaths. It is believed that the tragedy was caused by adulterated rape seed oil sold door to door as olive oil. For patients surviving the acute stage of the illness, there were 'problems of paralysis, atrophy, infection and subjective complaints, and families decimated by illness and death' (192). A third of those affected were referred to psychiatrists for help. Seventy-one per cent were women, and more than two-thirds were experiencing anguish, anxiety, sadness and depression; more than half were suffering irritability and insomnia; and 20 to 30 per cent were suffering changeable mood, loss of short term memory, loss of concentration, feelings of personal inadequacy or loss of vitality. Women showed greater sadness, depression, variable mood, loss of concentration and short term memory and eating difficulties. The extent to which the catastrophe itself was the key element in causing this disturbance is reflected in the fact that three-quarters of this group had no previous history of involvement with psychiatrists or reported being 'nervous'. Less than 10 per cent were judged as having a 'poor adaptation' to life prior to their illness. Also, those referred were not those with the most severe toxic oil syndrome.

Toxic accidents can generate massive anxieties in communities. A leak of toxic chemicals from a ship at Parnell in New Zealand (210) was given extensive media coverage, emphasising the hazardous nature of what had occurred. Many people came for medical help with symptoms of dizziness, headaches, weakness, sweating, nausea, confusion and anxiety. The doctors, however, could find no cases of actual organophosphate poisoning, and it seemed likely that the symptoms were a reflection of the high level of residents' anxiety.

Similarly, in January 1985, the town of Karlskoga in Sweden was affected by a leak of oleum gas from the town's large chemical industry. Since there was no wind, the cloud hung over the central part of the town. Although the gas was not highly toxic it was very irritating to the respiratory system, and some people were trapped in their homes for about twelve hours. Some had to consult doctors with respiratory problems, but no one was seriously injured. The central factor for the victims was therefore the sense of threat to life.

Various groups of people affected were interviewed about their experiences (200). Rescue personnel felt more prepared for the incident, but had a more unpleasant experience of the disaster. They were more preoccupied by thoughts and feelings about the events to the exclusion of other things than those residents who were directly affected. This group developed more depression and guilt feelings that they had let themselves or others down. Those who were trapped in their homes were worst affected, with more unpleasant feelings and thoughts about events, and a higher degree of depression, feeling less able to get over the experience. People with previous mental health problems felt less able to recover from the experience and had a more intense fear of dying and a high degree of depression, although not as high as those who had been trapped.

Nuclear accidents give another example of the anxieties that may arise. The nuclear accident at Three Mile Island, Pennsylvania, in 1979, has received a good deal of attention in terms of study of the reactions of various groups in the surrounding community. The accident began with the failure of several water pumps, which was compounded by equipment failures, inappropriate procedures, human errors and ignorance. Despite initial official assurances that there was no cause for concern, within two days all within ten miles (sixteen kilometres) of the plant were advised to remain indoors, and all pregnant women and pre-school children were advised to leave a five-mile (eight-kilometre) radius. The threat of a hydrogen explosion receded within days, but the threat in the minds of residents did not. The President's Commission concluded that 'the mental stress to which those living within the vicinity of the Three Mile Island were subjected was quite severe'. It also concluded that the distress was 'short-lived'.

The following are highlights of the major findings of the Task Force on Behavioural Effects (70) which reported to the President's Commission:

1   In the general population and sample of mothers of young children, the highest level of demoralisation was found in the month following the disaster, dropping swiftly in the second and third months. Only 14 per cent of the mothers sought professional help, the rest relying on their usual social supports (33).

2   People living in the five-mile (eight-kilometre) radius had significantly more psychological symptoms than people living five to ten miles (eight to sixteen kilometres) away from the plant.

3   Of the teenagers studied at the end of the second month, those who were most symptomatic tended to live within five miles (eight kilometres), had evacuated the area, and had a pre-school sibling. Levels of symptoms decreased over time in a pattern similar to that observed among the adults.

4   Workers, particularly non-supervisory employees, had significantly more distress than workers in an unaffected plant. The presence of a pre-school child at home enhanced the impact of the accident, particularly amongst supervisors, who had low job esteem. The potential for self-blame in the supervisor group therefore increased the severity of difficulties (163).

Another group that was studied was people with a history of psychiatric problems who lived in the vicinity (34). No overall differences could be found between such patients and a similar group of patients who lived near nuclear installations elsewhere, but two subgroups did, however, appear to be more at risk. Firstly, a group of patients who continued to believe that the nuclear facility was still actively dangerous, and secondly, a group who lacked a supportive social network.

One and a half years after the accident (85), residents of Three Mile Island continued to experience greater stress than people living elsewhere. They reported more distressing symptoms, including physical complaints, anxiety and alienation. The stress interfered with such behaviours as the ability to concentrate, and was also reflected in high levels of body chemicals (urinary catecholamines) which are associated with stress. Although the levels of these measures reflected mild stress, it had become persistent. Some residents experienced less stress than others, and these tended to be people who had the benefit of moderate or high levels of social support. This support reduced the psychological and behavioural effects of stress, but biochemical measures did not show any decrease. Lack of support therefore increased levels of physical arousal, but greater levels of support did not reduce them. Social support appears therefore to bolster the ability to cope and to minimise the unpleasantness of stress, but does not grant the ability to terminate it.

In summarising the TMI studies, two broad points can be made (32). Firstly, in contradiction of the early findings of the President's Commission, long term studies have revealed persistent elevations in psychological distress. Secondly, these levels are at the high end of the normal range, 'and the functioning of TMI residents appears not to have been impaired as a result of the stressors in the area'. No reports of PTSD appear in any of the studies, reflecting perhaps the absence of extreme trauma and overt damage experienced in the impact phase of other disasters.

PERSONAL DISASTER

Most trauma is caused on a daily basis by the disasters of everyday life, rather than by major catastrophes. These will include violent crime, car accidents, household fires and the like. The emotional consequences will be much the same even though the events do not necessarily cause banner headlines. A range of these will be examined.

Terrorism and mass shootings

'The Troubles' in Northern Ireland since 1969 with their larger and smaller scale acts of violence have created a 'creeping disaster'. In a group of 499 people in Northern Ireland who had been referred for medico-legal assessment following terrorist attacks (193), 23 per cent were found to be suffering from a full PTSD. After the 1974 Birmingham public house bombings, of 116 victims who sustained minor injuries, twenty were interviewed two years after the explosions: 70 per cent had suffered significant psychological symptoms, particularly in terms of anxiety and phobic reactions, and dependence on prescribed drugs and alcohol. Levels of absence from work were six times higher in the bomb-affected group in comparison with ordinary hospital out-patient clinic attenders (289).

Terrorist attacks differ from events such as the 1987 Hungerford shootings or the 1996 Dunblane massacre. The latter two can be seen as one-off events, the act of a 'maniac'; the former are known to have a strong likelihood of repetition and represent a clear intent to threaten and terrorise and are much more likely to be experienced as personally directed.

Two mass shootings occurred in Melbourne, Australia, within the space of four months, being the first two such events in that country's history. The first occurred on 9 August 1987, in Hoddle Street, Clifton Hill. A 19-year-old local man armed with three guns, including a semi-automatic rifle, embarked on a twenty-minute shooting spree, directed at pedestrians, motorists and cyclists. Six people died, two whilst assisting those who had been shot, and seventeen were wounded.

There were no long-lasting signs that a disaster had occurred, except in the minds of local residents and those who were passing through. It became very important for these people to understand what had happened, to know where everyone had been, and when and how they had been hurt or affected:

> They spoke of insensitive colleagues who didn't understand their feelings and even made cruel jokes. They expressed guilt at having survived when others died. They pondered deeper philosophical questions about how to live more fully having confronted their mortality. Disillusionment about the world in general and fears about personal safety were expressed. Anger was directed at television crews who filmed a dead man slumped over the wheel of his car announcing his death to his family in a brutally public way. Discussions also focused on practical issues such as compensation and car insurance (264).

In the second shooting, on 4 December 1987, a 22-year-old man entered the Australia Post building in Queen Street, took the lift to the fifth floor office of the Telecom Credit Union, and opened fire on a young female cashier after an argument with a friend. In the next fifteen minutes he killed seven and wounded five people on two other floors before falling to his death.

In debriefing the 900 building staff, many similarities with those affected on Hoddle Street appeared: shock, disbelief, survivor guilt, anger about inadequate security, the need for understanding, feelings about the confrontation with death and a loss of the sense of safety of the world and the workplace (54). Thirty-three per cent of employees were found to be suffering from PTSD. Those who had changed their priorities in life since the event had the best outcome.

A similar situation occurred in the Berkshire town of Hungerford, where on 19 August 1987, a young man called Michael Ryan shot his mother, set fire to her house, and armed with a variety of weapons, killed a further fifteen people. He later committed suicide in the local school. A young girl described her first sight of the killer: 'I saw Michael Ryan – I ducked – a horrible feeling went through me that he was going to kill me'. When encouraged to leave the house she was frozen, unable to decide what to do, and a stranger literally picked her up and carried her to safety. The inability to understand what was happening, and the shock, is conveyed by the words of one wounded elderly woman: 'I heard this banging, and I went into the garden and said to him "What's that noise? It's getting me down", and he turned round and shot me.' Even for those who saw none of the shooting, there was no escape from feelings about the massacre: 'the smell of cordite was everywhere – it was frightening – everybody was frightened', one survivor remarked.

One widowed woman, whose husband was shot dead in his car, 'knew' before she was told what had happened. Travelling to her mother's house later that day,

> we passed his car – I did the human thing and looked. That was the worst thing for me – the black bag was by the car and the police made us stop right behind it. I just wanted to go to him, but Mum made me put my head down . . . it was just so unreal.

As time went by, she became very angry with her husband's killer – 'I got to the stage where I was very angry. The press portrayed this madman as a Rambo figure, a star. It was just so wrong – he was nothing, nothing but a madman.' She began to dream of aspects of the events.

> When I go to bed at night I sometimes cry. It's then that I see the car, all covered up, and just his hand – that's all I can see of him. When they mention Hungerford on the news I have to look away in case they show the picture of the car. I sometimes wake up with it in my mind when I've dreamt about it – I think it will always be there.

By six months she described that 'the dreams got fewer and far between – one a week, then maybe once every two or three weeks'.

There was a general sense of lack of safety amongst townspeople, and particularly amongst the children. The mother of one young girl described how her daughter 'won't let me out of her sight, because she thinks I'm going to be shot'. One bereaved girl who attended the school where the killer shot himself said, 'I've never been up to the room Michael Ryan shot himself in. I think he's still alive and he's going to jump on me and kill me.' By six months this fear had modified: 'I think that was a silly thing to say.

But I'll still never go back into that room – it brings back too many bad memories.'

That those more on the periphery of such events may be strongly affected is also reflected in the aftermath of the 1984 San Ysidro McDonald's massacre, in which twenty-one people were killed. Immigrant Mexican–American women who were not directly involved were surveyed some six months later (144). One-third reported themselves as seriously affected with 12 per cent reporting mild to severe PTSD symptomatology, albeit half of these recovering over the time period. Those most affected were those who had relatives or friends involved, and those with 'general social vulnerability'. The women reported relatively little impact on their children.

However, the reactions of children directly involved in such events is intense. On 24 February 1984, as children from a Los Angeles elementary school were crossing the playground at the end of the school day, a disturbed young man whose parents and siblings had been involved in the Jonestown mass suicide opened fire from a house across the street. One young girl and an adult were killed, and thirteen others were injured. In the siege that followed children hid either in the school buildings or behind cover in the playground for several hours before it was discovered that the gunman had committed suicide. Of a group of 160 of the children, 'it became strikingly apparent that the majority of the youngsters had suffered PTSD. More than sixty per cent had at least a mild degree of PTSD' (94).

Violent crime

To what extent is the aftermath of an individual violent criminal assault any different from the terror of a mass shooting? In a study of the consequences of crime (64), three-quarters of victims experienced emotional distress during the first few weeks after the crime – even when they had experienced no contact with the offender, the fear generated by the invasion of private space was more significant than the loss of possessions.

The crime increased negative feelings and decreased positive feelings, and there was a strong sense of self-blame. The feeling of being safe in one's home or neighbourhood was sharply reduced.

The heightened fear among victims is evident in the case of Sam Brown, a fifty-four-year-old man who lived on public assistance. Sam Brown was robbed one night at knife-point by two youths who broke down the door to his apartment. When he told the youths that he only had $15, they forced him to disclose when he would receive his next cheque, and said that they would be back on that date. If he didn't have money then, they said they would kill him. As a result of the threat, Sam Brown slept with furniture stacked in front of his door and a large pair of scissors and a can of mace near his bed (97).

Victims found it necessary to take precautions both inside and outside the home.

The 'general distress reaction' was more common among women, those who were injured and those of lower socio-economic status. The 'instrumental response' (i.e. taking precautions at home and organising with friends and neighbours) was more common among younger individuals and those of higher socio-economic status. At four months all problems had declined substantially, but there were still prominent distress reactions 'that included components of PTSD, particularly sleep disturbances, constricted affected, feelings of estrangement from others, recurrent thoughts about the incident, and avoidance of situations that reminded them about the traumatic event', the latter two reactions being particularly prevalent – victims of crime, after all, often have good reason to fear a recurrence of the event. 'The recurrent thoughts and avoidance ... are probably more related to anticipation than to the salience of the trauma in and of itself' (64).

In a group of staff from financial institutions subjected to armed robbery (123), 50 per cent were above the cutoff for indicating 'psychiatric caseness' on measures of general psychological symptomatology at three weeks. At the same point in time, measures of post-traumatic intrusion and avoidance were at a level seen in those bereaved for two months. Scores returned to within normal limits at three months, and no individual appeared to be suffering from PTSD. Those who had stood face to face with the gunman had higher scores, as had those who experienced a gun being pointed directly at them. Nearly 60 per cent of staff experienced a significant threat to their lives, and the stronger the sense of threat, the more the individual was suffering at three weeks.

The experience of completed rape poses the greatest risk for developing PTSD. Almost 80 per cent of survivors who experienced a threat to life and were physically injured developed PTSD (265). However, half of survivors recover spontaneously, without treatment, and those who do not meet the criteria for PTSD at three months show steady improvement over time (271). However, at one year, 80 per cent of survivors report restriction of daily life, and fears are common, perhaps persisting over several years. Shame and guilt are notable emotions, as are self-esteem problems and sexual dysfunction.

The catastrophe of having a loved one murdered will bring the survivor face to face with many of the problems encountered in sudden violent death, as described in Chapter 1. A group of seventeen people, bereaved by murder, who attended a psychiatric out-patient clinic, were studied in depth (239). Whilst there was usually an initial numbness, there was also a high level of arousal, with restlessness, tension and pressure to talk. People who had witnessed the killing or discovered the body were haunted by intrusive imagery. Others had 'horrific images of what they imagined they would have seen', but had a strong need to find out exactly what had happened. Guilt and self-reproach were common, particularly where the killing had been carried out by a relative. This could become an obsessional preoccupation and sometimes led to self-punishment. One woman experienced her sister being stabbed to death in her presence, and when threatened herself, ran away. 'Her sister's face had been spotted with blood and she later inflicted injuries to her own face in an attempt to punish herself for her cowardice. She also engaged in compulsive hand washing.' Fears were pronounced as long as the killer remained at large. Psychotherapeutic treatment (only five of the seventeen had more than six sessions) led to clear improvement, but anger and self-reproach remained.

Clearly, post-traumatic stress and grief met together in these clients. The post-traumatic element contained fear, 'depressive avoidance and vivid mental imagery'. Also there was 'an intense rage towards the offender and all associated with him'. Trust in others, 'including the family, the police, the legal system and God', was undermined, underlining the violation of assumptions about life that is such a feature of trauma. Guilt, too, indicated the damage to assumptions about the self.

Road-traffic accidents

Road-traffic accidents (RTAs) cause ten deaths each day in the UK, and are probably the commonest source of post-traumatic reactions. Survivors receive little professional attention, unless of course they have been physically injured. As the survivors themselves see the events as a relatively common occurrence, they are often too embarrassed to discuss psychological symptoms.

One hundred and fourteen individuals who had been involved in RTAs, and admitted to a Sydney hospital, were interviewed during the first two weeks following their accident (37). One-third had scores on measures of trauma which mirrored those of survivors of major disaster. In one-third, anxiety levels were also high. Physical injury did not influence the degree of post-traumatic stress. The most important factor was fear, which points to 'the central role of perceived, rather than actual threat in the development of post-traumatic morbidity'.

In another study in the Netherlands (31), survivors of RTAs were assessed between one and six months after the accident. At one month half of the group had moderate to severe symptoms of intrusion and avoidance. These decreased with time, but at six months 8 per cent showed severe and another 10 to 17 per cent moderate symptoms. This indicates that there is a substantial natural recovery.

Re-experience phenomena are common, and hypervigilance particularly so. 'Patients often report that adjacent cars and intersections seem closer than they are in reality. Such illusions interfere with patients' judgement when they drive.' In one study, 33 per cent of survivors reported these phenomena, and nearly half stated that this had caused a hazardous or near-hazardous situation (41).

Again, assumptions about life are violated. Driving is inherently dangerous, yet the majority of us do not experience it as so. To drive at any significant speed makes us highly vulnerable to injury in the event of an accident – yet many drive above the national speed limit on the motorways each day. We believe that if we are careful and watch what others are doing, we will be able to avoid anything untoward. This of course is foolish, as the survivors of accidents realise. Following RTAs their sense of invulnerability when driving is gone, and their sense of the predictability of the dangers inherent in road use is damaged, becoming overpessimistic. The hypervigilance partly flows from these changed assumptions.

Survivors of RTAs often experience phobic anxiety, a fear of driving or car travel. The number reported as suffering from this varies from study to study, from 77 per cent (122) to 35 per cent (174) to 19 per cent (235). They are particularly prone to avoid situations that remind them of the trauma, be it certain locales, certain weather conditions, or they may avoid driving altogether.

One young pregnant woman became caught up in the middle of a police chase. Firstly she was struck by the escaping criminals' vehicle, and then by the pursuing police car. She thought she was going to die, and felt totally powerless: 'it was happening to me, and there was nothing I could do', she remarked. In the immediate aftermath all she wanted to do was to get home, where she could feel secure. Within four days she began to have nightmares, once about the accident itself, but mostly about car accidents in general. She began to worry about going to sleep in case she had nightmares. Whilst awake she would suffer intrusive flashbacks to the impacts. Although these lessened, she was reluctant to leave the house, and would only travel by taxi when she did. She had three spells during the following year when she was housebound. Three years later she still reported phenomena 'as if' the accident was happening again whilst she was driving or being driven. She would scan the road all the time for cars that might be veering towards her, steering towards the kerb if she suddenly felt someone might hit her. She had a strong startle reaction to the sound of any emergency service vehicle (the siren reminding her of the police vehicle that had crashed into her), and even as a pedestrian would walk down a side road to avoid what appeared to be a worrying situation further down the road.

3

ORGANISING FOR DISASTER

No group, community or organisation has ever been prepared for all the implications of disaster. Often, in terms of the psychosocial response, organisations have got caught up in a euphoric desire to help survivors Immediately after the disaster, resources are not a problem. Often for purely political reasons, jealously guarded money is made available during a period of massive media coverage. Ironically this help can be poorly targeted and woefully planned so that when the survivors actually need a service, one is not available. A primary purpose in the preparation of organisations is to make sure that the evolving systems ensure that survivors get what they need when they need it rather than being subject to a political whim or a gust of well-meaning euphoria.

Disasters have key features of threat, urgency and uncertainty (332), which affect not only the survivors themselves, but also the organisations that have to respond. All of these features provide challenges to the process of effective decision making. Organisations find themselves taking decisions which they have not anticipated, and many of the immediate decisions which are taken irrevocably shape the pattern of response for good or for ill. They are forced to take such decisions in areas where they have little knowledge, and in the heat of crisis when they themselves are undergoing extremely rapid organisational change.

The catalogue of catastrophes in the UK between 1985 and 1989 emphasised the total lack of preparedness of the health, social services and voluntary organisations for mounting long term psychosocial support. No social services department involved in any of these catastrophes had a plan which detailed possible mechanisms for a psychosocial response to survivors, despite the fact that such departments are run by local authorities which have a responsibility for emergency planning. Thus the social services in South-East Kent, which had to respond to the Zeebrugge disaster, had as its defined role in the county a major emergency plan to 'care and provide for those people who are made homeless because of the effects of a major emergency until they can return to their own accommodation, or be temporarily housed or provided with alternative facilities by another

71

authority'. Housing officials were therefore immediately sent across the Channel to the site of the disaster. Similarly, whilst general hospitals have disaster plans which allow for the emergency treatment of large numbers of casualties, no health authority had a plan which included psychosocial response beyond the reception of relatives. Further, there was no co-ordination between these two main statutory providers of care.

Why should caring agencies be in such a poor state of preparedness? Firstly, the public itself has little awareness of the problems posed by disaster (299). Disaster has a very low priority when compared with other community problems such as crime, or unemployment. Secondly, the same problem applies to caring agencies where there are tasks, especially statutory tasks such as child protection, which have a much higher everyday profile. Thirdly, individuals and organisations tend to believe that the probability of disaster occurring is too remote to warrant the effort of preparation. Fourthly, there may be no knowledge of the potential effects or of effective strategies for dealing with them. Lastly, there may have been no higher order (governmental) direction given, or funds associated.

The problem of disaster and its management can be divided into four areas (318):

1 Mitigation – activities designed to reduce the likelihood of disaster occurring, such as the banning of smoking on underground rail systems, or increasing security checks at airports; and strategies designed to reduce the magnitude of disaster impact, such as the siting of toxic waste processing facilities in remote areas.
2 Preparedness – including planning, public education and training potential service providers.
3 Response – the provision of emergency response such as evacuation, rescue and triage.
4 Recovery – longer term efforts to assist, or rebuild the affected community.

In this chapter we will consider the organisational aspects of psychosocial response during the preparedness, response and recovery phases. Organisation during the preparedness phase has a different character to that in the crisis of the response phase. The emotional and political impetus and the resource issues are different, yet the same issues of service organisation and provision remain the same.

The central questions that helping agencies need to ask of themselves in preparing for potential community disaster include the following:

1 What are the potential crisis situations? Helping agencies need to carry out a risk audit, to attempt to catalogue the more obvious potential hazards that may exist locally. Thus one English social

services department carrying out this exercise noted that it had sited close to its most densely populated area a dock, with its possibilities for accidents with dangerous cargoes; a chemical industry; two major motorways; an airport; a major high speed rail route; and two football grounds, merely to begin the list.

2 Who will be affected by them? Different incidents may affect different sections of the community. Thus the chemical industry described above may be sited near an area with a higher proportion of social problems, which may raise particular issues for the offering of help. From a positive point of view, if there was an escape of toxic products, and a particular geographical area was affected, a definable community could be targeted. A disaster at a football stadium, or a major fire in a shopping centre, would present very different scenarios for identifying and offering help to survivors.

3 What organisations are appropriately involved in psychosocial care following disasters? All local agencies need to identify what they have to offer to the provision of short and long term support in the aftermath of a major tragedy, and agree on a means of combining and co-ordinating these skills.

4 What are the various organisations' responsibilities? All agencies have a clearer picture of what they are bound to do rather than what they would like to do. In the face of community disaster, the social, education and health services may identify separate or communal responsibilities for psychosocial care based on what they perceive as their prime purpose.

5 What would be the effects of inaction? Each agency must consider what would be the effects on both the community and itself if no action was taken. This may range from the actual harm to the long term health of the community, to negative community attitudes towards the agencies for their apparent lack of concern.

6 How will the crisis affect normal workloads? If no action is taken, for example in a preventative mental health initiative, then agencies may face a serious increase in their workload at some point in the coming years.

7 What strategies will be effective, and when? Agencies must consider the alternative strategies that are available to respond to the crisis in both the short and long term, choose those which will be maximally effective, and implement them at the points in time they will be of optimal benefit.

8 Are the resources available to act and is the will to do so present?

9 What will be the financial cost of action?

10 Who in the various helping agencies are the appropriate disaster support workers? For instance, what roles should mental health social workers play in comparison with hospital or emergency duty social workers?

What are the comparative roles of psychologists and psychiatrists? What should teachers attempt and what should educational psychologists contribute? Who within the general practice setting is best suited to help a stricken family?

11 What are the necessary skills and resources? Which particular thera-peutic, counselling or other skills will be of most use, and is there a particular training or preparation which can enhance these skills?

12 What role does each organisation/person play in the crisis? Are there particular points in the immediate post-impact stage that particular agencies may be best suited to contribute to? Are some agencies not needed at all at this juncture?

13 What role does each organisation/person play in the long term, and how do these agencies work together?

Clearly, it will not be possible to plan for every disaster scenario. However, the real meaning of preparedness is not about being ready for every possible scenario, but of developing *core preparedness for crisis*. What actions are therefore needed to establish this core preparedness? Seven steps can be identified (180).

Convergence of ideas or interests

In order for a practical plan to develop, it is essential that it is not simply one agency alone which espouses the need for preparedness. A fallacy exists that the mere occurrence of disaster will automatically produce support for any attempt to give aid (346). In fact, those who are most likely to be supportive are those with 'non-competitive agency agendas', such as volun-tary counselling organisations, and those who are most likely to be obstructive are agencies or subsections of agencies who feel their 'turf' is being threatened, either by dilution of funds or by depletion of personnel. Following a flood in Eastern Missouri, the director of the local community mental health centre

> enthusiastically approached the director of the local Red Cross office, offering field workers who had helped out in a similar situa-tion a year earlier. This proposal was denied. The Red Cross director made it clear that she was in charge, and because existing agency agreements were lacking, she did not feel she had the time to consider a new programme. She deprecated crisis counselling, stating there was little need. Her first concerns, she contended, were the physical problems of victims (346).

Thus, various agencies may have different objectives, and may have little understanding of the potential interest of other agencies. 'Bureau politics' are a noted feature of disaster situations (332). Disasters create high profile political situations which can improve or worsen the position of the authorities and agencies. There may even be the added feature of tension between national and local agencies. Such features create intense rivalry which can only be mitigated by co-operative preparation.

Agency interests may converge for a variety of reasons: an accident elsewhere involving facilities similar to those existing locally, the personal interests of individual senior managers or clinicians, the desire for publicity even, but in order for a coherent plan to emerge, the convergence of interests must be multi-agency.

Initiation of activity

The preparation of a single agency for disaster, though laudable, runs the risk of being only partially effective, and encountering all manner of rivalry in the event of its preparations being put into practice. Similarly, any agency taking the lead in a community in terms of attempting to push forward the issue of disaster planning will be viewed with a certain amount of suspicion by other agencies, particularly in terms of establishing 'ownership' of something which seems to be prestigious. A way has to be found for the major agencies to come together to discuss the issue in an atmosphere of minimal rivalry. One way forward that has been employed in the UK, by health and social services departments, has been the joint engagement of external consultants, experienced in disaster organisation, to take the lead in initial stages. This takes the implication of ownership away from one particular agency and allows 'turf' issues to be described by an outsider and hence recognised and accepted more easily. Even if guidelines are developed for individual agencies, the need for truly co-operative planning will still exist.

Legitimisation and sponsorship

Essential in the development of disaster support services is their legitimisation, through key figures in the community recognising them, and their sponsorship, through the establishment of funding.

It is folly to think that because a well-prepared service exists, it will therefore be used. 'Because disaster intervention programmes are dependent on gatekeepers and established response networks, they have little chance of coming into being or helping victims unless sanctioned by primary intervention agents' (180). These are 'rarely experts or consultants, but rather are usually leaders from service clubs, business, the clergy, the schools, or other local constituencies, who often serve on a number of agency boards'. Service providers must accomplish their goals through, rather than over the heads of, gatekeeper organisations.

Professionals offer technical information, caring skills, counselling skills, specialist (e.g. medical or psychotherapeutic) skills, and resources. Their involvement is legitimate, but they have no *a priori* credibility, although it is often difficult for them to realise this. If the efforts they offer are not legitimised within the community, then a gap will emerge between survivors and professionals across which help simply will not travel. The involvement of existing community structures in the planning stage increases the chance that a bridge will exist in the event of tragedy across which help may travel more effectively. Following the Missouri floods described above, the community mental health centre director, learning from his mistake, 'approached the Red Cross before the next disaster hit, and instructed his board members to contact friends who served on the Red Cross board. This process produced a climate of reconciliation between the agencies' (346).

The establishment of funding is crucial. This is essentially a two-stage process, with the identification of funds in preparation, and the provision of funds after the event. It is typical in the aftermath of crisis that financially impoverished agencies immediately find all sorts of funds available. The director of Liverpool social services, speaking about the response to the 1989 Hillsborough disaster, described how:

> Our immediate calculations were that we needed £350,000 to run the central co-ordination activities to run our helpline, our database, our service and our training programme ... between 11 o'clock on Sunday morning the 16th and 10 o'clock on the following Monday, we had spent £100,000. We burnt out a new photocopier on the first day, and whereas usually we wait some considerable time whilst the repair man comes, it was pushed out into the corridor and the central purchasing department took a van round to a showroom, put a photocopier into the back of it and brought it back to the building. The same things happened with fax machines; telephone lines burnt out and we ended up with a GPO man in the building permanently (216).

But a cautionary note was added: 'if you don't act swiftly, people very soon forget, people who have to vote money'. Thus, the seeming river of money which initially flows from sources previously seen as dry, soon reduces in volume, and within a matter of weeks has reduced to a trickle.

Obviously, the situation for a social services department is that it has to turn to the elected members of the social services committee for further allocation of finance. Such people are obviously not helping professionals, but politicians. They have to understand the need of survivors (whom they must recognise as the very people who vote for them and keep them in power) and to be able to agree the necessary funds over the appropriate time-scale. On the Monday following the Hillsborough disaster of the previous Saturday, the social services department arranged for its disaster consultants to address the whole council on the issues involved, and within a week, council members had been provided with a half-day seminar.

Plan development

The various agencies, both statutory and voluntary, have to agree what sort of service is to be provided, and how they will relate to each other to achieve this. They must decide whether to join a consortium, providing a multi-agency crisis intervention network, or whether they will be part of a referral system to a support network provided by a single lead agency, or two main agencies. It must be decided what levels of response will be offered, although this may depend on the nature of the disaster. Five such levels can be described, each costing increasingly large amounts of money (180).

1 Public information. The wide dissemination of public information about the effects of disaster, and avenues for practical and emotional support, is a cost-effective technique for reaching the widest possible audience. It can be carried out both before and after the event.
2 Community education. The targeting of groups in the community for education can again be carried out both before and after the tragedy. Examples include public meetings and appropriate educational activities such as death education in schools.
3 Natural group crisis counselling. Such counselling involves group crisis intervention, with related groups of individuals, such as associations or staff groups affected by the event.
4 Individual and family outreach crisis counselling. This will involve the targeting of individuals and their families, and involve home-visiting.
5 Long term recovery counselling. This might involve the creation of a team of disaster support workers that would operate longer term in conjunction with other statutory and voluntary agencies.

Development of organisational structure

'Commitment by these parties cannot be assumed; it must be secured in an open discussion where reservations and fears can be expressed. Critical discussion items include involvement, control, resource identification, goals, policies, and the actual programme plan' (180). Participating organisations therefore require a much closer working relationship than frequently has previously existed, creating the joint funding of a crisis intervention network that is capable of working flexibly without some of the usual organisational constraints. Detailed recognition of this in planning terms is necessary to prevent inter-organisational conflict emerging at an early stage.

If the consortium or multi-agency crisis intervention team model is not adopted, then survivors' needs may be missed. Even if the consortium approach is taken, it will still be essential, for reasons to be considered throughout this chapter, to have a lead agency responsible for direction at an operational level, backed by a multi-agency co-ordinating group. In Figure 3.1, the potential relationships between survivors, community gatekeepers, a multi-agency disaster response team, specialist services, and the multi-agency co-ordinating group are outlined.

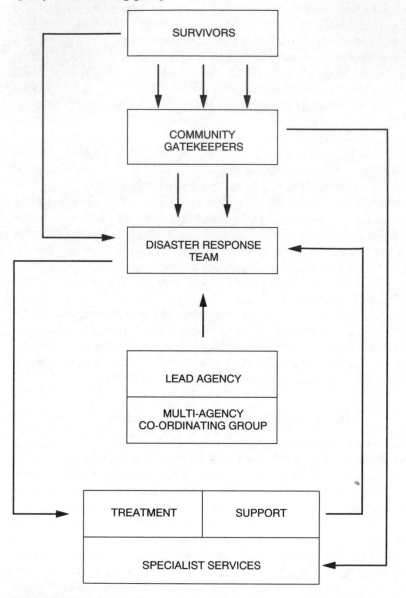

Figure 3.1 Relationships between elements of disaster response

Those involved in the aftermath of the King's Cross fire suggest that a co-ordinating group should include the following representatives (325):

* government advisor;
* local social services departments;
* local health authorities;
* chairperson of the disaster fund;
* relevant and involved voluntary agencies;
* representatives of emergency services;
* other involved groups, such as religious or community leaders.

It is clear that such a group, whether or not the composition outlined above is appropriate, could not by itself manage the response to disaster through co-ordination of the activities of the various agencies. The reasons, based on the experience of other co-ordinating groups in disaster situations (332), are of three sorts. Firstly, the individuals involved often frequently lack the abilities and skills to co-operate with each other. Secondly, they tend only to have the interests of the respective organisation that they represent in mind, trying to defend and promote these as much as possible. Thirdly, such a group tends to contain too many people and decisions are made not because they are really needed, but merely because decision makers are present. Such a group might be able to be a forum for broad discussion, but it simply could not take operational decisions. This must be delegated to a lead agency taking responsibility for direction of a multi-agency crisis intervention team.

In the late 1980s the UK Department of Health commissioned a report entitled 'Disasters: Planning for a caring response'. This recommended (5) that the lead role in managing psychosocial needs after a disaster be taken by the local authority social services department, and that the director of social services assume responsibility for the organisation and co-ordination of social and psychological support. Thus, responsibility was placed firmly at the local level.

The establishment of the social services department as the lead agency perhaps only confirmed what had already occurred. Although the emphasis on local service provision seems logical, this is only of use if services are actually provided. No one is actually mandated in the UK to provide such support as a statutory responsibility. Several years after the publication of this report, the fourteen English regional departments of public health were surveyed (1). Provision for psychosocial response was mentioned in most plans, but was general rather than specific, with the exception of three northern regions who had detailed plans. However, there was 'little evidence that the research findings of recent years [had] been translated into increased provision for victims', and that 'this did not appear to be simply a matter of economics. There appeared to be some reluctance on the part of professionals working in the field of emergency planning to accept the need to plan for psycho-social care.' Despite the recommendation that social services should be the lead agency, although this appeared to have been accepted in some regions, a number of health regions had little liaison with social services, seeing 'provision of psycho-social care as a health response'.

Implementation

If negotiations are taking place in the preparedness phase, a notional disaster response network cannot wait in mothballs to be used. It has to have a remit to work with the personal disasters of everyday life, the house fires and road accidents, in a way that is different to the limited functions of emergency duty teams in social services departments or hospital services. Unless this occurs then the team will have had no opportunity to establish working relations within itself and with other organisations, and in the event of major disaster it is possible that there might be as much interagency competition as would have occurred without the planning effort.

Evaluation

Evaluation of the function of the service, including uptake, is crucial to refining its further function.

A RESPONSE TO A MAJOR DISASTER

Before we go on to look at the duties of the lead agency, and the composition and function of a disaster support team, we will examine in detail a response to a major disaster. The immediate response in the post-impact phase has been called a 'phase 1 response' (325). This describes the process of triage and immediate medical care, and the emergency services and hospitals have detailed plans covering this first phase. The 'phase 2 response' is the longer term care of the psychosocial needs of survivors.

Phase 1 response following the Zeebrugge disaster

The Zeebrugge disaster is an example of multinational co-operation in the worst disaster scenario – a transportation disaster, outside the country of origin of the majority of those affected, a protracted rescue situation, many injured people, and a lengthy period of body recovery.

The *Herald of Free Enterprise* left the harbour of Zeebrugge at 7.10 p.m. on the evening of Friday 6 March 1987, with 543 people on board, including eighty crew. At 7.28 p.m. it was 1,400 metres outside the harbour when it leaned slightly to the port side, then towards starboard, and again towards port, capsizing. There was no time to send out a mayday call, but the accident was seen by a watchman on a sand dredger, whose captain alerted the port authorities. From there the information was transmitted to the pilot and rescue services and a pilot-boat was sent out. The radio message was also heard by two tugboats, who on reaching the scene, pushed the capsized ferry onto a sand bank (179).

The pilot service warned the search and rescue service, a Sea King helicopter service based at a nearby air force base, who transmitted an SOS message to ships in the Channel and North Sea. The regional alert centre was contacted by the port authorities, who at 7.45 p.m. declared a full alert and launched the OH Plan, the Organisatie Hulpverlening, which governs the organisation of rescue operations, a disaster plan for the region of Brugge and Zeebrugge. At 7.50 p.m. the medical rescue teams from the St Jan Hospital at Brugge, some twenty minutes inland, and from the hospital at Blankenberge on the coast, were called by the pilot service. The alert centre at Brugge sent its ambulances and called in the help of all available private ambulances. As directed by the disaster plan, the governor organised a crisis committee at 8.15 p.m. in the port building together with the senior fire and police officers and the port captain. By this time a Sea King helicopter was dropping divers onto the ship, and as the magnitude of the problem became evident, demanded a second Sea King. A helicopter was launched from a NATO flotilla, which was taking part in manoeuvres in the Channel, and the faster ships set out at full speed. More tugboats cast off from the Belgian and Dutch coasts.

At 8.25 p.m., the first triage centre was set up in the work port, the Britanniadock. The medical rescue team, consisting of a doctor and a nursing officer, formed a command post with a fire brigade and a pilot service officer to co-ordinate aid. They began to make order out of what promised to become chaos caused by thirty ambulances and several buses gathering and waiting for survivors on the pontoon. A briefing was held for three doctors, seven nurses and around 100 ambulancemen and people from the Red Cross and Flemish Cross Units. Information on the situation was constantly communicated to the emergency unit of St Jan's Hospital.

At 8.45 p.m., the first victims were brought ashore at triage post 1 in the Britanniadock. Two hundred and fifty victims were evacuated between 8.45 and 10.30 p.m. The uninjured were taken to the admission centres by buses – a holiday camp and two hotels had offered space for survivors and called up extra personnel. The injured were seen by the triage doctor and transferred to one of the hospitals. As not all ambulance personnel followed the instructions given by the triage doctor, the final spread of the victims over the involved hospitals did not develop exactly as planned. Haste, insufficient information and their preference to drive to the nearest hospital instead of making a longer journey to the hospital suggested were the causal factors. All access roads to Zeebrugge and the harbour were partially blocked with many sightseers and press attempting to view the terrible proceedings. At the triage posts nursing teams were seriously hindered in their work by the great number of press personnel pushing them aside and trying to break through. The flashguns from their cameras made such vital procedures as intubation and pupil control difficult.

From 9.45 p.m. onwards some thirty victims had been evacuated by helicopter and brought to triage post 2 at the marine base. Two more teams were dropped onto the ferry by helicopter, but by this point those remaining in the *Herald* were badly wounded, trapped or drowning. The presence of the navy divers became crucial in the race against time, and helicopters from the RAF, France and the Netherlands were on their way with extra personnel.

At the triage posts, four patients were resuscitated by the medical rescue teams, and two were transferred under external heart massage to St Jan's. One of these was a 14-year-old girl who had been partially immersed in ice-cold sea water for a long period. On recovery she was clinically dead, but the anaesthetist leading the medical rescue team on the quay decided to intubate and ventilate her. She was transferred to St Jan's and thirteen hours after the accident was conscious and able to spell her name. Incredibly, she survived.

Low tide disrupted operations at the Britanniadock, and triage post 3 was set up at the pilot and rescue service base. Seventy passengers, mostly slightly injured, came ashore via this post. The last few passengers were evacuated through two further triage posts. At 11.15 p.m. the last rescuable victims were brought ashore, and divers searching in and around the capsized vessel gave up their attempts to find survivors. However, at 3.00 a.m., three truck drivers were miraculously saved from an air pocket.

Twenty-one medical rescue teams, including twenty-four doctors and thirty-four nurses, were involved that night. One hundred and sixty-nine people received medical care, with three dying after resuscitation at Zeebrugge, two at St Jan's and one several months later in England.

At St Jan's Hospital, the alert came at 7.50 p.m., and two medical teams were sent out within twenty minutes. The senior nursing officer immediately set in motion phase 3 of the hospital disaster plan. The plan was a 200-page document containing organisational instructions for each member of hospital staff. Phase 3 meant that (i) the disaster is so complicated that national or even international assistance is required, and (ii) the number of casualties is so high and the degree of injury so serious, that additional personnel are required. When, at 8.15 p.m., phase 3 of the plan came into operation, the following instructions were executed:

1   The members of the hospital management, doctors and nurses were called up.

2   A co-ordination committee was installed, in effect a group of troubleshooters.
3   Additional personnel from the following services were called upon: reception, social services, mortuary, civil service, catering, central sterilising unit and pharmacy.
4   An information centre was organised.
5   Medical rescue teams from inside and outside the region were alerted and their operations co-ordinated.

The first survivors arrived at 9.15 p.m., the last at 11.15 p.m., and in that time five emergency medical teams had been sent to the scene, and fifty-one victims dealt with, nine with life-threatening injuries (one died), thirty-one seriously injured and eleven slightly injured. One hundred and fifty spare beds had been put on stand-by, and by means of computer listing free beds were indicated so that survivors could be transferred to a room of their own as soon as they had been seen by a doctor. Although a lot of personnel reported spontaneously, nursing officers were called up and took care of the British patients, so that the night shift could proceed with their normal nursing activities. Information on the survivors was communicated to all involved hospitals, and a press centre was organised.

Although it took an hour for the first survivors to reach dry land, and the rescue services had time to organise their reception, triage was effective, as indicated by the fact that hospitals were not flooded by uninjured victims. One hundred and sixty-six survivors were hospitalised, spread over seven hospitals.

Phase 2 response following the Zeebrugge disaster – Belgium

There is no easy separation between the phase 1 response and phase 2 in terms of timing, merely in terms of tasks. At 10.30 p.m. that Friday night the Social Intervention Service of the Belgian Red Cross became heavily involved in the relief work (66), as outlined in its agreement with the Ministry of Health. Its first priority was the setting up of an information centre, which collected and processed data from the hospitals and admission centres to which the survivors had been taken. Interestingly, however, the Emergency Operations Co-ordination and Control Centre rejected the offer of help, believing that the information centre it had set up with two policemen answering the telephone to the effect that 'we have no information' was sufficient.

Only after it had become clear that the EOCCC's own provisory information centre was not really functioning at all and after an episode of bureaupolitical in-fighting, which included the formation of an ad-hoc coalition between Red Cross and Gendarmerie representatives, did the EOCCC finally agree that the SIS team would take over the task of informing survivors and relatives (332).

Eight telephone lines were at their disposal (although they had their own portable communications equipment), and messengers were sent to the eleven locations involved. By 11.00 p.m. the number of the SIS helpline had been given to the press, a service which remained available for nine days. It was, however, only on the Saturday afternoon that lists began to be compiled of the deceased with the co-operation of the Gendarmerie. This was the point at which relatives began to arrive from England.

Meanwhile, at St Jan's Hospital, another aspect of the phase 2 response was underway. In conjunction with the hospital staff, members of the British Army, the British Consulate, the Kent Police and representatives of the ferry company visited all the survivors. Time and time again the same questions were asked: 'Did you have relatives on board?' If the answer was 'yes', the next question was 'Do you know where they are now?' If the answer was 'no', the inevitable questions followed: 'What is the colour of their hair, their eyes, have they false teeth, any scars, what is the make of their watch, on which fingers do they wear rings, what are the colours of their clothes . . . ?' Many became desperate for knowledge of their loved ones, and a senior nurse was assigned to each distressed patient.

At midday on the Saturday one mother and daughter had still not found their missing husband/father. The woman obstinately refused to give any description, because she was convinced that her husband had survived. A member of the troubleshooting co-ordination team started a search of all the hospitals and hotels, and after two hours the man was located. He was escorted to his wife's room and he arrived as she emerged through the door. She stopped dead and then literally leapt into his arms, crying uncontrollably. There were a number of such reunions, but for many there was no such joy. Anguished relatives came to the hospital searching for loved ones, and again and again they went over the lists of patients. The fear and desperation became stronger, and staff repeatedly became comforters for those involved in these painfully fruitless searches.

At 6.00 a.m. on the Saturday morning the SIS had begun to work in the admission centres. They set up two services, one to receive relatives and the other to accompany them on their hopeful, joyful or painful tasks. Relatives were registered and then given available information. If the person was known to be alive, the relatives were accompanied to the appropriate hospital, and were supported if there was bad news or no news at all. Simple acts of physical care, such as providing clothing or cigarettes, became very important. When the person was known or suspected to have died, relatives were interviewed by the Gendarmerie, with the support of an SIS volunteer and a representative of the ferry company. Afterwards they were accompanied to the mortuary. For the volunteers, the sense of powerlessness 'was often acute in front of people asking for help' (66).

After forty-eight hours, the nineteen unidentified bodies were brought to the St Jan's mortuary, and extra nursing staff were deployed there to receive relatives. For the survivors, small but basic needs had to continue to be met – broken spectacles repaired, shoes replaced. The head nurse personally visited the patients daily to ensure all such needs were being attended to. The entrance to the Intensive Care Unit remained guarded as the life of the captain of the *Herald* had been threatened. He was later smuggled out of the hospital.

As the week-end progressed relatives continued to arrive from England to talk with the remaining patients, showing pictures, hoping that they might meet someone who had seen or spoken to their loved ones on board, or had been sitting near them when the ship capsized. Eventually the relatives departed to sit and wait in England for the lifting of the ferry. However, it was twenty-four days later before the last survivor left the hospital for the UK.

The salvage of the ship began on 7 April 1987. The Disaster Victim Identification team based in the marine base at Zeebrugge autopsied, identified and embalmed bodies, whereupon they were transferred to the St Jan's mortuary. It was here that any viewing by relatives took place. Members of the Belgian Special Investigation Branch, the Kent police, the British Army and the social services formed a general co-ordination group. In each hotel support was available from chaplains, the SIS and the British Red Cross. During the first seventy-two hours five teams comprising these personnel worked in escorting relatives to the mortuary. The same medical staff and nurses who were on duty the night of the disaster were called in, and they remained with their former patients and families until they returned to the UK. The efforts of the SIS continued for twenty-two days.

This proved the most difficult time for the hospital staff, as relatives walked slowly through the lines of mahogany coffins laid out in the mortuary. One man came to see his sister. 'All that time', he said,

> I could think of nothing but her in that dark ship. I had to come back here as soon as they got the ship up. I would not give up those few seconds. I just stood there, seeing her in that mortuary and I was that close to the little girl I grew up with. I had to be there because of my mum, too. Now my mind is at rest.

When the last body had been returned to the UK, the protracted phase 2 activities in Belgium were over.

Phase 2 response following the Zeebrugge disaster – the UK

On the night of the *Herald*'s capsize, members of the Dover District Council housing department, the department indicated by the county emergency plan, were sent to Zeebrugge, thereby beginning the British contribution to the phase 2 response. The principle behind this department's selection in the emergency plan was 'disaster = homelessness'. These staff performed a heroic task, but not one for which they had any conceivable preparation, or were suited for. Four days elapsed between the disaster and the arrival of Kent social workers on Belgian soil. It was a further eight days before there was any meeting between Kent social services, the local health authority, the relevant voluntary agencies and the Dover council in terms of planning the longer term aspects of phase 2.

Within another seven days the skeletons of the two teams who would provide the basis of the long term phase 2 response were moving into the building that would become the Herald Assistance Unit. The unit's telephone number was given out publicly for the first time on the day the *Herald* was raised, some five weeks on from the disaster (although another telephone line to the local social services office had been operative within a few days of the capsize). Owing to problems related to the identification of the deceased, the collation of information about the number of survivors and the slow generation of trust between the police and the social services (partly due to previous breaches of trust and occasional breaches of trust in the current operation), it was at least two months before a computerised database was able to generate a reasonably reliable list of names of deceased, survivors and bereaved relatives. Hence it was two and a half months before those on the database began to receive personal letters informing them of the existence of the unit, enclosing the 'Coping with a Major Personal Crisis' leaflet, and before proactive visiting, rather than reactive responses to telephone contacts received on the helpline or to contacts with the social services team in Belgium, began in earnest. The whole process in retrospect seems painfully slow.

Two teams were formed (127): a 'Home Team', which worked with the crew survivors and bereaved who were clustered in South-East Kent; and an 'Away Team', which carried out an outreach programme to the passenger survivors and bereaved, who were spread out across England from Penzance to Newcastle. The disaster had many groups of victims, as can be seen in Table 3.1, and help was available to all during the course of the following fifteen months.

Nine health professionals made up the Away Team: four full-time social workers, one part-time social worker based in the Midlands, one psychologist, and three part-time nurses, based in London. It was truly multi-professional. In all the team comprised seven whole-time equivalents. The task given to this team was unique – never before in the response to a disaster had anyone attempted to mount an outreach service across an entire nation.

Excluding the military passengers, as the armed services elected to take care of their own, there were 263 passenger survivors. The outreach task

Table 3.1 The three at-risk groups from the Zeebrugge disaster

Bereaved	Survivors	Rescuers/carers
Multiply bereaved	Passengers	The immediate rescue/triage and support workers
Singly bereaved	Passengers who did not board the ship	
The other two *Herald* crews	Crew	Body recovery and identification teams
The ferry company	Crew who changed shift	
The Dover community		
	Those traumatised by media coverage	Long term carers

involved a minimum 205 visits, and an unspecifiable number of visits to the families of seventy-four individuals who had died alone, and the twenty-nine multiply bereaved families who accounted for the remaining eighty-one deceased. Once the database was deemed sufficiently accurate, the country was sectorised, each worker being allocated an area which included a slice of Greater London, where there was a large concentration of victims. A map of the UK was purchased and put on the office wall, different coloured pins representing deceased, survivors and other affected persons – the veritable forest of pins provided a depressing reminder of the enormity of the task.

Following the first mailshot, which included the educative leaflet, and indicated the team's intention to visit, a second personal letter was sent out, stating that a team member would visit on a given day and time, and that if the person did not wish a visit they should contact the unit beforehand. Decisions had to be made concerning prioritisation of contacts. Given that no information about the victim being at risk could be gleaned until a face-to-face meeting (a postal screening questionnaire was not actually considered), prioritisation was made on the basis of the following:

1   Those who made contact with the unit in distress received highest priority.
2   The survivors, whom it was felt might have more immediately unrecognised needs than the bereaved, received second highest priority.
3   The bereaved moved to highest priority after four months of work, with the approach of the inquests.

At the outset, it was recognised that victims might only be seen by the Away Team on a one-off basis, with referral on to local facilities. The large majority, however, declined this, preferring to remain in touch with the team, perhaps because it was under their control, and less invasive, and 25 per cent of clients who were seen as most at risk received at least a second visit. To assess risk, the team used a structured interview schedule which approximated the format of a psychological debriefing. The interview involved a recounting of the story of the capsize and subsequent events, elaborating thoughts and emotions both at the time of the event and currently; reviewing relevant previous life events which might be increasing the severity of current feelings, and detailing action which might be taken to mitigate these. No support was provided during the public inquiry, which coincided with the unit mobilising its efforts, but visits were suspended during the three weeks of the inquests, when both teams worked together in court, mounting a continual presence of never less than five helpers. Visiting was completed after nine months.

The overall figures for contact with victims are shown in Table 3.2 (127). As can be seen, 85 per cent of the bereaved, 72 per cent of the survivors and 80 per cent of the bereaved survivors accepted a visit. It is interesting that the bereaved accepted outreach contact at a higher rate than the survivors. This possibly reflects an attitude of 'I should feel lucky to have survived – I have no need of/right to support when so many were bereaved', on the part of the survivor, and the more widespread acceptance that bereavement is a recognised difficulty, for which support is acceptable. The importance of the time at which outreach was offered is reflected in a six-month cutoff for survivors, after which they declined outreach visits in greater numbers, a factor which did not appear to operate for the bereaved. The six-month point was one also at which survivors appeared to begin to mobilise their own resources.

Of those who were not visited, Table 3.3 shows that 12 per cent proved to be uncontactable, and 13 per cent declined specifically because their existing support was adequate. Three-quarters of the group who were not visited therefore made an active choice not to meet with a helping professional, and three-quarters of the active decliners actually rang the team to refuse – they did not simply avoid the issue by going out. When the visit acceptance rate is adjusted to take account of these factors, the overall acceptance figure is 85 per cent. This of course begs a question. Are the 15 per cent who decline unaffected, moderately or badly affected?

Of those who were seen, Table 3.4 shows that men and women accepted visits on an equal basis. However, twice as many men as women rejected a visit, indicating that male stereotypes may have a powerful influence over

Table 3.2 Percentage of clients seen in the Zeebrugge disaster outreach programme in each of the three primary survivor groups

Bereaved		*Survivors*		*Bereaved survivors*	
Seen	Not seen	Seen	Not seen	Seen	Not seen
85%	15%	72%	28%	80%	20%

Table 3.3 Reasons for survivors not having been visited in the Zeebrugge outreach
programme

Seen by others	Declined	Not in	Not contactable
13%	58%	17%	12%

accepting help. This needs to be taken into account in any educative material, and in the phrasing of the offer of outreach. Of those visited 31 per
cent initiated telephone contact with the unit, and in this group, women
were represented twice as often as men, indicating yet again that women find
it easier to talk about their thoughts and emotions.

The pattern of level of contacts with the Herald Assistance Unit varied
during the first year (see Figure 3.2). As time elapsed following the
disaster, requests for contact decreased, although this may have been
connected with the outreach programme getting underway. Requests for
contact from the bereaved rose in the weeks before and the months after
the inquests, but Christmas was a very quiet time, as was the period
between Christmas and the anniversary, although requests for contact rose
again after this point. At Christmas there was not one single call to the
helpline. It appeared as if the survivors were avoiding any contact with
the outside world that would confirm their loss and make the emotional
pain unbearably real. As many victims said, 'we just sat tight, hoping that
Christmas would pass quickly'.

The Home Team meanwhile engaged in individual counselling and
groupwork with crew survivors, parents who had lost adult children, and
staff of the ferry company who had worked as welfare staff in Belgium. The
two teams joined together at the time of the anniversary, staffing the unit for
three days, and splitting into three groups, on the sailing to the disaster site,
the church service in Dover, and keeping the unit itself open for those who
could face neither. The Away Team finished its work some three weeks after
the anniversary, the Home Team finishing some three months later. These
decisions were not taken on clinical grounds, but for largely financial
reasons – the service had cost £320,000 in fifteen months.

Table 3.4 Sex differences in uptake of the Zeebrugge outreach programme

	Male	Female
Seen	183	176
Not seen	56	27
Telephone support	35	71

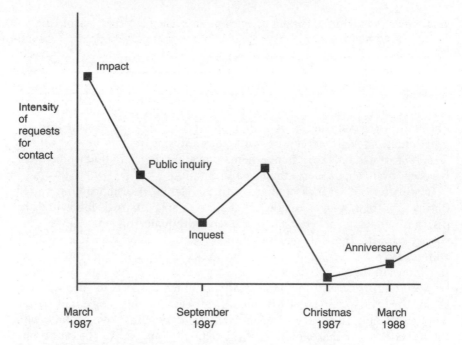

Figure 3.2 Pattern of requests for contact with the 'Away Team' following the
Zeebrugge disaster

THE ROLE OF THE LEAD AGENCY

Those planning the response to the Zeebrugge disaster took one central
lesson from the psychosocial response to the Bradford fire: that of the
crucial importance of there being a lead agency for the co-ordination of
psychosocial support. The presence of a lead agency reduced, although it
did not eliminate, the likelihood of 'convergence' on survivors, the
phenomenon whereby a variety of helping agencies, both statutory and
voluntary, descend upon the unwitting individual, compounding their
victimisation. One survivor of the Clapham train crash, who whilst living in
Dorset was in hospital in London following the loss of a hand, was
subjected to six approaches by different counselling agencies in one day. She
naturally told them all to go away. When she was approached by a member
of the disaster support team provided by the local social services, the agency
most appropriately sited to help her, her reaction was one of anger.

What is at the root of convergence? It is almost certainly not purely the
desire to help the victim. The most painful feature of the initial period
following disaster is the intense interagency and interprofessional rivalry
that quickly emerges which leads to agency competing with agency for
access to the survivor population. Disasters, being high profile events,

provide an opportunity for showing what an agency can do. This is often at the expense of the others. Therapeutic omnipotence and political advantage may merge in the most counterproductive of tussles, where each agency, for instance the health and social services, or different professional groups within a single agency, seem to struggle for primacy in the disaster response. With a veneer of co-operation, each plans services separately. Thus on the day a social services department reported its plans for setting up disaster support teams in response to the Clapham train crash, the news item that announced this was followed by one in which a local health facility literally advertised 'psychotherapy groups' (whatever that meant to the early morning business commuter!). Within weeks the victims had been circulated with an offer of therapy groups from a London teaching hospital.

Interagency and interprofessional rivalry is natural. Under normal circumstances it spurs people and organisations to do just that little bit better. In crisis it serves to drive them apart. Thus there is a danger that the agency which becomes identified as the lead agency will become exclusive, guarding its information closely, and the agencies not so identified will feel, and actually be, excluded. In the aftermath of a school bus disaster in Israel, a variety of interagency problems emerged. Firstly, the local mental health agencies arrived. Within a short period of time, representatives of Shefi, the school psychology service, appeared. The perception of the local agencies was that Shefi took over, sent the 'well-meaning' locals home, and undermined everyone's self-confidence (321). The perception of Shefi was that it arrived to find the local agencies in chaos, and their prime aim was to assist them in organising themselves (169).

Figure 3.3 shows the percentages of people contacting, or being contacted by, each of the main independent agencies after the King's Cross fire (325) (based on an initial sample of forty-three people seeking help, including survivors and bereaved and emergency services personnel). The range is wide, and the numbers in contact with each high. They can be categorised in four ways: (i) official contacts, including the police and the inquiry; (ii) practical support contacts, including the disaster fund, solicitors, and London Regional Transport; (iii) psychosocial support/medical care, including the King's Cross Support Team, general practitioners, counselling agencies, the hospital, religious groups and social workers; and (iv) the media. It is interesting to note that the greatest proliferation of agencies is in the area of psychosocial/medical support.

'Disasters: Planning for a caring response' (5) accorded social services the role of lead agency. The more specialist resources of mental health units of health authorities seem ideally suited to form, as suggested in Figure 3.1 in this chapter, a second-line service, engaged in specific tasks with specific groups of those affected and those who work with them.

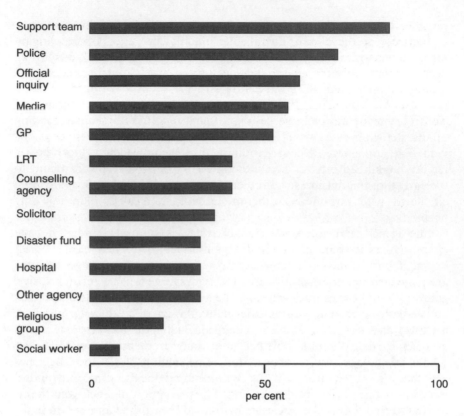

Figure 3.3 Percentages of survivors contacting/being contacted by agencies after the King's Cross fire

The lead agency has to do the following things:

1   Accept responsibility for fronting a service. In the absence of pre-planning, accepting responsibility in the short term has generally occurred with little hesitation. This, however, is the least important period – the responsibility for providing the service must extend to the long term, a minimum time-scale for which should be estimated at eighteen to twenty-four months. In this planning, one maxim holds good. Planning for the long term allows the short term to fall into place, because it will naturally be taken into account. Planning for the short term alone may be of no benefit to the long term at all, when different systems and strategies may be needed.

2   Liaise with other agencies. The lead agency has to take responsibility for creating, within and outside of the multi-agency co-ordinating group, channels of liaison with other agencies, both statutory and voluntary. In the absence of pre-planning, the 1989 Hillsborough disaster was unique in that at the very first meeting of helping professionals, twenty hours

after the event, health and social services departments were actively planning together from the outset for the very first time. The sharing of confidential information is a key issue that has had to be dealt with at this point, not only between helping agencies, but between helping agencies and the police.

3 Plan and define the service to be provided. In the forum of the multi-agency co-ordinating group, the lead agency has to head the planning of the shape of the front-line service with which most of those affected will come into contact. Decisions have had to be taken about the shape of the team (e.g. 'core' v 'core and cluster'); its size; its management; its support; its base in the affected community; its philosophy (i.e. pro-active as distinct from reactive contact with clients); its brief (e.g. contact and referral on v longer term counselling); and its methods (e.g. use of leaflets, newsletters).

4 Establish the service. The lead agency has to arrange selection and training of disaster support workers. Again, in the absence of pre-planning, the 1988 Piper Alpha disaster was unique in that for the very first time a disaster support team was provided with training and team-building at the outset. However, one of the problems that the lead and other agencies have had to face is the organisational resistance and resource problems attached to replacing the workers they have drafted into the disaster response.

5 Promote the service. The lead agency has to use the media and other sources of community promotion to promulgate the service, ensuring that the message of its existence has reached the largest number of those affected.

6 Monitor the service. Monitoring of the service by the lead agency is crucial for a number of different reasons. Firstly, it is necessary, for purposes of quality assurance, to know that the service planned is actually being delivered. Secondly, it has proved essential to collect detailed data to justify within the agencies the extent of usage of the service, to ensure a continued flow of funds. Thirdly, information about the usage of the service, when made public, has increased the acceptability of it for those who have not yet used it to come forward for help.

7 Provide a clear ending. Helping professionals are very good at making their clients dependent on them. It is therefore important to decide at the outset when the service will be withdrawn. This is helpful both for the worker, who knows when the difficult task will be coming to an end, and for the user, who is not faced with a sudden loss.

The value of multi-agency pre-planning is reflected in the problems encountered in planning the phase 2 response after the King's Cross fire. These were categorised as the following (325):

1   Arrangements for psychosocial care were made in an *ad hoc* fashion owing to lack of planning.
2   Energy was wasted in the task of forming a cohesive team approach.
3   Lack of knowledge existed about who was affected/involved.
4   Convergence of helping agencies upon the victims occurred.
5   None of those involved knew what might be the most effective treatment approaches.
6   There was no natural source of funding for the helping efforts.

Three periods of the phase 2 response have been identified (325):

1   The immediate aftermath. Here there are four main tasks:

   (a) The provision of comfort and support.
   (b) Meeting the social needs of victims who may have been displaced.
   (c) Identification of all involved.
   (d) The institution of a telephone support and counselling service.

The question arises as to how many of the tasks in this period need the attention of helping professionals. A member of the Department of Psychiatry at University College Hospital described how senior members of the department found that one of their most useful roles in the immediate aftermath was making cups of tea and comforting relatives. Well-briefed volunteers could carry out such a task equally, if not more, capably! Similarly, the staffing of the telephone helpline can be provided by lay counsellors with professional support. Again, it may even be preferable for volunteer counsellors with training in telephone technique, and who are free from the mental constraints of imagining they are working for a statutory agency, to do this. One social services employee who was in the burning stand at Bradford found herself very distressed several days later. She rang the helpline which had been established by the social services department, only to find herself very quickly being asked how many children she had. Realising that she was being made into a 'social work case' she rang off, and it was some two years before she asked for help again, by which time her problems were deeply entrenched.

2   The reactive period. The reactive period will involve working with the immediate emotional needs of:

   (a) Those injured in hospital and their relatives.
   (b) The bereaved.
   (c) Survivors and others, such as helpers, who make contact via the helpline.

The service is reactive during the initial few weeks, and at other periods, such as the inquiry and inquest. During the reactive period the compilation of the database of those affected will be continuing, and preparation for outreach will be made through contact with the press, the promulgation of leaflets and posters. The establishment of the database is of high priority, and it is essential that its accuracy is unimpeachable. To send a letter intended to be of help to a household addressed to the deceased person may result in intense and justified anger, and a loss of confidence in the helping agency.

3   The outreach programme. The duration of the outreach programme will last between the first months and several years. It involves proactive visiting of all those involved, and screening for inclusion in counselling or more formal therapy programmes.

SERVICE CHARACTERISTICS

The service offered needs to have the following seven characteristics if it is to be used by the maximum number of those affected who may need it.

1   *Credibility.* The service must be seen by survivors as offering something that will be of use, and that makes sense to them. Thus if the helper cannot answer the question 'How will this help me?' in a way that the survivor will both understand and believe, the opportunity, at least for the meanwhile, will be lost. The survivor must believe that becoming a client of a mental health professional is worthwhile given the stigma that may follow.

2   *Acceptability.* Help must be offered in a way that the survivor does not feel demeaned. Users of the helping services normally have little choice in who they see, and are often kept waiting in unpleasant waiting rooms with no facilities for children or refreshment. Seldom is there any privacy and poorly paid and undertrained clerical staff can behave in an offhand manner. If clients can avoid this experience, they will.

3   *Accessibility.* The location of help must be in a place that is geographically accessible, in the heart of the community affected, and presents no institutional or organisational barriers in terms of procedures. Clients must not have to argue their eligibility.

4   *Proactivity.* The service must reach out to those affected, rather than wait for clients to arrive on its doorstep, as do the vast bulk of helping services.

5   *Continuance.* The service must be guaranteed to be present over a sufficient period, perhaps two years in a decreasing form. This is not because it will be carrying dependent clients throughout that time span, but because people will ask for help during the second year who have not done so during the first year.

6   *Terminability*. The service must be seen as having an end point, signalling to clients that they will not become endlessly dependent, and that recovery is a distinct possibility. In particular, clients must continually be enabled to understand that they can end the relationship at any time.

7   *Confidentiality*. Many people fear the lack of confidentiality possibly caused by their being transformed into an 'agency case'. Consequently they need reassurance of confidentiality. One young man who lost his wife on the *Herald of Free Enterprise* had fought a court battle for the custody of his son with his in-laws. He would only ring the helpline anonymously, for fear that if he was seen not to be coping, social services would take his son into care.

If the lead agency does not take the appropriate steps outlined above, and ensure that these seven characteristics are met, then the following may happen.

1   *Confusion*. Both workers and clients will not understand what is being offered by whom, to whom.

2   *Wasted energy*. Confusion will lead to duplication of services and wasted precious energy on the part of the worker.

3   *Wrong services*. The perpetuation of confusion will lead to the generation of wrongly conceived services.

4   *Resentment*. Wrongly conceived and badly offered services will cause resentment in the very population the agency is trying to help.

5   *Unfulfilled needs*. Wrongly conceived services will leave large gaps in provision, and confusion and resentment on the part of the client will lead to failure to utilise services. Both will leave unfulfilled needs.

There is thus a gap between that which professionals have to offer and the sorts of help that victims need. Figure 3.4 portrays the issues, and the gap that outreach must bridge. This gap has to be bridged by people and organisations, such as community workers, family doctors, health visitors, youth workers, teachers, librarians and voluntary organisations such as Relate (marriage guidance), Cruse (bereavement), Victim Support, addiction counselling services (alcohol and drugs) as well as specific disaster support workers and health professionals such as psychologists and psychiatrists.

For effective decision making, the lead agency will need to establish a crisis management team, a group of three or four senior managers who will take the lead role in operational management of the response to the disaster. A variety of management styles have been suggested as being of use in such a group (263):

1   The ability to generate creative solutions.
2   The ability to communicate or sell such ideas.
3   The ability to see the flaws in every creative solution.
4   The ability to translate creative ideas into practical plans in a more painstaking, orderly fashion.

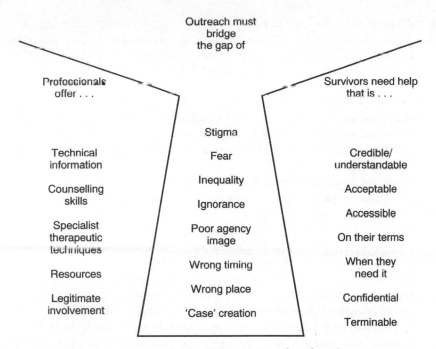

Figure 3.4 The gap between professional help and survivors' needs

This group would have roles delegated before, during and after the crisis. Before such an event has occurred, its primary roles would be that of crisis audit and the detailed development of policies and strategies. During the disaster response period, it would have delegated to it from the multi-agency co-ordinating group day-to-day direction and quality assurance functions. In the post-response period, it would be responsible for operational review.

PROACTIVITY

Proactivity means to reach out to those affected rather than waiting for them to come and ask for help. The work of the Zeebrugge Away Team, described above, demonstrates a proactive response.

Such an outreach has been described as being to a 'reluctant population' (190). Following the 1977 Beverly Hills Supper Club fire, in which 165 people died, a Fire Aftermath Center was opened in the affected community of Cincinnati. Formal outreach work began some six months after the fire, and was directed towards survivors, injured and uninjured; the bereaved; and rescue workers who lived within a forty-mile (sixty-four-kilometre) radius of the town. Effective outreach was seen as requiring three steps: (i) identification of the affected population; (ii) communication of the availability of mental health resources; and (iii) willingness on the part of survivors to follow through. Four methods of outreach were devised.

1 *Use of the media.* The media effort involved statements in newspapers and magazines, and on radio and television, with both a health education element and a service information element. The main media activity occurred seven to eight months post-fire, and at the time of the first anniversary.

2 *Community case finding.* This involved contacting leaders in pre-existing community support systems including general practitioners, private mental health professionals, community mental health centres, social agencies, clergy, lawyers, schools and others. The outreach team made itself available to see individual survivors, conduct workshops and provide consultation on ongoing work with survivors. The period of greatest effort in this area was at the ten/eleven-month mark.

3 *Outreach to special populations.* Workers attempted to tailor outreach to special groups, such as those hospitalised, those who identified bodies in the mortuary, and organised groups attending the dinner. As with the previous area, the period of greatest effort was at around ten to eleven months.

4 *The phone contact team.* Fifteen clinicians formed a team that contacted 500 patrons and employees of the club, and forty next of kin. Each survivor was prepared for the call by letter and given the opportunity to refuse it. The decision was taken to emphasise the research element of the centre's activities, rather than the mental health role.

The estimated number of those affected by the fire within the chosen area was 2,500. Each generalised mode of outreach brought in less than 1 per cent of the estimated survivor population, although some specific modes of outreach were more successful than others. Thus contacting special groups resulted in a 7 per cent positive response rate, and telephone outreach resulted in a 14 per cent positive response. Overall, only 5 per cent of survivors formally engaged with the centre. The contrast with the Zeebrugge Away Team's formal engagement figure of just under 80 per cent shows the value of the prompt proactive approach adopted.

If we compare this with the figure of 50 per cent who overall may need professional help, proactive outreach appears to be overinclusive. Professionals will be visiting people who will not need their help. There is, of course, in the absence of reliable risk indicators which can be identified without a face-to-face meeting, no other way of assessing risk.

Factors affecting the take-up of outreach services include the following:

1   *The nature and severity of the disaster.* Not all disasters have the same extent of effects on those involved. In some, a large proportion of those involved may recover more quickly, for instance if the direct threat to them was less.

2   *The post-disaster recovery environment.* Those surrounding the disaster survivor (forming the 'trauma membrane') need to see the mental health effort as potentially helpful before they allow access to the person within the membrane.

3   *Cultural attitudes towards mental health.* Many survivors see their reactions as indicative of weakness and expect themselves and others to cope without professional help. Some environments can be caring, others can be less so. In the aftermath of the Supper Club fire, particularly appalling was 'the reaction of several fundamentalist ministers who refused to acknowledge survivors as members of their congregations because the fire represented "God's punishment for the wickedness of drinking, dancing and music" ' (190).

4   *Timing of outreach.* Outreach should begin in the first three months, and preferably as soon as possible. This probably accounts for part of the poor response to the Fire Aftermath Center.

5   *Intra-psychic factors in survivors.* Many survivors cope by sealing off their pain, and 'many survivors who continue to be at risk simply cannot allow intervention' (190) for fear of reactivating the trauma (despite the fact that it is continually with them). As one of the fire survivors, who had lost a mother and brother, said in response to telephone contact: 'I think of the fire twenty-four hours a day; I can't afford to let it get the best of me. I have to keep working; no, I won't come to your center, I have to forget it.'

Helping agencies in disaster situations often have difficulties with the notion of proactivity. Firstly, such agencies rarely act proactively and in a preventative mental health capacity in their everyday work, and such a way of working is alien to them. Secondly, given the sense of enormity of the event, agencies feel anxious about intruding. Such questions as 'What have we got to offer at this time?', 'What right have we to intrude?', 'Will we make things worse?', 'Surely it's better to wait?' are frequently heard. Those who come from a counselling background often have a particular reluctance to go out to potential clients who have not specifically requested their arrival, as if it breaks some mystical tenet of counselling that clients can only accept help if they come and ask for it. Proactivity does not 'force counselling' on anyone. What it does do is to form the solid groundwork on which the person may at a later point decide whether they wish, or even whether it is safe, to enter a 'counselling' relationship with a helper. If proactive contact is not made, the victim may not be able to make that decision at all.

Four points can be made about proactivity in the aftermath of disaster:

1 Proactivity validates the normality of experience when it carries the message 'these feelings are understandable and frequent reactions to an abnormal situation'. It therefore decreases anxiety and isolation.
2 Proactivity increases the take-up of offers of help, thus bringing more of the at-risk population into contact with those who may be able to help them before their reactions become entrenched.
3 Contact with survivors will rarely be 'too soon'. A frequent basis for rejection of contact is that it has been offered in the wrong way, or is in the context of competition with other help (convergence). Even if these problems are absent help may well still be rejected, but this does not mean that it is rejected for ever. If the helper returns, their face is familiar. One social worker in Lockerbie made two calls on an elderly couple, being rejected on both occasions. When, a few weeks later, another official arrived with some specific questions he was told 'No, you go and see Mr X at the social services, he'll deal with this'. Despite the rejection, the social worker's name was remembered, and he was made use of when it was needed.
4 Engaging proactively at a very early stage means that the worker will be providing help with a very wide range of practical tasks. Providing practical help in the early stages forms the basis for a future relationship.

THE DISASTER RESPONSE TEAM

The membership of a multi-agency disaster response team must include the following: (i) social services personnel, (ii) health service personnel, (iii) education department personnel, and (iv) relevant voluntary agency workers. They must be skilled, trained practitioners, with an ability to communicate. They must have trained together, and preferably had the experience of working together in some (perhaps lesser) crisis situation. They must have a clear idea of their role and its limitations. They must not simply become 'counsellors', to be sucked into a morass of need. They are not there in place of any other service, rather they are an adjunct to existing services. They will have five main functions:

1 *Immediate post-impact function.* Inevitably some, but not necessarily all, of the team will have some role near to the site of the event. They will be liaising with those involved, collecting information, and giving information, particularly about future points of help. Inevitably they will have contact with the media. An important role for helpers at this and subsequent points will be 'advocacy', enabling survivors to ask the things that the situation and their position have disadvantaged them in asking.

2   *Debriefing.* They will be able to offer debriefing to those workers involved in the immediate post-impact, and as engagement begins, to the survivors themselves.

3   *Education.* The team is a repository of knowledge, which will be invaluable to others. Education of a whole range of 'community gatekeepers' must take place, including general practitioners, clergy and community leaders. Such gatekeepers will require an understanding of what will now confront them.

4   *Crisis counselling.* As a necessary follow-up to debriefing, the team will offer limited crisis counselling to some survivors and their families.

5   *Screening and referral.* In the course of debriefing and crisis counselling, the team will constantly be assessing the problems individuals present. With clear ideas about their limitations, they will refer on to specialist services. These may be psychological in the form of cognitive behaviour therapy or psychotherapy; psychiatric in terms of assessment for medication; or require specialist social services response, for example child or disability.

Some agencies have questioned the setting up of such teams. Some social service departments see such work as a normal part of any social worker's function. That there does have to be an identified team follows from two main points, one clinical, one organisational. Firstly, those who are identified as the 'disaster workers', who see a large number of victims, come to understand the pain and uniqueness of the disaster in a way that other workers will not. Hence they become more credible to those who may wish to ask for help. As one Zeebrugge counsellor commented, 'I've escaped from every part of the *Herald*', indicating how he had become a rich repository of experiences which victims could readily relate to.

Secondly, outreach to disaster victims requires organisation, and the support of workers doing it requires special organisation. This is best provided within a team of individuals dedicated to the same task. Various models of teams have been employed; thus, as has been described, after the Zeebrugge disaster, two 'core' teams were established. An alternative team model is the 'core and cluster' model. Here there is a central team with additional workers scattered over the area where the victims originate from, each of whom has a small number of clients, and all of whom are supervised from the core team. Such a model functioned well in the Grampian region of Scotland following the Piper Alpha disaster (323).

The operation of a disaster response team will need certain facilities. Most importantly, it should have an operations room, which should have facilities for communication and information processing. With regard to communication, the following facilities should be available:

1   An ex-directory dedicated incoming line, which allows assured incoming communication from other agencies.
2   A dedicated outgoing line, assuring communication to the outside when all other available lines are blocked by incoming calls.
3   Internal telephone lines.
4   A facsimile machine.
5   Mobile telephones.

With respect to information processing, the following facilities should be available:

1   A PC with a database for recording information about those affected by the disaster.
2   Word processing facilities.
3   A photocopier.
4   Wallboards.
5   Pre-printed stationery.

SERVICE PROMOTION – USING THE MEDIA

Should helping professionals shun the media as exploiting ghoulish preoccupations, as potentially damaging to those directly or indirectly involved in the tragedy, or should they view the media as a potential asset? The media may have a definite role to play in proactive outreach, despite the fact that their position in the aftermath of disaster is inevitably controversial (301). Organisations are, however, capable of producing a long list of arguments for *not* using the media. These may include:

•   'We don't have a spokesperson/press officer available.'
•   'No one here just at the moment has much experience in dealing with the media.'
•   'We can't commit ourselves just yet.'
•   'We don't know what to do.'
•   'You can't trust them, remember when they . . . '

The media do, of course, present certain problems for helping agencies in the aftermath of disaster. Firstly, they simplify and trivialise complex emotional issues. Secondly, they personalise issues, and this raises problems of confidentiality for helping agencies. The disaster worker will be approached with a 'shopping list' of types of victims needed to produce good copy: 'Do you know a parent who lost several children?' It may be implied that the helper's own comments and observations will be featured if the survivors are supplied. Approaches from the media are seductive, creating a sense of great personal importance. Whilst it is clear that there are survivors who wish to talk to the media because they wish the world to learn about their suffering, or, more frequently, about injustices that have been allowed to happen, helpers need to be clear that they are quite able to tell the media to go away and find their own material themselves. Thirdly, the media are invasive and workers may feel that they have no time. However, this attitude runs the risk of losing the positive benefits gained by using the media.

In the immediate post-impact phase, the primary need of the survivors and their relatives is for accurate information about what has happened and what is about to happen. The first useful role for the media is conveying this accurate information. In terms of helping professionals, two types of information are important to convey repeatedly over the following days: information concerning the types of reactions those affected are liable to begin to experience, and details of where support may be obtained. The first type of information, about emotional reactions, is important in order simply to validate the feelings of those affected. To see someone on the television naming the sorts of feelings you are experiencing inside, but have feared to tell anyone else about, is a powerful reassurance, and serves to reduce the sense of isolation.

The initial message that helping professionals give should contain four points. The first point is about the identification of key feelings, whilst emphasising individuality. This may be made in the format

> X, Y and Z are feelings that are very common at this point in time – some people may not be experiencing them, others may be experiencing them intensely – these feelings may subside or they may stay for quite a while. They are understandable reactions to abnormal events.

The second point concerns simple advice about sharing thoughts and feelings – the victim should be encouraged to talk, and their social supports, their family and friends should be encouraged to listen. The third point that should be communicated is the helpline telephone number: 'If you would like to talk to a helper, a person is available on this number now'. Fourthly, it is crucial to convey that help will continue: 'help will be available for a long time to come'.

There are a number of key steps in using the media – many of which must be ensured beforehand:

1   *Locating the media.* The lead agency's press office should ensure that it has the telephone numbers of editors and key journalists in the major national and local media. Thus they can turn immediately and directly to an individual.

2   *Having facilities for a press conference.* Television crews bring a huge volume of electric equipment with them. At the first social services press conference following the Piper Alpha disaster, Grampian social services were able to use facilities in the council offices that had been prepared for a press conference in the event of an occurrence in the North Sea. Thus accommodating four television crews and a number of radio journalists with tape recorders in one room presented no difficulty from the simple point of view of electrical points.

3   *Holding daily press conferences.* Bradford and Liverpool social services departments used the daily press conference to great effect. It is usual that the media attempt to 'control' the helping professionals by making them fit into the media time schedules. The press conference means that the helping professionals make the media fit into their own schedules, and thus reduces anxiety by focusing the press contact. Such an approach may be unusual to helping professionals, who may doubt that they have this sort of power to summon the media – but it must not be forgotten that they have the information that the media want. Such conferences have the added value of sharpening the thinking of the agency – if it says publicly that it is going to do something, it has an additional incentive to carry it through.

Two sorts of uses may be made of press conferences: briefings and issue interviews. The agency is able to brief the media and hence the public on the development of its response to events. To say 'Ninety people phoned the helpline yesterday, in comparison with sixty the day before' is a message to potential users that it is acceptable to use the telephone number that they have written down but been afraid to use, because other people are clearly doing so. Secondly, the helping professionals can give 'issue interviews', interviews in which they can discuss in detail particular aspects of the disaster (such as missing bodies) which may pose particular problems, hence allowing them to reach out to a specifically affected group.

4   *Appointing a spokesperson.* One spokesperson should be appointed to speak from beginning to end with authority. Viewers will bond with one person who becomes the 'face of the agency', in a way that it will be difficult to bond with a succession of different faces. Also, one person may make a mistake, and be able to correct it. If two people say different things, this is much more difficult to correct. Of course, it is crucial to ensure that everyone, notably the switchboard, knows who the spokesperson is.

5   *Using press releases.* As summaries of briefings, press releases are important, as they reduce the likelihood of idiosyncratic interpretations of statements. They are also important to be able to give to press who come late.

6   *Encouraging press responsibility.* It is important to tackle the press directly about the way they will report the disaster. One useful strategy is for the helping agency to have a seminar with the press, held as an 'off the record' briefing following the initial press conference, to discuss how they may cover the events, in terms of a responsible attitude to reporting which serves the function of providing copy for the media but at the same time helping the community in doing so. This is particularly important with local press, radio or television, who will continue to be interested after the main networks and daily papers have moved on to other items of interest. It is crucial that the continuing work of the agency is publicised, as some people will decide to seek help long after the initial awareness of avenues of help may have been lost from the public eye.

DISASTER AND SCHOOLS

Disasters: Planning for a caring response (5) noted that 'the special needs of children following disasters have often been underestimated or unrecognised . . . more attention to this in teachers' training has been suggested as likely to be very beneficial'. Whilst this cannot be gainsaid, only a partial understanding of the position of schools facing tragedy is demonstrated.

Experience of many multi-disciplinary preparatory meetings to explore disaster response has found that the education services are not represented in the majority of cases. Sometimes this is due to the organisers having forgotten to send an invitation, but mostly, the education services have simply failed to attend. This may be because schools are very well-defined communities within communities, whose boundaries are well drawn. The contact between them and other local authority services and health services is restricted. They view themselves as basically self-sufficient. In a study of the effects of disaster on schools (43) the occurrence of tragedy started a 'fierce debate among staff on the question "To intervene or not to intervene?" '. Lack of knowledge about the effects of trauma combined with certain myths militated against an active approach. Key myths, found in all countries, included the following:

- 'Children under seven don't understand and aren't affected.'
- 'We must get back to normal and continue the normal timetable.
- 'Our students weren't killed so there's no need to mention the event in school.'
- 'We don't need outsiders helping us – our students/school/community is special, we have a wonderful pastoral system'.

This last problem has manifested itself in several tragedies involving schools in the UK in recent years, where well-meaning external resources have ended up in bitter conflict with internal resources over 'turf' issues.

Organisationally, within the school, as elsewhere, preparation must begin before the crisis, with a legitimisation of the activity through the appropriate training of teachers and the establishment of a within-school crisis response team, working in concert with the school governors and head teacher, supporting class teachers and the students themselves (43). A second aspect of this is appropriate curriculum planning, including 'looking at life, death, bereavement and other rites of passage within a multi-cultural and multi-faith framework' (354). In the north of Israel, a preparatory stress inoculation programme was designed by psychologists for teachers to run in schools with adolescents, in an area repeatedly subject to terrorist incursion. Psychologists taught teachers to administer the programme; teachers then used it in the classroom (177).

Critically, however, the school has to accept and use the help of external resources including (43):

- the local education department;
- specialist student support services (educational psychologists, specialist teachers, etc.);
- parents and community;
- the local disaster response team;
- non-education agencies.

A number of key steps in the process of responding to a disaster that affects a school can be identified. After obtaining the necessary factual information, the school management will need to meet with the school's crisis intervention team. Families will then have to be contacted and a general staff meeting called to give information. The students themselves will need to be informed in small groups. A debriefing meeting should be held for the staff involved in the disaster, followed by a debriefing for the students involved. The order of this is based on the principle that teachers need to be functioning as well as possible to help their students effectively. Over the days that follow, it is recommended that, as far as possible, a normal routine should be followed (354) – to close a school out of 'respect' is simply to deny access to support systems. Some children, notably those injured, will require assistance back into school, with staff visiting them, maintaining contact and reintroducing them to work and relationships. Others, within school, who may be seen as being at risk, will need monitoring within school, and one forum for doing this is observing the response to class discussion of the events. Some schools have established a special, safe 'quiet area' for affected children to retreat to if stressed. The structure of schools provides certain advantages. Scheduled gatherings being an accepted part of the day's events normally, special assemblies and memorials are acceptably easy to arrange.

Any treatment that is found necessary can be arranged through the educational psychology services or the local disaster response team, whose role will have been to support the school's internal recovery process through advice and teacher support.

4

CRISIS INTERVENTION, DEBRIEFING AND OUTREACH

The process of crisis intervention and outreach challenges professionals who are not used to going out from their agencies and selling their services to clients who have not requested their attention. Normally clients are referred, or they refer themselves. This transaction has certain important underlying characteristics which are crucial to our understanding of the problems which the concept and practice of outreach present for the professional helper.

Firstly, people do not usually ask for help unless they are desperate. Readers will have to address this assertion for themselves. In what circumstances would they be prepared to go to a professional helper and discuss personal matters, especially where they feel a sense of failure? Who would they go to? To what sort of agency? What would their expectations be? How do they think they would feel ... embarrassed, ashamed, angry? Would they feel comfortable and confident going to their own agency? If not, why not? Unless these questions are addressed, it will not be easy for the helper to understand the position that the client is in. If this perceptual gap is not bridged then disaster outreach may be abortive.

In this chapter, after placing our activities within the province of crisis intervention, we will consider a number of the important elements of disaster outreach: psychological debriefing and consulting to groups, engaging clients in sessions, telephone support, educative leaflets, and newsletters. Throughout each of these, the thread of dealing with the difficulty in asking for help must be considered to run. Firstly, however, it may be helpful to place these activities within the framework of the main methods of disaster outreach.

METHODS OF DISASTER OUTREACH

Immediate post-impact

1   The provision of disaster site support, giving 'emotional triage', information, comfort and practical assistance.

2 Immediate use of the media to inform the affected public about likely reactions and available help.
3 The immediate commencement of a twenty-four-hour telephone helpline, continuing for eighteen months to two years.
4 Immediate distribution (both at the disaster site and in the wider community) of literature concerning emotional reactions.
5 Debriefing of the emergency services involved on the disaster site.

The first month

6 Establishment of a database of those affected in co-operation with the police.
7 Debriefing of crisis workers involved in the 'emotional triage' period.
8 Education of local professionals/volunteers in the effects of trauma and bereavement by sudden death.
9 Proactive visiting by a front-line disaster response team, including the debriefing of survivors, crisis counselling, at-risk assessment and providing referral networking.
10 Provision of short term practical help, with benefits, official procedures, funeral arrangements, etc.
11 The provision of support at memorial services.

The long term

12 The provision of support at the public inquiry.
13 The provision of support at the inquests.
14 The facilitation of public meetings.
15 The establishment of a community drop-in centre.
16 Individual recovery counselling.
17 Groupwork with key survivor groups.
18 Community education, such as death education, in schools, etc.
19 The establishment of a community newsletter.
20 The support of self-help initiatives.
21 Provision of specialist therapeutic approaches.
22 The assistance of responsible television companies in the making of documentaries.
23 Provision of a focus for discussing memorialisation.
24 Provision of support at anniversary events.
25 Preparation for and marking of withdrawal of service.

Thus in order to meet the needs of the maximum number of survivors, the response must be broad based, allowing those affected to choose what they want, and when they want it.

CRISIS INTERVENTION

Crisis theory (44) suggests that as people attempt to adapt to a problem they try known solutions first, and if these do not work, a window of opportunity opens to assistance. If no new strategies are generated, then the person becomes stuck with maladaptive solutions. The interventions described in this chapter address this 'window of opportunity'. They describe strategies which are preventative, not in terms of preventing reactions themselves, but preventative through minimising the problems that the presence of these reactions causes, through the fostering of resilience.

One of the first examples of the success of a crisis intervention approach was given by work with relatives of patients in the emergency admissions ward of a hospital (39). In a randomised controlled trial, relatives were given a brief counselling session which was supportive and empathic. 'The subjects were encouraged to express their feelings and concerns about the crisis. Information about the injury or illness and its prognosis was provided.' During the period under study, anxiety levels decreased in the counselled group, and increased in the non-counselled group. Cognitive measures of anxiety improved, and it was concluded that 'apparently, without counselling they experienced increased difficulty in meaningfully integrating the traumatic events whereas the counselled subjects were better able to gain cognitive control over their unfamiliar and confusing circumstances'. Other studies of crisis intervention have found positive results, for example with widows (255). However, it must be noted that one very early, acute, brief intervention with bereaved people (246) was not shown to be effective.

The principles of crisis intervention have long been recognised by the military in relation to the treatment of acute stress reactions arising from combat (274, 9). Front-line treatment for such problems is the norm for many armies. Three principles of treatment are employed: (i) proximity – close physical proximity to the combat zone; (ii) immediacy – as soon as possible after symptoms develop; and (iii) expectancy – the expectation of a quick return to combat.

If these principles are reframed as taking place in the community where the trauma occurred, as soon as possible, and with the assumption that normal functioning will be quickly resumed, then they can be seen as the principles underlying all disaster crisis intervention. Their use is described in a therapeutic unit of the Israel Defence Force during the Lebanon War of 1982 (320). The unit was situated near the front line, allowed for a stay of a few days, and had a one-to-one therapist:soldier ratio. Each soldier was told by his commanding officer that after a short period of rest, he would become an active soldier again, capable of returning to the front. The living environment confirmed this, in that the soldiers lived in field conditions, wore uniforms and attended physical training. They had a personal meeting with the therapist–commander twice a day and attended group therapy twice a day.

The main treatment strategies were: (i) the creation of a space where the soldiers could deal with the physical aspects of the stress – restoration of sleep, rest, food and calm; (ii) the achievement of the resumption of military life in a military setting; (iii) continued contact with former officers and comrades; (iv) opportunity for the sharing of battle experiences and the ventilation of disturbing feelings; and (v) the expectation that the problem is short term.

In the group sessions, the men reconstructed the main events that had occurred before, during and after the battle, very much in the style of a psychological debriefing. They described the feelings associated with the events, and these shared revelations decreased the sense of guilt and shame they felt about being evacuated from the front. Some soldiers immediately announced their intention to return to the front, thus modelling constructive behaviour for the others. The results of this programme were successful – all soldiers returned to their units within thirty-six to seventy-two hours, and only one was referred for further treatment. Three years later, only two of the men had subsequently become disturbed.

The role of the three principles in treatment has been evaluated for all the soldiers who developed combat stress reactions during the Lebanon War (297). Return to military unit showed a strong association with proximity; thus those treated at the front returned to active duty more frequently than those airlifted to the rear or treated initially at the rear. Similarly, the same relationship held for immediacy: those treated immediately had the highest return rate, with those treated after the ceasefire the lowest. The most impressive result was with expectancy: the return to active duty rate was double in the group that had been given the expectation that they would soon be able to return to duty. The development of PTSD was less widespread in those treated at the front. It was immediacy, however, which had the greatest association with low levels of PTSD, especially for those treated immediately or within two days.

The overall picture of these studies leads us towards the conclusion that if principles of crisis intervention are used, people may return to normal functioning quicker and may have a reduced likelihood of developing long term problems. The question is *what* should be done, and *when*, to achieve this.

PSYCHOLOGICAL DEBRIEFING

Those who worked with the survivors of the disasters that occurred in the 1980s in the UK often observed that the survivors were frightened by the unfamiliarity of their symptoms. Many thought they were going mad as they experienced feelings that were both extreme and unpredictable. Some became withdrawn in order to hide from social view and to escape the

111

stigma. Fear and shame were often reinforced by a complete lack of understanding in their family and friends, expressed at times as impatience or censure. This predicament was based on ignorance.

An example will illustrate. A 30-year-old bank employee was referred after a senior personnel manager had reviewed the employee's status as this person had been off work for almost a year, asking for an opinion before a final decision was made to retire the employee. During the course of the interview, it was discovered that the client had been in an armed raid. She described a series of problems and symptoms which were consistent with a post-traumatic reaction. The rest of the session followed closely the format of a psychological debriefing. The client was able to recognise that the picture she was outlining of herself was typical. What she gained was an account, a clear and structured description, of her progress from the event to the present state of affairs. She now understood the direct link between the incident and what she had become. This insight changed everything and was the trigger for her recovery. She was greatly relieved, but, more significantly, she was very angry that so much time had been wasted in this state. Within the week she had returned to work.

Normally, psychological debriefing aims to reproduce this effect at a much earlier stage. Essentially, the goal, if applied to the case above, would have been to construct a cognitive model at the earliest opportunity, preventing the client from developing the depressive symptoms that arose as a reaction to the entirely normal, predictable, post-traumatic symptoms. Some models of debriefing place almost exclusive emphasis on the information-giving role. 'Didactic debriefing' (74), where participants are educated about stress, ways to recognise it, and techniques of self-management, have been recommended with emergency workers.

While debriefing does not eradicate these symptoms, it helps *to set the agenda for recovery*. It is not in itself a treatment but a heuristic model which enables people to build an account of their experience, highlighting predictable and manageable features and thereby moving them on to a more confident outlook. This presents a certain difficulty for anyone carrying out research into the efficacy of this model for its success lies not in the removal but in the better management of psychological reactions.

Debriefing is normally carried out as a group procedure. Its individual objectives include the following:

1   The ventilation of impressions, reactions and feelings.
2   The promotion of cognitive organisation, through clear understanding of both events and reactions.
3   Decrease in the sense of uniqueness or abnormality of reactions, achieving normalisation through sharing.
4   Mobilisation of resources within and outside the group, increasing group support, solidarity and cohesion.

5   Preparation for experiences such as symptoms or reactions which may arise.
6   Identification of avenues of further assistance if required.

Practical considerations

1   When? Debriefings may be held from about forty-eight or seventy-two hours after the event onwards. It is often the case that those involved will pass through a period of little reaction immediately afterwards, and the value of the session is reduced. It is even possible that debriefing carried out too early may have negative results. Debriefings may be held any time after the event, of course, but may lose some of their thrust. However, the authors carried out a series of sessions with a couple who lost five children in a house fire. In the ensuing nine years the couple had never talked about what happened that day. The first session approximated to the narrative phase of a debriefing, and the couple found it particularly useful (see below). A debriefing following a family death would probably not be best held until several weeks later.

    Particular types of incidents raise particular issues about timing, as is observed with survivors of terrorist bombing. Experience has shown that where there is extensive physical damage the meeting should be delayed for a few days longer than usual (perhaps up to a week after the incident) because people are usually preoccupied with this damage and do not find it easy to concentrate on what is happening internally. In a sense, they need to be given time to 'clear up'. After the 1996 Manchester terrorist bomb, people were concerned initially about the belongings that they had to abandon, the car they could not retrieve, or whether they had a job to go back to. These matters had to be resolved before they could deal with their emotional wounds. The initial period of disbelief and unreality is extended until they have taken in the visual information before them. Similarly, the psychological debriefing of someone who had been bereaved by a traumatic death would probably best not take place until several weeks had passed, and certainly not until several weeks after the funeral.

2   Where? The ideal setting for a debriefing is a room away from interruptions, notably the telephone. The group could be seated round a table rather than using the traditional group therapy model of a circle with an empty space in the centre, which some people may be unfamiliar with and threatened by.

3   How many participants? Fifteen to twenty participants are probably a maximum number unless there are unusual circumstances. If working, for instance, with a large number of emergency service personnel engaged at a major incident, groups of participants can be debriefed by

several teams of debriefers concurrently or sequentially. Those involved may not necessarily normally work together – they may have shared a common task, but not be a team. If, however, there is a clear team, and the numbers exceed twenty, it may be preferable to have a larger debriefing so that no artificial divide of small groups is created, and everyone hears and potentially experiences the same things, especially if there are important facts to cover. One of the authors carried out a debriefing with forty survivors of a fire together, because he was aware in advance that there would be certain aspects of the events that would arise in the narrative phase and it would be essential that all experienced together. This was traded off against the possibility that less people would have a chance to speak about their reactions.

4   How many debriefers? Those who carry out debriefings require a number of skills: they have to be familiar with groupwork, anxiety-based problems and their management, trauma and grief. They have to be confident and at ease with intensity of emotion. When there is the luxury of two facilitators, both should be used, one being the identified leader. Practical considerations, such as financial resources, training, availability of personnel at the time of a crisis, and the size of a group, may determine how many facilitators there will be to do the job.

However many are used, there are certain tasks to be completed. The leader's task is to facilitate the debriefing itself. This involves questioning, listening, following the process, giving information, and bringing the meeting to a satisfactory conclusion. The functions of any co-leader will include noting the group dynamics, watching to see if the leader misses anything, facilitating movement in and out of the room, and , if necessary, spending time with individuals who are distressed.

Process

Debriefing as originally defined (222, 75) was described as having seven identifiable phases:

1   introductory phase;
2   fact phase;
3   thought phase;
4   reaction phase;
5   symptom phase;
6   preparation phase;
7   re-entry phase.

This presentation was somewhat overelaborate in its description of the internal processes. In practice, debriefing has four identifiable phases rather than seven. These are:

1   introduction;
2   narrative;
3   reactions;
4   education.

The introduction

It must be assumed that this procedure will be used with many people for whom psychological intervention is rare or indeed absent in their lives. This places a special and significant burden on the introductory phase. Firstly there is the question of what people are expecting and whether they have developed any negative anticipation. They may be wary or afraid, intimidated, dubious or cynical. They may be anxious about how long it will take. They may wonder if it will take some toll on them, and that it will upset them or change them in some sinister way. Some may feel tainted by the idea, not familiar with the notion of psychological support as positive and enhancing but rather seeing it as stigmatising and shameful. It is possible that one or two people will actually have had a disappointing encounter with a psychologist or a psychiatrist. There is very likely to be a mixture of these attitudes in any average group. Therefore the clinician must cultivate a willingness to name these fears and anxieties and to give assurances.

There is also the question of the group and its dynamics. Some groups will have been brought together specially for debriefing and have no history at all. Every workgroup, however, will have its own history and dynamic makeup. The quality of management and professional development will vary and personal and social intimacies will have their impact. The leadership style of those in charge will either liberate or constrict expression. All of this and more will influence not only the impact of events but also the path and pace of recovery itself, and this theme will be developed further in this chapter.

In some organisations, preparation for the possibility of debriefing will be in place. In situations where it is not, some preparation is always possible and must not be viewed as an unwelcome irritation. Minimum standards include making sure that there is a suitable venue available, that the seating is appropriate, and that interruptions will not take place. Moving furniture about and making the place look tidy and pleasant may not be on the curriculum of the best clinical institutes but attention to this sort of detail makes a difference. Nobody likes a mess and it shows respect.

The introduction should not follow a script slavishly, but should include the following elements to be adapted to the personal style of the clinician:

1   A statement of who you are and how you come to be there. Introducing yourself is important. Not only do participants not know you, but they have no reason to believe in you. They are not familiar with your

training or professional experience, or your competence. Without dishing out copies of your curriculum vitae you must give them assurances that you are competent and that they can trust you.

2   The addressing of fears and misconceptions. The facilitator must acknowledge briefly the range of anticipatory fears that members of the group may be harbouring, and indicate that they are understandable, but unjustified. This gesture demonstrates that you are sensitive to their situation and keen to reassure them.

3   An outline of the session, including goals and rules. Any outline should include an estimate of the time the session is likely to take. This will be approximate, but on average the debriefing should not normally last longer than two hours. Certain types of incident may take longer, for example hostage-taking, as these usually involve a long narrative phase. If the group is larger than twenty or so the meeting may last longer. In these cases a short break in the middle may be advisable. It is up to the clinician to estimate times and to negotiate changes to the schedule. It is important to remember that people will have plans and appointments of their own. Indeed, they may have to leave the session before it is finished. These issues must be addressed at the beginning. It may be explained that in addition to the introductory phase, now in progress, there will be a narrative phase in which everyone will have the opportunity to 'tell their story', a reaction phase when the group will be looking at how everyone has been affected, and finally an education phase in which the clinician will pull things together, and prepare people for what may come next, including the arrangements for a follow-up session.

The goal of the session should be stated simply and realistically. The aim of the group meeting is to help people to understand what is happening to them and why, so that they can manage their symptoms with a minimum of anxiety and disruption. It should not be stated or implied that this is a treatment to get rid of symptoms. A fundamental principle underpinning the procedure is the proposition that any post-traumatic symptoms experienced at this stage are 'to be expected' or 'normal in the circumstances'. Similarly, if participants do not have any significant symptoms, they must not be made to feel abnormal, or that their deterioration is inevitable.

The objective of having rules is to help the process run smoothly and not for reasons of regimentation and control. Rules give a sense of boundaries and order, and contain the fear that matters may get out of control. The following should be stated:

(a) Apart from a brief telling of their story, nobody will be coerced into speaking although participation should be encouraged.

(b) The intention of the meeting is not to lay blame or to ascertain what went wrong and participants should therefore refrain from making judgements about others.

(c) Everyone should agree to listen to one another and to let people have their say. The clinician will actively prevent any individual from dominating proceedings. Participants should be requested to speak for themselves, rather than on behalf of others.

(d) Everyone is expected to keep confidentiality. Many will be unclear as to what this really means. 'No gossip' is a rather simpler way of putting it. If, in a workgroup, any management figure is present for the debriefing, it is important to stress the special obligation on them to protect the interests of their more junior colleagues. In a gentle but firm sense they are reminded not to abuse their position of power.

(e) Participants are allowed to leave at any time but they are requested to return promptly if they are taking a comfort break, or if they are departing by prior arrangement they should do so without fuss or disruption. If they are leaving for any other reason they should let the group know so as to reduce anxiety or speculation. Sometimes people leave because they are upset and feel they cannot contain or control their emotions. Having left they then feel too embarrassed to return and face their colleagues. It is important at this introductory stage to say that telling the story of the incident can make people feel upset but it is better to remain in the group and to confront any difficult feelings. However, this point should not at the same time be overemphasised as it may provoke unnecessary fantasies that everyone is going to shed tears. Where there has been a death of a family member or colleague, tears are to be expected, and the introduction is a time to give encouragement and reassurance that crying will not harm anyone and that giving support is fine. If the facilitator is working with an occupational group there may be an atmosphere of restricted convention concerning how people usually react or behave with each other. This can be for a whole variety of reasons, including cultural and professional.

4 An opportunity for questions. At the end of the introductory phase it will be necessary to ask if there are any questions and deal with them.

The narrative phase

This is the first section of the debriefing in which the participants take an active part. The principal objective is to share the facts, and promote the first stage of cognitive organisation. It breaks the ice for everyone, lets them hear their own voice and allows them to build confidence in speaking.

Starting with one person (anyone will do) the participants give an account of what happened, concentrating on their own particular experience rather than giving an overall view. The simple question 'Who would like to start?' will generally be sufficient. Some debriefers, however, will go round the group in an orderly way.

Participants are encouraged to refrain from getting into an account of psychological reactions at this point although there will inevitably be a spilling-over into this area. When this occurs the clinician will gently steer attention back to the facts. It is often the case that not everyone knows what happened, because they were not present; could not see what was happening; or they were so frightened they did not notice. Sometimes there is a small but highly significant detail which simply has not previously been mentioned and may have been only available to one or two members of the group.

An example of this is given by a debriefing with a group of staff who had been attacked at work by an arsonist. In escaping they had apparently left behind a colleague to burn to death, not knowing that he had been in his office. They felt tremendous guilt. One member of staff had, however, accompanied the dying man to hospital. As the week-end had intervened between incident and debriefing, this person had not seen their colleagues, and not known of this developing belief. They were now able to describe how, in his last lucid moments, the dying man had described how he had talked to the arsonist, and been next to him, disbelieving, as he set the fire. In deciding how to escape, he had taken a wrong decision, and slipped and fallen in the flames. His colleagues now knew that they could have done nothing to save him.

Sometimes a person's memory of what they did or said is different from that recollected by others. This is usually because they underestimate or trivialise their contribution to events and this perception is rectified by others. Some degree of factual cross-questioning is useful during the narrative phase as it teases out key pieces of the jigsaw, as long as it does not become argumentative. Participants must remember the rule that the debriefing is not a tribunal and that people should listen.

If the incident has actually spanned a large tract of time or if it has involved a number of identifiable chapters, with different things happening to different people in different locations, then the narrative phase can take some time and really must not be rushed. An example would be a protracted struggle for survival, or a hostage-taking. In these sorts of incidents it is usually the case that one or more of the group will have a very different kind of experience to everyone else. In one incident a woman was held by members of a gang for over twenty-four hours while her family desperately tried to arrange for her release. For the woman, this period of time not only seemed endless, but represented various distinct phases of factual and psychological content. Much of this was also new factual ground for others in the debriefing and although difficult to hear, reduced their speculation.

They now knew what had happened rather than having to consider a number of alternative scenarios, which only served to multiply distress.

Another good example of the usefulness of this part of the debriefing is given by the occurrence of suicide. In a workgroup, when a colleague has committed suicide, it is often the case that people are perplexed as to how it could have happened, under their noses, without anyone being in a position to prevent it. Most believe they ought to have done something – hence the awful sense of guilt that people share. The narrative stage of the debriefing session usually reveals that no one person had access to all the relevant information that would have led to the view that suicide was either possible or likely, but that such information was shared by everyone in bits and pieces. One senior member of a staff team who, it turned out, was an alcoholic, committed suicide. No one actually knew he had this drink problem. It was not until they began to pool their knowledge of him that his drinking history was made obvious and that his alcoholism was a contributory factor in his tragic death. Debriefing following a suicide has been described as a 'psychological autopsy' (277) in that it helps to assemble facts and hence explain the conditions that led to it. The narrative section of the session assumes greater importance as the pieces of the jigsaw are drawn together. It is often found that by the end of the session the sharing of information enables the group to resolve some of the conflicts inevitably caused by this terrible act, including issues of guilt and responsibility.

With the couple who had lost their five children in the house fire, and who had not discussed the events of that day in the nine years that followed (a fact of which the facilitators were aware before the meeting), the first session followed closely the narrative phase of a debriefing, including elements of the reaction phase. The couple each went through in great detail, step by step, the events of that tragic day. The father, who had not been present, was able to understand at last how everything had happened, the mother having withheld these out of guilt and shame. When the couple returned to the next session, they described how two days later they had taken a picnic to the local park, and gone through the events again, just to make sure that nothing had been missed. Thus, the narrative phase lays the groundwork for cognitive formulation. It gives participants access to all the available facts, forms a picture, and corrects any unhelpful speculation. It permits them to think more objectively.

The reaction phase

Cognitive formulation develops further in this phase. Reactions and symptoms could all come out in a rush, and the clinician should avoid this. It is best to generate a simple chronological structure which then sorts symptoms into what is a generally accepted pattern of developing reactions over the first days. A suggested pattern is as follows:

119

1   Reactions during the incident itself.
2   Reactions in the immediate aftermath.
3   Immediate reactions of family or other significant people.
4   Reactions overnight.
5   Reactions the next and subsequent days.

If the debriefing has not taken place at an early enough stage, for instance for several more days or even weeks, then further increments are added to the chronology:

6   Reactions in the rest of the first week.
7   Reactions in the second week and so on.

This structure provides us with a sort of symptom topography which helps participants to recognise where they are located, almost as though they had entered into a map area. During the education phase of the debriefing this theme is expanded. For the moment, the clinician is helping to build a picture which will make more sense later on.

Previous renditions of the debriefing model have divided thoughts, reactions and symptoms into separate sections as though they had been experienced quite separately. In this formulation, reactions and symptoms are set out in sequential chronological sections. This is merely because clinical experience has shown that the development of symptoms does seem to occur in these sequences, but, of course, not always. This should be stressed to people as the session progresses. They should not be made to feel odd because they are not fitting into a set pattern. Again, the imagery suggested by the 'map' idea is helpful here. The symptoms are features that may or may not be encountered within the *experience as journey*. Though the map has been charted by those who have experience of the journey, the participant may take a different route, miss certain parts altogether, move faster than others, linger a little longer in certain places, etc. Nobody has to conform, though experience does tend to bear out that it is unusual to be completely symptom free.

It has been observed that debriefing is a cognitive procedure. In the session itself, the facilitator should phrase questions that ask for thoughts before asking about feelings. This is because asking questions in this order creates the direction of the link between the two, establishing the notion of thoughts during the incident and after being the precursor of feelings, and placing cognitive change as the precursor of change in emotions.

1   Reactions during the incident. A suitable simple introductory question is 'What were your first thoughts when it happened?' One of the first reactions that participants describe is disbelief, disorientation, not at first realising the nature of the event, a sense of slow motion, thinking

that someone is playing a joke, a sense of physical separation from the scene, lack of any emotional involvement, the sensation of watching as though one was in a movie, etc. Sometimes participants are reluctant to share these first thoughts because they seem bizarre. The group principle of universality ensures that someone else has had a similar reaction, and that the individual will be reassured.

Further questions along the lines of 'And what did you think next?' may bring forth responses such as that participants believed they were going to die, would never see their children again, etc. Note that it is not the fear related to this that is focused upon. The power of this thought may be challenged simply by concentrating on the fact that, for instance, a weapon was implied but not real. Encouraging the person to state 'I thought I was going to die but I know now that there was no weapon' leads to 'objectification' (209). 'The telling becomes, as it is produced, an object', assuming a reality which it does not have when held internally. If participants can objectify something, they can 'begin to regard it as an event which [they] can now move away from in time. As long as an experience remains a wash of unstructured emotion, it remains a part of our directly experienced present.'

Either the description of the incident, or the answer to this question, may be the occasion for distress. The occurrence of emotion is not a necessary aspect of debriefing – a debriefer should not feel that if 'No one got upset then it wasn't real because they weren't in touch with their feelings'. Debriefing is cognitive rather than emotion orientated. However, the exhibition of distress will need careful handling. Such outbursts should not be accorded reverence. To give them too much attention would be time consuming, not to mention drawing an attention to the participant that they might not wish. The debriefer may respond 'I can see that thinking about this is upsetting, we will come back to you in a minute', and mobilise peer support by signalling a neighbour to put an arm round the person. When the debriefer returns to the person, they should ask 'You got upset when you were describing X. . . . What thought was it that made you upset?', thus anchoring the process firmly in the cognitive realm, focusing on the causative thought, rather than the feeling itself.

The question 'What did you do then?' often leads to the report that people felt sick with fear and expected that at any moment they would collapse. However, the norm is that people do whatever is necessary to survive. In one bank raid where a cashier was shot dead, the colleague standing nearest actually retrieved a bag of cash from the clutches of the dying victim in order to hand it over to the raider. Subsequently people may review their behaviour in these circumstances and think themselves cold and callous, or uncaring. They report that their behaviour does not fit their previous expectations of themselves.

Sometimes in a debriefing participants say they panicked, but this is exceptional, and is often contradicted by others who go on to describe what really happened. This demonstrates one of the values of group debriefing, and how others can correct a cognitive distortion, when an individual is describing their feelings rather than their actions and putting more emphasis on what they see as the negative part.

Debriefers should note participants who seem to suffer a lot, or who are silent. Silence must, under the established rules, be respected, but it is part of the assessment function to note this for the follow-up. If a person is particularly upset, but it is not clear why, a useful question may be 'What was the worst thing about the experience for you?' This may identify the cause of the distress, which the participant has felt as yet unable to verbalise.

2   Reactions in the immediate aftermath. The question 'What did you do and how did you feel after the event was over?' summons a different range of reactions. Help is summoned and people comfort each other. To begin with, participants may report a sense of relief, even euphoria, that the danger has passed. In retrospect they may feel this euphoria was inappropriate. Individuals may report that they had a release of energy and could not contain their enthusiasm to get on with their tasks (if the incident happened in a work context) or devote their time to helping others. There has literally been a surge of adrenaline, which promotes activity and a feeling of well-being. It is usually quite short-lived and is followed by feelings of exhaustion and negative outlook. In this sense it is misleading to outsiders who fail to recognise it as a symptom and instead interpret it as a benevolent sign.

For others there may be intensity of distress, a sense of collapse, and a need to be taken care of. Different styles of coping emerge. Some will report becoming busy with tasks, others will find a place to be quiet. As the minutes and hours tick by, and people begin to reflect on the violation perpetrated on them, whether it is a crime, an accident or a random act of a natural phenomenon, many individuals will report feeling angry. This anger, as time goes by, may be directed at a number of targets, perhaps focusing initially on whoever caused the hurt but gradually moving out in ever-increasing circles to include those who may have been neglectful, who failed to protect, who seem not to understand, who make light of it or who seem unconcerned. Sometimes this may encompass whole classes of people – men, for example, if a woman has been sexually violated.

For some there quickly develops an immediate awareness of danger and threat so that from day 1 there is difficulty in being alone. Victims of crime will describe a nervousness of being attacked or threatened even as they return home within a short time of the incident. Detailed knowledge on the part of the debriefer is crucial in knowing how to shape questions that will allow participants to contribute these reactions. It is the skilfully shaped question that indicates that a particular symptom is not unusual and that it is appropriate to disclose it.

3   Reactions of family or other significant people. In debriefing it is important to ask about how the survivor was received by their loved ones when reunited (if the traumatic event occurred whilst they were not together), or how they were received by significant others such as work colleagues or friends. The description of this point of contact may be the signal for another outburst of distress, as this may be the point that people first realise what they might have lost. Participants may say 'Well, it was then that I thought I might not have been cuddling my children again'.

Survivors can be isolated by the reaction of their family or others who are close to them and this is simply because it is very difficult for, say, family to relate to the severity of an incident that occurred at work if they have not been involved and experienced the sense of threat. Participants often report that when they told their story to those at home they were met with an air of indifference or matter-of-factness which did not meet their expectations. This was a very common experience of those hundreds of young Saturday workers who were affected by the 1996 Manchester bombing. This often happens because those not involved have no idea of the seriousness of the event. They may only know that no one was killed or injured. Later on as the gravity and extent of this bombing percolated through the media to ordinary citizens, reactions went to the other extreme. Some parents wanted their sons and daughters to give up their jobs and keep out of the city centre, further undermining their sense of security. The importance of concentrating on this in debriefing is that the group itself becomes the reference point for validating the survivor's feelings either that the incident was indeed frightening, or that the environment is now safe again. When this occurs, a lack of understanding in the family, or an anxiety-provoking overconcern may be mitigated.

4   Reactions overnight. The next questions should focus on 'How did you react that evening? What happened in the night?' Some participants will describe how they talked continuously about their experience to friends or relatives, spending long periods on the phone. Others will report getting drunk, and 'trying to forget'. On the first night people often report difficulty in getting off to sleep through fear, hypervigilance, repeated rumination over the event, or flashbacks. Fear is a frequent consequence of a violent or threatening episode in which the victim harbours a fantasy that the perpetrator will stalk them at night. The person concerned often realises how unlikely this is but feels the tension none the less, even after redoubling their security arrangements. They may then become hypervigilant, interpreting every sound or movement

as evidence that their fear is being realised. One man, on returning to his home after an armed raid, was convinced after a while that the raider would find him and kill him. After retiring to bed the intensity of his fear reached crescendo when he heard a car pull up outside. He remained in a terrified state until dawn fearing that if the raider did not get him then he would succumb to a heart attack. That morning he discovered that his next-door neighbours had returned late from an evening out. Another woman reported feeling so petrified that first night after a similar incident that she did not even have the courage to put her hand up to turn on the bedside light, lest it be grabbed. These are the incidents that it is crucial to share, because, inevitably, others will be experiencing them as well.

It is often during the first night that participants will describe the commencement of rumination. One grief-stricken father whose son had been knocked down and killed by a car near their home became convinced during a sleepless first night that he should not have bought the dark-green jumper his boy was wearing at the time. A man came upon a violent scene which he could see through the opaque glass of an office door. Instead of going to the aid of the victim, he hid in an adjoining room. At night, lying awake, he ruminated endlessly over what he believed he ought to have done. It is also often during the first night that participants will report the start of key mental images associated with the event intruding as flashbacks. One young girl, in the aftermath of the 1996 Manchester bomb, became distressed during periods of silence in the night, as it was then that she was reminded of the uncanny moment following an explosion when all seems quiet.

The value of group debriefing is that as these fears are recognised as commonplace within the group, rather than unique, they lose the power to cause secondary anxiety about the fact that they occur at all. Similarly, as the participant learns that sleep disruption is a common, short term reaction, they lose their secondary anxiety about it, which reduces the likelihood of sleep further.

5   Reactions next day. Questions such as 'How did you begin to react on the day after?' reveal that this is the point at which symptoms begin to gather momentum, and this part of the debriefing will contain the bulk of the continuing problematic reactions. Participants may report feeling tired, vigilant, low in mood or simply labile. Furthermore, they are often nervous if they have to return to the scene of the incident. Having time to reflect on the experience frequently brings on thoughts of anger.

Adrenaline-induced activity and disturbed sleep contrive to produce tiredness. This is often combined with the inability to concentrate as images continue to intrude and the person ruminates over the event. Vigilance or watchfulness is common after most traumatic and unexpected events. Participants who have been involved in a bomb explosion or scare will notice cars parked in odd places or on double yellow lines or experience a reaction on seeing a briefcase seemingly unattended. One woman found herself scanning a marketplace to see if she could see a man who had just raided a building society in which she was a cashier. Family members who have been subjected to the ordeal of a kidnapping become extra careful in answering a knock on the door or take the numbers of suspicious vehicles as they enter the vicinity of their home.

Participants will describe how feelings can oscillate. One moment all may seem fine as the person gets on with ordinary, everyday tasks either at work or in the home when suddenly there are tears without any obvious provocation. Being emotionally labile then makes people feel out of control and incompetent and they then worry about the opinions and reactions of family or colleagues. They become embarrassed at their vulnerability, and these feelings themselves, in turn, often generate upsurges of anger and resentment. These are aimed primarily at the perpetrator but also at others, such as an employer or a relative. However, the primary cause of such anger is the violation inflicted whether by another human being or random circumstances.

One young university student was date-raped by a fellow student. When she told her parents, both psychologists, they at first reacted in a low key way as if she was exaggerating her account. They then developed a somewhat critical tone as if the incident had been her fault, as if she had provoked it. In the end they stopped talking about it. She was enraged. In the workplace a colleague or a boss may say the wrong thing through lack of tact or pure ignorance, provoking an angry backlash. In fact, there are times when it seems impossible to do the right thing, when the best efforts still reap painful anger and the victim is left seeming ungrateful or at best unreasonable. Anger is a ubiquitous response to violation.

The education phase

The education phase is formally introduced at this point in the debriefing process but has in fact been going on virtually throughout the session. The whole reaction phase is akin to the development of a shared inventory of symptoms and the primary vehicle for this ongoing learning is the universalising of symptoms through the simple expedient of hearing about other people's problems. Many participants begin the debriefing with a sense of isolation, believing that they alone are frightened and sleepless, watchful and uneasy, anxious and tearful. To find that others have similar stories to tell is a great relief. Throughout the narrative and symptom phases the clinician will have been drawing attention to an emerging picture, making connections and allowing people to respond with their variation or, at times, deviation so that the picture is not forced. The main thrust of the education phase is the summarising of the session, the bringing together of the various elements, narrative and symptomatology so that participants can see if it fits their experience.

This bringing together can be facilitated by the use of carefully selected written material. One clinical team within the UK works extensively in the aftermath of armed raids and has therefore developed a highly effective booklet which represents an account of post-raid symptomatology. Another such account was developed after the 1996 Canary Wharf terrorist bombings specifically for bomb victims. The value of written material is that it authenticates people's accounts of their experience drawing as it must from the accounts of others, thereby universalising beyond the physical boundaries of the debriefing session. A booklet is, of course, not necessary to achieve this goal. The experienced clinician can verbally present the same material, but the value of a booklet is that it can be studied later or shown to family members.

This phase continues with some forward planning. Attention is drawn to the fact that symptoms will not now disappear as if by magic and that other symptoms may yet be to come. Again, the aim of psychological debriefing is not to eliminate symptoms but to normalise them and to make them manageable. The clinician reiterates that the symptoms experienced are normal in the circumstances and will eventually cease. In the meantime there has to be a recognition that they will cause some difficulties but usually only for a limited period of time. Realism is important.

Forewarned is forearmed. Knowing what to expect restores participants' confidence. Assured anticipation replaces anxiety and reduces the negative impact of recurring symptoms. Participants may ask how long symptoms will last, and a realistic response will depend on a number of factors. For example, the authors' experience of working with kidnap or hostage clients is that difficulties will normally last for about a year whereas, in general, survivors of armed raids can expect a diminishing of reactions within a few weeks and only a small minority will suffer symptoms after three months.

In this phase of the debriefing it is important to attempt to identify those who may need immediate help. In some cases it is possible to discuss coping strategies that will help with certain difficulties, for example dealing with specific phobic reactions that arise from the incident. In the aftermath of armed raids, for instance, it is not uncommon for a participant to develop a fear of going back into the workplace where it happened, or, more frequently, to work at the till. A simple, structured desensitisation will normally solve this problem. The group, if it is a workgroup or a group that may continue to meet regularly, is itself a reservoir of resources. By the end of the debriefing participants will recognise that they have been able to talk with their colleagues about their ordeal in a supportive and understanding atmosphere. For some it is the only place where they feel free to discuss their experience. At follow-up, young survivors of the 1996 Manchester bombing reported they were happier to get back to their workplace because they were with people who understood each other, having felt isolated at home. It is important to stimulate discussion on what support participants feel they will need from each other.

At the end of the session the subject of follow-up is introduced and a date and time is normally set. The rationale behind this second session is explained to the group as a review of progress rather than a revisit to the incident itself. During these final minutes, there is the opportunity to outline the availability of further help and how it is to accessed. For example, is there to be telephone support? Will individual sessions be provided if requested?

Follow-up to the debriefing

Follow-up is essential. It may take place anytime from a couple of weeks later onwards. It provides an opportunity to track recovery, identify positive elements which have been helpful or negative elements which may have slowed down expected progress, and then to address any difficulties that may require further clinical intervention. It has less structure than the debriefing itself, its prime task being simply to review group members' progress. Additionally, the follow-up procedure promotes the positive message that clinical oversight continues. Very often, victims of catastrophic or traumatic events feel forgotten after the initial flush of interest in their predicament has passed.

The follow-up continues the process of assessment. More serious problems are not usually evident at the time of the debriefing itself since the symptoms described are generally regarded as normal. At the follow-up they are often more obvious, and it is at this point that a decision about further action will need to be taken. This may simply be the decision to hold a further follow-up. A series of follow-ups is normally required for more severe events such as a kidnapping where it is possible to predict more long term problems which respond well to continued clinical intervention. Alternatively it may be decided after the first follow-up that individual intervention is necessary.

The debriefing continuum

Group debriefing is only applicable in certain circumstances. When people experience an individual tragedy, there may be no group to debrief. This does not of course mean that the model is inappropriate, merely that some of its advantages may be lost. Alternatively, very large groups or communities may be traumatised. Setting up small group debriefings may be impossible to organise immediately. Here a different sort of debriefing, called a 'crisis seminar', may be used, which enables the information-giving and the relationship-forming elements of debriefing to be retained.

Debriefing activities may therefore be viewed as lying on a continuum governed by the numbers involved, as Table 4.1 shows (132). Each of the processes of debriefing has differing weights in each of the three debriefing activities.

The crisis seminar

The crisis seminar is a two-stage public meeting for any number of individuals, combining education and survivor networking (possibly for the creation of debriefing groups). It is a quite innocuous way of introducing people to the idea of receiving help. They are able to see for themselves that there are others in the same or similar position to themselves. They are quite free to turn up if they wish and once there they can leave whenever they want to. There is no pressure on anyone to speak.

The first stage of the crisis seminar is a presentation. This can be by a survivor of some other tragedy, who is credible and readily identifiable with, and who can speak to their own experiences (the educative element) and about the pros and cons of help. It could also be done by a professional person with experience in the field of trauma. This minimal formality gives people a familiar model with which many will feel comfortable. Nothing is actually required of them except to sit and listen. They are not exposed to a threatening therapeutic encounter, nor are they confronting each other. After the presentation, questions are invited from the 'audience' and this again means that people can frame their contributions in as general and

Table 4.1 The debriefing continuum

	Crisis seminar	Group debrief	Individual debrief
Number of participants	N = 20+	N = 2 to 20	N = 1
Preparation	High	Moderate	Low
Survivor personal involvement	Low	Moderate	High
Facilitation	Low	Moderate	High
Event-specific processing	Low	Moderate	High
Centrality of education	High	Moderate	Moderate
Centrality of previous experience	Low	Low	Moderate

non-personal a way as they wish. Strong emotions do surface, so it is important that they are appropriately facilitated by a professional helper at the front of the audience with the survivor/presenter. A number of other helpers will need to be present to follow an agreed strategy. During the first stage, they need to keep a low but obvious profile, perhaps wearing name tags so they can be identified but not standing apart as a separate group. If someone is seen to leave in a very distressed state they are able to approach them and offer the opportunity to talk.

In the second stage, participants get together over refreshments. They invariably form into small groups. Workers are now available to mingle, answer questions, make introductions, hand out leaflets and phone numbers, and explain who they are and what they may be able to offer. A list can be made of those who might like to meet again.

There are risks involved in such meetings. There can be a very poor attendance or it is possible that one or two vociferous survivors will dominate the meeting or that the whole event becomes dedicated to anger and rage alone with no constructive movement at all. The structure described should prevent this. Awareness of the probability of media intrusion is also important.

Two such meetings were arranged following the Hillsborough disaster in 1989. There was a higher than expected turnout to each of them. It was discovered that a number of those who attended had travelled quite long distances, and they described their isolation and were introduced to others. They had previously been unable to approach any agency for help but the idea of a public meeting was attractive.

Individual debriefing

The debriefing model is applicable to individuals. Exactly the same process can be followed. Specific event-related material can be processed, and information can be given about patterns of responses. What is lost, of course, is the key element of groupwork, the ability to identify with what other group members say, and benefit from universality. What is gained is the space for individuals to examine current experiences and reactions in the light of past events and reactions. The individual is therefore able to refer to their previous history, how it shaped their perceptions of themselves, and explore how it relates to their current reactions.

It is possible to put together a pattern and time-scale of debriefing activities as shown in Figure 4.1. These will range from activities such as on-site intervention, where, for instance, stress may be detected amongst body recovery personnel during an operation, to defusing, a gentle non-structured grouping immediately after such an activity, through to individual therapy.

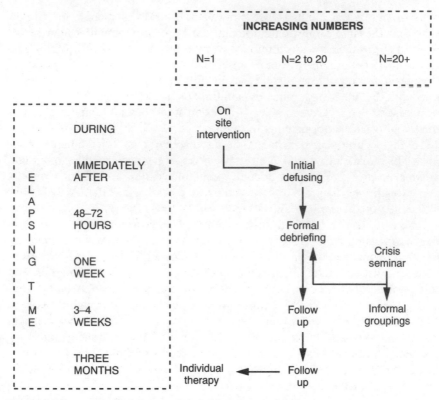

Figure 4.1 A pattern and time-scale of debriefing activities

Does debriefing work?

Debriefing has become a popular activity in recent years, yet little research has been conducted into its effectiveness. Support for the process has been largely anecdotal, and better conducted studies have produced mixed results. These studies can be grouped according to the main theme of their findings. Firstly, there are those which demonstrate that participants value debriefings highly. Secondly, there are studies which show no effects of debriefing. Thirdly, there are those which show a negative effect; and lastly, studies which show positive results.

An Australian study followed up emergency services personnel who had participated in psychological debriefings (269). There was a significant lowering of measures of the impact of the event on the personnel two weeks later. However, as there was no control group, it was impossible to gauge whether this might simply reflect spontaneous improvement. The debriefings were rated as being of considerable value, and the greater the initial rating of the impact of the event, the greater the rating of the value of the debriefing. Talking about the incident, notably with others, and greater understanding of the self were cited as the primary benefits. A series of studies of victims of armed crime (123) found between 97 and 99 per cent of participants experiencing debriefing as helpful (split approximately into thirds finding the debriefings as 'helpful', 'very helpful' or 'of very much help'). Less than 1 per cent required further support. Symptom levels were within broadly normal limits at three months, with the subjective perception of participants indicating that the bulk of recovery began immediately after the debriefing. However, this again may simply be tapping a natural recovery process.

Out of a group of hospital staff who had been assaulted and offered debriefing (84), 69 per cent of staff reported 'regaining a sense of control' within ten days and only seven out of sixty-two required further support. Thirty-two psychological debriefings with helpers took place after the Hillsborough disaster, between four and thirteen days on, and 68 per cent of recipients found these of help. However, some found them unhelpful, and respondents suggested that more than one method of providing support should be available (281).

A study of emergency personnel involved in bus crashes (109) found that those who attended debriefings had significantly higher levels of symptoms at twelve months than those who had not attended. However, those who attended debriefings were those who had experienced greater distress and they were more likely to have perceived the debriefing as more helpful – a self-selection of those more affected into the debriefing group seemed therefore to have occurred. A study of fire-fighters exposed to a bush fire (204) found that individuals who were not debriefed afterwards were more likely to develop an acute post-traumatic stress reaction than those who were. However, individuals who developed a delayed onset post-traumatic reaction were more likely to have attended a debriefing (although this relationship was much weaker than that concerning reduced acute stress). Again, attendance at debriefing was not randomised, and this may simply reflect a feature of the individuals who opted for debriefing. Another study of disaster workers involved in an earthquake, who were followed over two years, found no evidence of improved rates of recovery in those who were debriefed. Given that there was no control over who was debriefed, the authors noted that 'it may be that those who were debriefed in some way self-selected for debriefing because they were at risk'. Thus, the debriefing may have stopped them from getting worse, or if the more psychologically affected individuals opted for debriefing, their symptom levels may have actually been reduced to the level of those less affected, who did not opt for debriefing. A study of soldiers acting as gravediggers in the Gulf War (65), who were given debriefing and assessed at nine months, also found no difference between those debriefed and those who did not receive debriefing. Further, a study of non-professional fire-fighters found no difference two weeks later between those formally debriefed and those who had simply talked with colleagues (146), and lastly, a randomised study of burns victims found no preventative effect for debriefing (21).

One study has reported negative effects for debriefing (121). Here, a group of road-traffic accident victims were allocated randomly to debriefing or no intervention. (The individuals in the debriefing group were more severely injured, and stayed longer in hospital, but levels of psychological symptoms were similar.)

> Interventions were undertaken within 24–48 hours of the accident in most cases; they comprised an hour's debriefing combining a review of the traumatic experience, encouragement of emotional expression, and promotion of cognitive processing of the experience. Advice was provided about common emotional reactions, the value of talking about the experience, and early graded return to normal road travel.

Four months later, neither group showed a significant reduction in psychological symptoms, with the intervention group showing some evidence of increases in certain symptoms, although there was no effect on long term outcome. The authors concluded that a single intervention might not have been sufficient, and that selective interventions directed at specific problems might have been preferable. Importantly, they noted that the early nature of the intervention may have disturbed natural defences, with some patients 'still too numbed or distressed to be receptive'. Separately, the main author wrote of doubt about the value of 'individual debriefing when conducted very early post-trauma by inexperienced debriefers' (120). Indeed, it seems that far too much was attempted within the hour. 'Encouragement of emotional expression' is not part of the debriefing process as described above. Indeed, within such a short space of time this would actively militate against cognitive processing. Further, the survivors were given brief advice about self-desensitisation to car travel, and hence might have been experiencing increased anxiety as a result of this, the non-intervention group protecting themselves through avoidance. Another study has found an increase in symptoms over time in police officers after an aircraft disaster when they had participated in debriefing (45).

The most positive support for debriefing was provided by a controlled study of road accident victims who had been hospitalised for a week. One group received no intervention, a second received the equivalent of a debriefing, and the third group received the debriefing plus two to ten hours of further psychological input. This last group, followed up three to four months later, had fewer psychological symptoms than the debriefing-only group, who in turn had fewer symptoms than the 'no intervention' group (25).

In all these studies, a clear problem is that debriefing has been poorly defined – very few studies actually describe what was carried out, and by whom. Most lacked the follow-up session described above as vital, that is they did not imply extended care. Debriefings have been carried out at various points in time, degrees of trauma have varied, and outcomes have been assessed in different ways. The difference between a group and an individual debriefing is an important issue. Despite this, given the fact that debriefing is a form of crisis intervention, and crisis intervention (brief and early intervention) is of demonstrated efficacy (255, 296, 21), it is puzzling that debriefing has not up to now been demonstrated to be more effective.

Some authors have suggested that 'at best psychological debriefing affords some protection against later sequelae, and at worst makes no difference' (20). The as-yet lack of demonstrated value has been linked to a variety of issues, including the possibility that

> it does not take account of subjects' levels of arousal, defensive styles and coping processes, cognitive impairments associated with acute trauma, dissociative phenomena relating to the traumatic experience, and other pathogenic influences such as past trauma, past psychological morbidity, and current and recent life stresses. Debriefing has typically been used as though all the trauma comprised a single element – for instance, a threat to life – whereas loss, separation and dislocation are separate stressors that probably need different interventions and timing.

However, it must be remembered, as noted above, that debriefing has been found in a number of studies to be very well received. This would hardly be the case if it made people worse.

Debriefing has never been seen as a 'cure all'. Its users must be circumspect concerning its use and limitations. It must also be acknowledged that it has potential risks, but these are probably no more than the risks attached to any intervention which is not done well. It must be carried out with careful thought in relation to the population involved, not with blind enthusiasm; it must not be forced on people, which would damage their existing coping mechanisms; and it must not be seen as an end but as a potential opening for some, that is it must not obscure pathology by the assumption that, the intervention having been carried out, all will be well.

The originators of psychological debriefing (223) caution that 'many times' individuals 'will need more help than a debriefing alone can provide', and where crisis intervention has been proven to be effective, it has always provided a more extensive intervention than the single debriefing session. Indeed, in the study referred to above with victims of armed crime in the workplace (123), the package of help included management support within an hour of the attack; preparation for debriefing; a group debriefing at forty-eight to seventy-two hours, focusing on cognitive rather than emotional issues; access to individual help over the telephone; further management support; a follow-up meeting at three weeks; individual coun-selling of a cognitive–behavioural nature if necessary; and a third follow-up if needed.

If debriefing is to be effective, it will probably be so as one element of a crisis intervention package. Messianic fervour for it is undoubtedly misplaced. In major disaster situations debriefing may simply act as a means of engaging as many survivors as possible as soon as can be achieved – it is therefore an initial outreach tool. Similarly, the quality of those who use it must be high. Debriefing is a simple tool which requires a great deal of expe-rience and skill to apply, not least of all because this grants knowledge of limitations. Further, it is very easy for the least skilled of counsellors to stim-ulate emotion, yet it requires far more skill to work with the cognitions and issues that underlie distress.

It is possible to see in certain circumstances how debriefing itself (rather than debriefing done badly) might make people worse. Thus, if a group of unconnected individuals who had experienced the same disaster, but who had had widely different experiences, were brought together for debriefing, it is possible that those who had had the worst experiences might vicari-ously traumatise those whose experiences were less traumatic, by virtue of stimulating 'What if . . . ?' thinking. This effect may well be worsened by persons leaving the group and going back to a social context which has not experienced debriefing, in which these thoughts cannot be discussed. The full model of debriefing may best be carried out with natural groups, who have a life together outside of the group, that is they have a continued recovery context, such as workgroups or families. If disparate individuals are brought together, either a continued recovery context must be created, in the form of additional meetings, or the debriefing model should be modified, particularly in respect of the narrative phase, with more emphasis on education.

In summary, the following cautionary points may be made:

1   Debriefing should be carried out as part of an overall crisis intervention programme, and never without a follow-up.
2   It should be carried out with careful thought in regard of the group involved, and modified if necessary.
3   It should be carried out only by experienced clinicians, focusing on cognitive aspects and education.
4   It should not be carried out too early, that is within forty-eight hours.
5   Sessions should not attempt to achieve too much, and should not be too short.
6   It should be seen partly as an assessment procedure to identify those who are at risk, and as a way of establishing engagement with such indi-viduals.

CONSULTING TO GROUPS AFTER TRAUMA

Many disasters happen to groups of unconnected individuals, such as passengers on an aeroplane, or those on an underground platform. Others happen to groups of individuals who are connected, for example they work together. Examples include the crew of the ferry *Herald of Free Enterprise*, a platoon of soldiers suffering a fatal accident whilst training, a group of factory workers involved in an industrial accident, or a group of bank employees who have been held hostage.

Groups like these have a history, an existing pattern of relationships, a group identity, and a relationship with their leader or manager. This forms what has been referred to as the 'recovery context' (83). The group will have strengths and weaknesses in the way people give and receive support and there will be a variety of relationships of differing quality between the leader and the others. The role of the leader is particularly important in the way the group is enabled to recover, requiring a skill which has been called 'grief leadership' (148).

The following example highlights the crucial role of the leader's attitudes. A financial institution was subjected to a particularly unpleasant armed raid. A drunken raider smashed a shotgun repeatedly against the glass screen whilst being foully abusive. The cashiers were terrified, convinced they were going to die, describing it as 'the most terrifying thing we have ever experienced'. The manager was out of the office, and returned a half hour later to discover what had happened. He refused to close the branch and made all the staff resume their positions. Four days later in the debriefing, one member of staff said of the manager's actions: 'That was a worse assault than the raid itself – I've never come so close to hitting anyone in my life before'. The others agreed. The manager for his part described privately how helpless he had felt. 'I just didn't know what to do. Anything I could say seemed pointless. I thought it was just better for everyone to get back to the job.' Bad decisions which on the surface seem crassly insensitive are quite simply often the result of lack of knowledge about what to do for the best. However, they may jeopardise recovery.

Organisations often wish, in the heat of the crisis, to bring an 'expert' in to work with particular individuals who may be 'most affected'. They want the problems localised and eliminated. Clinicians may collude with this attitude as they are often geared towards identifying and treating individual pathology. For optimal recovery, the consultant must bear in mind that

> the norms and social processes that operated prior to the tragic event will influence how the group functions as it strives toward a new equilibrium . . . before offering advice, it is very important to

look for the positive, sustaining dynamics already existing in the group (102).

The approach assumes that the group, whilst not responsible for its plight, is responsible for its own recovery. This promotes active attempts to regain mastery.

A prime technique of consultancy is to work through the leader. A picture of group functioning must be created for the mutual benefit of the leader and the consultant. They have a joint task to clarify what it is about the group that will help or hinder recovery. Before this is achieved, the leader's predicament must be identified. Leaders are often those who are most affected. They feel a natural sense of responsibility for those they manage, and may feel an irrational sense of responsibility for the damage that has occurred – 'If I hadn't sent them in there to do that at that moment, no-one would have been hurt when the bomb went off'. It is also likely that the leader will feel lonely and isolated, without natural support for these reactions. Often, they feel they have to appear strong at all times.

The first task of the consultant is therefore to carry out some sort of individual debriefing with the leader. This process validates the leader's emotions, shows that expression of feelings is not destructive (intense feelings may be reframed as reflecting the extent of the leader's concern and humanity), develops a positive view on intervention, and allows the development of a realistic perspective on the possible reactions of others. In this, the leader must be helped to look at the group at two levels, firstly as a whole, in terms of overall strengths and weaknesses, and secondly at an individual level, in terms of which group members cause most concern and for what reasons.

Various dimensions of coping strategies can be borne in mind when assessing the coping skills of individuals and groups. One such set of dimensions derived from work with communities under stress has been described by the mnemonic 'BASIC Ph' (176):

- B is for beliefs. Some groups will rely on beliefs and values to guide them through times of crisis. This includes not only religious beliefs, but political stances and the sense of mission or meaning in their task. In times of crisis, families and communities may reject the need for outside help by adopting the belief that they have 'always managed'.
- A is for affect or emotions. Some groups will cope by very open sharing of emotion, by crying and laughing together.
- S is for social. Some groups draw a lot of support from their group identity, its structure, and their roles and shared skills.
- I is for imagination. Some individuals and groups will use their creative imagination to mask the brutal facts by diverting their attention in some way, such as by fantasising or daydreaming.

- C is for cognition. Some individuals and groups will cope using cognitive strategies, by gathering information, problem solving and planning.
- Ph is for physical. Some individuals will cope by using physical strategies, such as games and exercise.

Obviously, people and groups react in more than one of these modes, and everyone has the potential to cope in all six modes, but each person or group develops its own special combination. The task of the consultant is to help the leader identify the group's coping strategies, perhaps by using these dimensions, to recognise which coping strategies can be capitalised upon, and which can be encouraged.

'Leaders will have two broad areas of concern: taking care of the emotional needs of the members of the group and restoring the group's level of functioning. Leaders will typically see these as separate tasks to be completed sequentially' (102). Organisations are generally not at ease with emotion, and the consultant must enable the leader to understand that emotion is only destructive if it is not recognised, and that grieving and returning to work are not separate phases, one of which must be passed through before the other is possible. The leader must accept that the dichotomy between personal (emotion) and work (practical) is false and unhelpful. Work obviously has to be resumed, but the way it happens is crucial. If the leader expects people to 'get back down to it' immediately without acknowledgement of grief or pain, by modelling strength, this will be seen as insensitive and will cause resentment. The leader must understand that showing emotion is not a sign of weakness, but a sign of strength, and far from undermining their leadership, it may strengthen their credibility.

Leaders can facilitate a number of things which will aid recovery:

1   Ensure a formal psychological debriefing takes place. Organisational preparation creates the ground for the clinical work to be undertaken and enhances the likelihood of a successful intervention. However, this is really only feasible where there exists an appropriate structure. Ideally, when interventions in organisations following trauma are planned for, there should be a policy which sets out the commitment of the organisation, describes the operational procedure and the standards which govern its operation, and ensures that appropriate non-clinical functions are carried out by trained in-house staff. In the case of large organisations, where debriefings will be carried out frequently, it is essential that there should be a well-developed policy; strong, unambiguous management commitment; workable procedures; and clear liaison with the clinical providers. In organisations where no such preparation has been made, debriefing has to be carefully explained to those who may participate.
2   Enable the group to meet a new challenge. Army units who have suffered a fatal accident are observed to restore their morale quickly if

they can successfully complete a difficult training task soon after the tragedy (102). After a workplace arson attack, one of the authors who was acting as consultant noted that a team who normally worked in one big office had been split into a number of different rooms across the building. This reduced opportunities for support. The managers agreed to a further relocation to another large office, with staff organising the removal of the materials, computers, etc., which had previously been done for them when they were absent.

3   Facilitate small groupings. Workers will naturally select other workers with whom they feel greater comfort and affinity in expressing their feelings. The leader must allow such groups to come together. By allowing this to happen during, rather than after, work time, the organisation is signalling that it cares. Again, after the workplace arson, the consultant encouraged mangers to allow small workgroups to convene to discuss anxieties about safety in the workplace.

4   Mix with the group. The aftermath of tragedy is often a point where leaders become separate from the group, because they feel isolated, or because of sudden demands of administrative tasks related to the accident. The leader who mixes with the group becomes more identified as part of the group, and is less likely to have group feelings projected onto them. There is almost bound to be anger about management – 'the powers that be' – whenever things go wrong. This can be confronted and mitigated.

5   Provide accurate information. Rumours and gossip abound after tragedy. These may undermine group functioning, and the best way to combat them is for the leader to provide accurate information as soon as is practicably possible. There is information about not only what has happened, but what is to come, possibly in the shape of an inquiry or inquests. Workers need to know what they will be expected to do or say, with whom, when and why. The legal process holds particular terrors.

6   Enable rituals. Rituals help people come to terms with things by providing a structure: when a group carries out a ritual, it strengthens the common links between members (10). Rituals can be more or less formal. After the Zeebrugge disaster a group of relatives went out in a tugboat and held a small memorial service close to the capsized ferry. Videos of this were later made available to other bereaved relatives who were not present. On the anniversary several hundred relatives sailed to the site of the disaster for a service and to throw wreaths into the water.

    Other rituals may be more personal. After an avalanche disaster which killed a number of soldiers on a NATO exercise, the surviving platoon members made up books about the military service of each of those who died, and presented it to their families (117). It must be remembered that there is no one correct formula for memorialisation –

there are many. The most useful thing the leader may be able to do is to create space for group discussion about the issue.

INDIVIDUAL CRISIS COUNSELLING

Disasters of course very often affect groups of people who are completely unconnected with each other. After their exposure to tragedy they return individually to their homes. After the disasters of recent years in the UK, lead agencies established a programme of proactive visiting to such individuals to establish crisis counselling. Most disaster workers reported considerable difficulties with their initial visits, feeling helpless, hopeless and deskilled, with nearly all revealing that they were anxious about how they would be received. Many made sure they had a tight script to follow. Some made the arranging phone call in private lest they be overheard by a colleague. Others repeated their script as they drove around in their cars. One worker, on his first visit to a survivor, drove past the house several times before finally stopping to complete the task. This anxiety contains not only fear of rejection, but also fear of the unknown. There is of course reality to this, as disaster is generally personally unknown – there is nothing to compare it with. Therefore, if helpers say they lack adequate information and preparation, and feel uncertain about their purpose and role, this is an authentic position to be in. In many cases the client has been through a catastrophic experience about which, in the main, nothing very much can actually be done. Both client and helper remind each other of their helplessness. The question 'What can I offer to this client?' is a legitimate one to ask.

Both helper and client will be anxious, threatened with loss of control and failure. This can all too easily happen when the worker feels overwhelmed by what they are confronted with. One warning sign is the length of the interview. It was not uncommon for relatively inexperienced disaster workers to boast that they had spent three or four hours with a client – several clients a day, every day. Nothing will lead to burnout more quickly than this level of exposure to extreme distress. Only structure can ameliorate this problem, and the psychological debriefing process sets out such a structure.

Introductions

Bearing in mind that the client is largely reluctant and that the helper totally lacks credibility, the first few minutes take on a great deal of importance. It is this initial encounter which strikes such fear in the hearts of support workers. They will have sent a carefully worded letter of intention to call, perhaps backed up with a phone call, and their opening gambit should run along the lines described in the introduction to debriefing: 'My name is . . . and I work with the . . . team. I am the person who wrote/phoned.'

Identification may be desirable. After the Hillsborough disaster, it was rumoured that members of the press were actually posing as social workers on Merseyside in order to gain access to survivors. As a result social workers were issued with cards.

Additional preliminary ground to be covered in the first few minutes of the interview includes an explanation that all survivors are being offered a service. This will have the effect of destigmatising the process. The client's likely feelings of awkwardness, embarrassment, worry or even anger at having to have a visit in the first place must be addressed, and shows sensitivity and confidence on the part of the helper. Experience has shown that survivors have their own novel way of dealing with this unusual situation. Helpers are often taken completely by surprise when the client expresses concern that they have such a very difficult job to do and wonder if anyone is looking after their interests. A large pile of sandwiches, cakes and tea may be waiting. This concern is probably genuine, but also strategically restores what the client perceives as a loss of balance in the relationship. The response to this solicitous overture must, above all, be credible. The survivor knows disaster is harrowing – the worker knows the work is harrowing. Simple acknowledgement is called for.

Time boundaries

At the beginning of the interview, it is also wise to tackle the issue of time boundaries. A time limit should be agreed for the interview and this should accord with what is commonly agreed among professional helpers as sensible. A time limit creates a convenient break; otherwise the experience can be negative and draining and the client may eventually be unwilling or unable to bear any more.

Providing information

How much the support worker follows the debriefing model is a matter of training, and the agreed aim of the service of which they are a part. However, the education element will certainly be appropriate in an initial session. The information that the helper can give is primarily of three sorts. The first is factual information, such as about the process of coroners' courts. Secondly, there is information about the reactions that the survivor may experience. Thirdly, the survivor must be presented with the potential benefits of the service. Information will be of value even if there is no further contact.

The helper brings to the interview the ability to help move pieces of the jigsaw of reactions. Whereas in group debriefing other participants would confer normality on reactions, here the burden is on the helper to do so. The helper knows the same things have happened to others in similar situations, and must be able to give a thorough, informative account of reactions that can be anticipated in these circumstances, and what may be expected in the future. They will often find it helpful to share other survivors' stories and reactions to build credibility. Literature, as in debriefing, augments any verbal account, and may be even more important in this individual situation.

The notion of 'selling' implies presenting a service to the client in a way that they understand what is being offered and can make an informed choice. Most sales training works on the principle that the essential point is to establish that there is a need. Only then is it possible to offer a service. It is possible to isolate those factors which are considered to be positive and helpful in the experience of 'purchasers' from those which are offensive and negative. Negative experiences include insincerity, being 'pushy', hesitancy, anger at resistance, overfamiliarity, presumption, hastiness, being hard to get rid of, and being disrespectful. Positive experiences include good knowledge of the product, honesty about disadvantages, inspired confidence, allowing time to reflect, respectfulness, creating a sense of choice, and being non-threatening. High on the list of important factors in the selling process is knowing the product well and having the capacity to demonstrate it. Unless this is present, the client has no real choice. The first choice the client can – and often does – exercise is to refuse a service. So a major undertaking for the professional is to develop a good presentation of what is on offer.

Following the Bradford fire, one of the authors found himself in the sitting room of his first disaster client. He had written a carefully worded letter in which he had sensitively suggested a visit. After a cup of tea, he went on to state that he was 'here to help'. The client pounced mercilessly. 'Go on, then', he said in a quiet, deliberate tone. Helpers are often poor at giving a clear, simple account of what they do. They use inaccessible language, woolly expressions, all of which refer to little that is concrete. Unless we can tell our clients in concrete terms what it is that we are offering to them, we cannot expect them to feel it will be worthwhile. The introduction to debriefing set out above attempts to achieve these sorts of things briefly, realistically and with clarity.

Coping with emotion

It may well be that during the initial session the client will begin to describe their experiences, or they may wait until a proper 'contract' has been set out. Either way, at some point, emotional anguish will surface – the recounting of the incident will create numerous triggers which will bring on bouts of crying, anger and despair. As with debriefing, it is not the objective of such a session either to 'squeeze out' or pass over the survivor's pain. Indeed, great care should be taken in eliciting emotion – the notion that 'it is good to experience and express feelings' may simply reinforce for the survivor how awful things are, and that 'counselling' is simply the pointless recycling of feelings that cannot be dealt with. The helping process may be choked off at this point, the survivor retreating to attempt to repress their feelings. The structure of the interview must allow the client to express feelings in doses, and the provision of information about the normality of reactions goes part way towards helping contain them.

In individual sessions the worker does not necessarily (unless other family members are present) have the opportunity as in debriefing to leave the person for a moment, move to another person and encourage comforting by a neighbouring participant. The response of the worker must be authentic – the survivor will be sharply aware of any insincerity and guesswork. They may say 'But you cannot understand . . . ', to which the only honest reply is: 'No, I cannot understand, but I know how what you are saying makes me feel . . . '. The issue of the cognitive causation of feelings will be as important in an individual session as in a group. In the event that the survivor does enter into strong feelings, the helper must observe the need for a period of gentle debriefing at the end of the session.

The helper as 'witness'

Given the circumstances, it is entirely authentic that the helper should subside in humble acknowledgement. At times, the professional task may be to do no more than listen and witness. These are the delicate moments when the professional's credibility is on the line. So-called therapeutic techniques like acceptance here mean to restrain the temptation to make things right with reassuring words. There are times when the survivor needs to know that what they are going through is awful and there is nothing that can be done or said to alter the fact. The helper's behaviour needs to say 'I accept that you are going through a dreadful experience and there is nothing I can do to prevent it, but I am willing to be a witness so that you are not alone'. Family, friends, colleagues and neighbours, partners in ordinary daily sharing, often cannot witness in quite this way.

Helpers often feel a sense of uselessness in these circumstances because they believe their training should equip them to put things right, to make a difference in some palpable way. Their disappointment in themselves is a reflection perhaps of their failure to understand what is required of them. The real task is to allow pain, to witness and not to deny. This is help and it is useful.

Agreeing a second interview

The question of arranging a further interview is crucial. Indeed, it might be said that one of the main aims of the first interview is to arrange a second (providing of course that the helper and survivor both see it as desirable – a second meeting must not be a reflection of the helper's helplessness and inability to 'leave alone').

We must consider whether such visits are helpful or harmful. Table 4.2 shows perceptions of helpfulness of such visits made by staff from the Herald Assistance Unit after the Zeebrugge disaster (133): 6 per cent of survivors and 4 per cent of the bereaved found the visits either 'harmful' or 'very harmful', whereas 70 per cent of survivors and 62 per cent of the bereaved found them either 'helpful' or 'very helpful'. Largely, therefore, such visits appear worthwhile to survivors and run little risk of causing harm.

Further sessions

This section was entitled 'crisis counselling'. However, as the review of treatment in the next chapter indicates, there is little evidence that 'supportive counselling' makes any marked impact on post-traumatic symptoms. Such sessions may be satisfying to the counsellor, and even to the survivor, but little real progress may be made. Even if a debriefing approach is taken in the initial session, the literature reviewed indicates that any crisis counselling must include the following components:

1 Detailed review of the event, constructing an account and allowing 'exposure'.
2 Education.
3 The use of cognitive techniques to foster restructuring of distorted beliefs.

LITERATURE

The use of literature has been recommended as part of the debriefing process, and it is in itself a tool of outreach. Indeed, the Supper Club Fire Aftermath Center found the use of printed matter had a 9:1 superiority over television as a means of communicating information (190). It was suggested that many factors probably contributed to this – quality, style, source, timing and trusted authorship – and that

this finding is also consistent with the internal experience of the survivor, namely, the struggle to contain fearful intrusive thoughts and images connected with the trauma. Survivors repeatedly told us that the unexpected message over TV or radio is yet another

Table 4.2 Perceptions of helpfulness of visits by the Herald Assistance Unit

	Very harmful	Harmful	Mixed feelings	Helpful	Very helpful
Survivors	4%	2%	24%	33%	37%
Bereaved	2%	2%	34%	33%	29%

unwarranted intrusion, while the printed message could be discarded when overstimulating, yet retained when manageable.

The history of the use of literature in the field of health education is long. One such example, devised for use after disaster, was the leaflet 'Coping with a Major Personal Crisis', which was constructed by three doctors following the 1983 Ash Wednesday bush fires in Australia. This leaflet, couched in simple, everyday language with an avoidance of jargon, sent to the Mayor of Bradford after the football stadium fire, served four main functions:

1 It provided those affected with information about the sorts of emotions and physical sensations often experienced.
2 It gave a list of simple 'do's and don'ts'.
3 It suggested when it might be appropriate to seek professional help.
4 It indicated where professional help might be obtained.

The self-report of those receiving the leaflet testifies to its effectiveness. One widow of the Piper Alpha disaster, when asked what she thought of the leaflet, replied that she did not know because she had not really seen it as her 10-year-old son slept with it under his pillow each night. Only one project has looked at its effectiveness in an organised way, following the Red Arrows' crash on a village in Lincolnshire (178). The leaflet was posted through the doors of 300 people who lived closest to where the two planes crashed: 91 per cent who had received the pamphlet had made some effort to read it, and just over a quarter had continued to keep it. By and large most people felt that it had been a good idea and helpful to circulate it, 'although many of them remarked that they themselves had not needed the information contained, but that they felt that there were obviously other people who were going to benefit from this sort of help'. To a certain extent this must represent a defence against feelings, because clearly a quarter had kept the leaflet because it meant something to them.

Women were more likely to rate the leaflet positively than men. This may well have been due to those younger women having been at home and hence having experienced a more direct sense of threat from the crash. Younger residents of the village were more likely to rate the pamphlet positively than those who were older or retired, who often commented that they had lived through the war without any support. Those who were younger, and hence with less life experience, found it useful to have their strange new feelings validated without judgemental 'condemnation or a look of consternation'. It was suggested that whilst the leaflet suited the needs of a severely traumatised group, with its focus on post-traumatic reactions, it lacked an emphasis of coping with non-fatal events. Overall, however, the arrival of the leaflet was experienced as a sense that someone cared.

Is such material harmful? Table 4.3 shows perceptions of helpfulness of the 'Coping with a Major Personal Crisis' leaflet distributed after the Zeebrugge disaster (133). Whilst there is a sizeable percentage of mixed feelings, no survivor found the leaflet 'harmful' or 'very harmful', whilst only 3 per cent of the bereaved did so.

It is clear that a range of literature can be usefully developed, covering major to non-fatal incidents. Further, there is a need to develop different material for children than for adults. With the increase in the establishment of local disaster response teams, stocks of such material may be established with contact numbers included, for immediate distribution. Indeed, in 1995, when a cargo aircraft narrowly missed crashing onto a housing estate outside Coventry airport, such a leaflet was posted through the door of everyone on the estate within twenty-four hours.

TELEPHONE HELPLINES

The survivors of disaster, their relatives and the bereaved may make their first contact with helpers on the disaster site itself. The helper's role here is not counselling, but the provision of information, comfort and assistance with such tasks as identification of bodies and notification of death. The relationships formed on the disaster site are often strong and long lasting. Many people, however, will leave the disaster site having spoken to no one, returning to a home where those they love may find it very difficult to listen to their experiences. The telephone helpline may therefore literally be a lifeline, and the first point of contact with a helper, offering immediate access. The establishment of a such a line, that is not a service simply offering information but offering a listening ear to anyone who wishes to share their experiences, has been a feature of the aftercare provided after most major disasters in the UK.

Many who occasionally used the helpline at the Herald Assistance Unit, which was available twenty-four hours a day for twelve months, remarked that 'we didn't use it much, but knowing it was there, and that we could ring at any time, was so important'. The telephone outreach (although this involved helper ringing survivor, rather than vice versa) following the Beverly Hills Supper Club fire was the most effective form of outreach.

Table 4.3 Perceptions of helpfulness of the leaflet 'Coping with a Major Personal Crisis'

	Very harmful	Harmful	Mixed feelings	Helpful	Very helpful	Never read
Survivors	0%	0%	21%	35%	23%	21%
Bereaved	1.5%	1.5%	36%	36%	12%	13%

Whilst most of the survivors contacted by our telephone team failed to come to the Centre, they generally expressed appreciation and support of our outreach effort. Many responded with pressured accounts of their experiences in the fire, subsequent sleeplessness, difficulties at work, phobias, and nightmares (190).

Following the Hillsborough disaster, speedy work enabled the helpline number to be given out twenty-one hours following the disaster. By the end of that day, some seventy calls had been received. Within ten days the helpline had taken 1,650 calls from people who actually wanted counselling (216).

Some workers have hoped that helplines could soon be scaled down or terminated. Thus the Piper Alpha helpline took 594 calls in the first four weeks (just over a third requesting information, just under a third requesting a counsellor's visit), but only forty-five calls in the following ten days (323). However, after this, there is generally a small but definite use. For some, this route of communication was an important tool. The Herald Assistance Unit helpline was available twenty-four hours a day, switched after 5.00 p.m. into team members' homes. Despite anxieties about this, it was never burdensome. There was a small group of clients who would sometimes ring at about 2.00 a.m. Clearly they had been unable to sleep and had dwelt more and more upon their difficulties until it became unbearable in the loneliness of the night. One young man, who would never give his name, who rang regularly during this period had lost his common-law wife. There had been a custody battle between him and his wife's parents for his son, which he had won. He found it impossible to approach the unit formally to talk about his anguish, because he believed that his son would be taken away if social workers knew who he was, and how badly he was coping. The relative anonymity of the telephone allows people to disengage, removing as it does the sense of any long term commitment.

A model for a helpline is one which becomes integrated into the everyday work of the disaster response team, and is available twenty-four hours a day for at least eighteen months. The skills needed are simple and yet difficult for many professionals because the task is unusual for them. Volunteers may well be equally or better equipped for this task, especially those with a Samaritans background. Because visual cues are absent, careful listening becomes essential, as do other traditional counselling skills such as reflection. Callers are easily put off by an overprofessional approach which seems to be converting them into a 'case', or appears intrusive by suggesting a face-to-face contact too early in the interaction.

Helplines, however, have disadvantages. Firstly, there is no way of guaranteeing that the person will actually get through to someone at the moment they need to, and such moments are easily lost. Secondly, the telephone may inadvertently discriminate against certain groups, and setting up a freephone arrangement may be desirable.

NEWSLETTERS

Individual work and groupwork are possible with an identified survivor population which is willing to work in these ways. Newsletters are a useful means of keeping in contact with survivors in a non-obtrusive way, while at the same time keeping the door to help open should they feel like taking it up at any future date. The Bradford newsletter, *City Link*, was a model which was later adopted in the wake of other disasters. It was the brainchild of a social worker whose aim was to mobilise the resources of survivors themselves and to reach out to those who were too ashamed to make themselves known to counsellors. It was to become for many the only acceptable place to share a feeling, divulge a problem, or ask a question. Once again it was important that survivors could communicate with survivors. There are five main functions of a newsletter:

1 Distribution of information to the widest possible group, either about the outreach effort, or about other aspects.
2 Provision of a vehicle for seeking views about particular issues, for example different forms of memorialisation, from the widest range of people.
3 Provision of a forum whereby those affected can share thoughts, feelings and experiences about the disaster.
4 Provision of a place where educative material about coping may be located.
5 Provision of a forum whereby survivors can ask questions which they failed to ask at the time – 'Who was the lorry driver in the tartan jumper who kept me out of the water? I never thanked him for saving my life and would like to be able to do so now.' Similarly, the bereaved can pursue questions that remain unanswered – 'This photograph is of my husband whose body has never been recovered. Did anyone see or talk to him, who could tell me how he died, or what he was doing?' These will be recognised as important steps in formulation.

The editors of *City Link* were survivors. Five were bereaved, five had suffered burns; hence the newsletter had extraordinary credibility. *City Link* was to be independent editorially from its sponsor, the social services department, and this enabled it to respond freely and honestly to the needs of its audience. It was a self-help project and the editorial group took their work very seriously. The whole point for them would have been missed if the editorial function had been directed by professionals. First and foremost, it preserved their credibility with their readership. Secondly, and hardly less important, it preserved their dignity. They were not dependent on welfare, they were in control. The social workers on the editorial board did not get their own way – the survivors had the majority of the votes so decisions were invariably biased away from the professional perspective on things.

The newsletter created a reciprocity in the giving and taking of help. The letter, so helpful to the writer, was help to the reader, perhaps because it gave permission to express something similar. Anger was such a feeling. The need to share with those who understood became more important as time went on. As outside interest turned to ambivalence and then to indifference, *City Link* remained a steady focus for survivors' concerns. The editors knew that people moved at their own pace, in their own time and in their own way. People were not encouraged to get better – they were simply encouraged.

The editors were also able to recognise when it was time to move on. They were all too aware of how easy it would be to become more or less a permanent victim of disaster. They ended the newsletter at the beginning of the summer of 1988, three years on. *City Link* won a national social work award. Whilst not all those on the editorial board felt that they could take part in the celebratory award ceremony, there was a sense of intense achievement for non-professionals to receive an award alongside professionals.

There is divided opinion about whether it is absolutely necessary that the newsletter should be run only by survivors. After the Piper Alpha explosion in the North Sea, the oil company involved began to publish *Piper Link*. This was viewed with some cynicism by survivors and professionals alike. The newsletter had been published by those who were an apparent legitimate source of anger, and this created difficulties for the establishment of a newsletter that had more chance of acceptance. *Piper Line*, started by the Piper Outreach Team, published eight editions during the eighteen months of the team's existence, thereafter being taken over by the Piper Alpha Families and Survivors Association. A newsletter published following the King's Cross fire was subsequently taken over by the Families Action Group (323). These newsletters have developed particular characteristics. Whilst appealing for material from children, *Heraldlink* (established after the Zeebrugge disaster) received none. *Piper Line* developed a character called Bosey Badger to appeal to children. This produced a good response, and the drawings and letters were powerfully moving. Another feature of such newsletters is the tendency of those affected to express themselves in verse – men and women of all ages who had never written poetry before suddenly began to write simple, unsophisticated, but powerful poems, which expressed their feelings more keenly than many pages of letters.

Heraldlink was distributed, of course, to crew survivors and bereaved as well as passenger survivors and bereaved. It was sometimes difficult for the crew to cope with the anger expressed therein towards themselves by a small handful of contributors. Further, many of the survivors felt that the newsletter was more the province of the bereaved. However, *Heraldlink* had a mailing list numbering 686 individuals, and during the year of its circulation there was only a 1.5 per cent refusal rate. Given the 15 per cent overall visit refusal rate, it truly went where professionals could not go.

Again, we must consider whether this material is helpful or harmful. Table 4.4 sets out perceptions of the helpfulness of the *Heraldlink* newsletter: 5 per cent of survivors found it 'harmful' or 'very harmful', whereas 4 per cent of the bereaved did so; 63 per cent of survivors found it 'helpful' or 'very helpful', as did 62 per cent of the bereaved.

Table 4.4 Perceptions of helpfulness of the *Heraldlink* newsletter

	Very harmful	Harmful	Mixed feelings	Helpful	Very helpful	Never read
Survivors	1%	4%	26%	18%	45%	6%
Bereaved	4%	0%	31%	26%	36%	3%

5

TREATING
POST-TRAUMATIC STRESS
AND ABNORMAL GRIEF

Crisis intervention is intended to minimise the likelihood that unnecessary disturbed and disturbing psychological reactions will develop. In this chapter we will explore therapies for those individuals in whom post-traumatic reactions become entrenched.

Treatment strategies must be able to address the following areas of post-traumatic responses:

1   The traumatic event – recollection. Emotional processing must begin with the events themselves. Any treatment package must therefore begin with a full exploration of the traumatic events in immediate debriefing or later in psychotherapy or behavioural therapy. This may start at the point of assessment, be repeated in more detail, and become very detailed and repeated if an exposure treatment approach is adopted, such as imaginal systematic desensitisation or flooding. For those who still find thoughts (or images) difficult to manage, distraction techniques can be employed.

2   Cognitive appraisal and dysfunctional beliefs. Cognitive therapy can be employed to attempt to identify and modify distorted thinking, automatic negative thoughts or irrational beliefs.

3   Intense emotion and overarousal. Relaxation (aided if necessary by biofeedback techniques) can be employed to reduce arousal in general, and may be part of a behavioural exposure treatment approach. Medication may be used with some individuals to reduce bodily arousal. Techniques of anger management can be utilised to combat raised levels of irritability.

4   Avoidance. Exposure treatments such as *in vivo* graded exposure or flooding may be an important tool in allowing the person to return to the situation where the trauma occurred and achieve some mastery of their anxiety.

5   Emotional numbing and depression. Anti-depressant medication may be necessary to treat a concurrent depression before intensive psychological treatment begins. Activity structuring may reduce both

150

depressive helplessness and the withdrawal from normal activities. Couple counselling or family therapy may be used to tackle the relationship difficulties that the person's withdrawal and irritability creates.

EXPOSURE TREATMENT OF PTSD

Behavioural treatments involve the exposure of the person, either in imagination or real life, to the feared situation, allowing them to experience a decrease in anxiety. This can be done in a graded, hierarchical way (systematic desensitisation) or without a graded approach (flooding). Behavioural treatments are based on the idea that fears are learnt, and are maintained by avoidance. The notion of learning, or rather maladaptive learning, does explain some elements of PTSD. All sorts of stimuli present during the trauma become attached, or 'conditioned', to the anxiety of the event. These may include the place, other people present, the time of day, or even thoughts, which become powerful triggers of anxiety in their own right.

Unlike other fears, post-traumatic stress has the particular feature of constant reliving in the form of intrusive thoughts, flashbacks or nightmares. Despite this re-experiencing, the fear does not go away, or extinguish. This may well be because victims (i) learn to avoid painful memories or things which stimulate them, (ii) allow other emotions (such as anger) or behaviours to become more prominent, or (iii) simply do not have access to memories because they are attached to a very high state of arousal, so-called 'state-dependent learning' (166). All successful treatments of PTSD involve some element of controlled exposure to trauma-related stimuli (82).

Systematic desensitisation

Systematic desensitisation involves pairing the stimulus, the memory of the traumatic event, with the incompatible response of relaxation, which should lead to the extinction of the arousal connected to the thoughts and memories. An example is provided by the treatment of a recurring nightmare in a Vietnam veteran of an incident some nine years earlier where he had seen the virtual disintegration of a fellow soldier who had stepped on a mine (276). Progressive relaxation was taught and a seven-stage hierarchy was constructed that followed the progression of the dream.

1   A convoy is preparing to deliver supplies and the road is being swept for mines.

2   The patient is at the end of the convoy on the machine gun turret of a truck. There are three soldiers behind.
3   Two Viet Cong flags are seen – the area is checked but no mines are found.
4   The patient asks if one of the foot soldiers wants a ride. The reply is negative because of orders to walk.
5   Further on, another flag is found. A soldier steps on it, setting off a mine and a crossfire ambush.
6   The patient tells the truck driver to back up in order to rescue the soldiers on foot.
7   Only two men get on, and a crater is found with the charred remains of the third. The patient reports the gruesome smell of 'burnt meat'.

The patient progressed up the hierarchy in imagination, using relaxation whilst imagining each scene, and when anxiety was rated as nil, progressed to the next scene. Self-administered desensitisation was carried out at home (further habituation of anxiety between sessions being considered an important part of the technique). In all, there were five bi-weekly sessions of thirty minutes. At three- and seven-month follow-up there had been no instances of the dream, and although there were several partial recurrences before reserve duty, they were essentially anxiety free.

   In a study of nine cases of survivors of rape (324) systematic desensitisation brought about improvements in measures of anxiety, depression, fear and social adjustment. In a larger, controlled study of survivors of this particular trauma (91), between 67 and 75 per cent of patients showed improvement in fears with systematic desensitisation. In a group of ten veterans (26), systematic desensitisation was effective in reducing autonomic nervous system arousal associated with intrusive re-experiencing, as indicated by drops in measures of heart rate and muscle tension. In a study of seventeen trauma survivors (90), fourteen sessions of systematic desensitisation led to decreases in anxiety and fear, as well as measures of social adjustment. However, 75 per cent of the patients in this study voluntarily began *in vivo* desensitisation, that is they began to carry out desensitisation in the actual feared situation without being bidden.

   There is a general trend throughout the literature on exposure therapy to favour flooding, it being not only quicker, but also generally more effective. It has been suggested that the images evoked in flooding are not only more intense, but also involve 'stimulus, response and meaning elements, and therefore allow for more complete emotional processing' (111). Relaxation is not viewed as a necessary component of flooding treatment. However, as this represents a skill which can be used in situations of prolonged stress (e.g. a person suffering from a phobia of car travel undergoing self-exposure), it seems unwise to ignore this strategy. This should follow the usual format (18) of muscular relaxation in which as the technique is learned, cue words become associated with the feelings of relaxation, and the muscular exercises are omitted. This can be coupled with pleasant imagery training, which increases the sense of relaxation and the person's skill in maintaining positive images.

Imaginal flooding

Flooding aims to lead to habituation of fear by simple exposure to the highly feared stimulus straight away, with avoidance prevented. An example is given by the treatment of a Vietnam veteran who had panic attacks, depression, alcohol problems, traumatic nightmares and other intrusive phenomena, sleep problems and social anxiety (165). Three war events were related to the flashbacks, nightmares and intrusive thoughts: the accidental death of a fellow soldier whilst a rifle was being cleaned, the death of another in an ambush, and feelings of helplessness and anxiety whilst on night duty with orders not to fire until fired on. Treatment proceeded with ten minutes of relaxation at the start of each ninety-minute session, followed by forty minutes of flooding, where the patient focused on traumatic imagery.

> A scene began by instructing the patient to imagine the weather conditions, terrain, the specific locale, the accompanying individuals, and the patient's emotional status prior to the occurrence of the trauma. The details of the event were then slowly and gradually presented by the therapist who regularly elicited feedback from the patient regarding the next chronological event in the sequence. When the patient became visibly anxious, especially during the most disturbing aspects of his memory, he was encouraged to retain the image as long as possible until it was no longer anxiety provoking. All scenes were concluded by eliciting the events and emotions associated with the time immediately following the trauma.

Treatment was carried out over twenty-two days. During treatment anxiety ratings declined, and sleep improved. At three- and twelve-month follow-up, anxiety levels were still low, there was no alcohol abuse and social behaviour had greatly improved. Nightmares and flashbacks were rarely experienced.

In a controlled study of Vietnam veterans (167) flooding sessions of ninety minutes' duration were used, including fifteen minutes of introduction, ten minutes of relaxation, forty-five minutes of flooding, ten minutes of relaxation and ten minutes of concluding integration. Not only did anxiety and fears improve, but re-experiencing, startle responses, and memory and concentration difficulties decreased as well, as did measures of depression. These gains were maintained at six-month follow-up.

Combined imaginal and *in vivo* treatment approaches

As behavioural treatments for PTSD have developed, so the tendency has been to develop combined treatment approaches, involving a number of different behavioural strategies. One such programme (267) centred around imaginal treatment sessions lasting ninety minutes, of which sixty involved exposure. The patient imagined and recounted the traumatic experience in the first person, present tense, as if it was actually happening. The therapist would ask the patient to hold distressing scenes in their mind until reported distress levels dropped. Sessions were audiotaped, and the patient was required to listen to this at home, four times per week, thus essentially repeating the session in home work. New tapes were generated for each treatment session. Relaxation was not a necessary component of treatment. Residual phobic avoidance was eliminated with *in vivo* exposure, but such treatment was ineffective or only partly effective if attempted first, perhaps because of an increase in concurrent depression. All patients improved, achieving 'resolution of all major PTSD symptoms'.

The use of audiotaped sessions as home work has become a widespread adjunct to treatment. A variant of this, named image habituation training (333), involved patients providing six brief descriptions of recurrent images. Each description was followed by a thirty-second silence during which the patient was asked to 'visualise as intensely as possible the meaning that the description evoked'. Subsequently, the patient listened to the tape for one hour each day. Decreases in anxiety were noted both within and between sessions, anxiety being highest in the first session, dropping to a plateau until session 4, and habituating by session 10. Of ten consecutive patients treated with the technique, six improved considerably after ten sessions (none worsened), and gains were maintained at six months. Patients suffering from alcohol abuse, high arousal levels, irritability, low levels of intrusion, and an inability to focus on the stimulus were regarded as less likely to benefit.

A further development of these methods (315) has been called CEASE (Conditioning pairing, Engram formation, Arousal, Stimulus generalisation and Extinction). Treatment began with a non-time-limited 'debriefing session' (although with a stronger emphasis on imaginal exposure than the account of debriefing given in the previous chapter). Subsequent sessions lasted ninety minutes, once weekly. Imaginal exposure was then initiated, as described above, with the patient 'reliving' the traumatic events, recounting them in the first person and present tense, including as much detail as possible, across all sensory modalities. The account was audiotaped during each session, and patients were asked to listen to this at least three times a week between sessions. A 'rewinding and holding' technique was used to get the patient to focus on particularly distressing aspects. For instance, the therapist may have asked the person to stop and repeat themselves, prompting for more detail (stimulus, response or meaning). Alternatively they may be asked to hold or freeze a particular distressing image or scene in their mind, without trying to avoid or neutralise the accompanying emotional reactions.

After imaginal exposure was underway, graded in vivo exposure was begun, although it was noted that it was sometimes difficult to develop a strict hierarchy. Thus whilst it might be easier to produce a graded hierarchy in a survivor of an RTA, it was more difficult in the case of someone subjected to violent crime. 'Where necessary, separate hierarchies were constructed for different sorts of external traumatic stimuli.' Lastly, cognitive restructuring was employed, specifically 'Socratic questioning to elicit attributions and beliefs surrounding the trauma, training in identifying and challenging automatic thoughts, and behavioural experiments'.

Twenty-three patients were treated with this package, and there was a low drop-out rate, although home work compliance was variable. On the measures used, reductions of between 35 and 61 per cent were achieved. Half of those who suffered PTSD no longer qualified for this diagnosis at the end of treatment. Alcohol abuse was seen as a contraindication for this sort of therapy.

In vivo exposure has formed a part of several of the programmes described. Survivors of the Zeebrugge disaster were accompanied on ferry trips across the Channel. This was done in a graded way with survivors initially taken to the docks, then onto a ship in dock, and only then across the Channel. One interesting example of an in vivo exposure technique is described (147) in the treatment of a pilot involved in a helicopter crash, who had developed guilt feelings, nightmares and a fear of not being able to fly. Nine days after the crash the pilot was introduced to a helicopter accident simulator as part of a course over two and a half days, the first day of which involved theory. On the second day he elected to enter the simulator last, and was initially distressed. However, after re-emerging he immediately felt substantial change and symptom measures then dropped with time. The treatment involved desensitisation (the first day of the course), modelling (seeing others enter the simulator) and flooding, enabling the pilot to recover 'feelings of mastery and control'.

A warning note must be sounded concerning potential under-recognised complications in flooding treatment. These are listed as (245) exacerbation of depression, relapse of alcoholism and precipitation of panic disorder. The mechanism for this is the mobilisation of negative post-trauma appraisal, accompanied by shame, guilt and anger. It therefore behoves therapists to make a thorough assessment (although alcohol abuse is often not evident on assessment), and to treat depression beforehand.

The relative values of imaginal and in vivo exposure have been tested (268). Fourteen patients with PTSD were randomly assigned to two groups. One group had four, weekly, hour-long sessions of imaginal exposure followed by four, weekly, hour-long sessions of live exposure. The second group had the same treatments, but in reverse order. Patients were also asked to do at least one hour of home work daily between sessions, taking charge of their self-treatment programme. This usually involved repeating exercises carried out within the sessions. Home work compliance was 70 per cent. The imaginal exposure used the methods described above, and it was noted that in most cases within-session reductions in subjective units of discomfort (SUDs) would be of the order of 25 to 50 per cent by the end of the hour, with audiotape home work producing SUDs reductions of 50 to 75 per cent between sessions. *In vivo* exposure was not always to 'exactly the same situations as the trauma since many traumatised patients avoid a wide range of situations, for example survivors of shipwrecks often avoid other forms of public transport'. Exposure was carried out until SUDs reduced by 50 per cent, or at least one hour of exposure had been completed. 'Therapists remained with patients, ensuring no distraction took place, and asked for SUDs ratings every five minutes.' Both groups improved significantly on measures of both post-traumatic and general symptoms, by between 65 and 80 per cent. No patients met the criteria for diagnosing PTSD at the end of treatment, and there were no relapses by one-year follow-up. The order of delivery of imaginal or *in vivo* exposure made no difference to rate or extent of recovery, but *in vivo* exposure provided greater improvement on measures of trauma-specific behavioural avoidance whether delivered first or second.

Finally, some qualitative analysis has been made of the changes of accounts of the traumatic incident during imaginal exposure (89). In a group of fourteen survivors of rape who underwent the exposure treatments described above, which led to substantial improvements on measures of PTSD and depression, the following changes were observed. During nine sessions, the survivors had relived their accounts anywhere between thirty-five and one-hundred times. Firstly, the narratives as a whole tended to become longer, 'perhaps reflecting the victims' increased ability or willing-ness to engage in the processing of the trauma as anxiety decreases over the course of treatment'. Secondly, the percentage of thoughts and feelings increased whilst the percentage of actions and dialogue decreased. 'These changes may indicate a shift in emphasis toward greater processing of emotions and meaning associated with the trauma and reduced attention to the details of the assault itself, which become less relevant as the memory becomes less threatening.' Thus without directly focusing on a cognitive perspective, cognitive changes take place. Reliving produces 'a more organ-ised memory record that can be more readily integrated with existing schemata' (272). There was a particular increase in 'organised thoughts' (thoughts 'indicating attempts to understand the events of the assault'), which were negatively correlated with measures of depression. Decreases in cognitive 'fragmentation' were highly related to improvement. Those who benefited least from treatment were those whose accounts contained more negative feelings, particularly helplessness, and whose accounts contained more repetitions, an indication of fragmentation, 'further suggesting fragmented narratives reflect the absence of emotional processing'.

In concluding, the following observations can be made about exposure therapy:

1   There is good evidence that exposure treatment leads to improvement in PTSD symptoms, as well as other associated symptoms such as depression. Imaginal flooding leads to more rapid improvement than desensitisation. Where there is a strong element of behavioural avoidance of feared situations, *in vivo* exposure should also be used.

2   Individuals should be carefully assessed as alcohol or drug misuse is a contraindication for such treatment. Any concurrent depression should be treated first, and patients with high arousal levels should be taught management techniques for these, as should those with a tendency to dissociate. Those who have poor skills at using imagery may have difficulty with the technique, and those who have little or no re-experiencing symptoms are unlikely to benefit.

3   Those entering therapy should be given a thorough explanation of the therapy techniques to be used, and their rationale. Many are naturally reluctant to relive their traumatic events. They should be provided with written information concerning these to consider outside the session. Clients should also be clear that their reactions may temporarily worsen rather than improving.

4   Average therapies of eight to ten sessions are typical, although as few as four sessions may be effective.

5   Care should be taken that clients should approach the reliving of a trauma gradually in the first session (and it is important to emphasise that it is reliving rather than retelling that is required). To attempt to progress too fast may lead to the client feeling out of control. More detail may be encouraged in subsequent sessions. Clients must not be left at the end of a session with high levels of anxiety as indicated by their SUDs. Sessions should last for sixty minutes.

6   Home work sessions utilising taped material from sessions with the therapist are essential for rapid improvement. Steps should therefore be taken to maximise compliance. Firstly, home work must be linked in the client's eyes to treatment goals. Secondly, a contract can be drawn up, anticipating reasons for non-adherence to tasks. Thirdly, written material can be used for the client to record home work, and fourthly, home work must be reviewed and progress praised.

7   Exposure therapy does lead to cognitive changes. These are not necessarily therapeutically sufficient, and more direct cognitive therapy may be required.

COGNITIVE THERAPY OF PTSD

Cognitive therapy techniques enable clients to monitor negative automatic thoughts, to recognise the connections between thoughts, feelings and behaviour, to identify dysfunctional or irrational beliefs which lead to distorted perception, to examine evidence for and against automatic thoughts, and to substitute reality-oriented interpretations (79,115).

Beliefs dispose people towards certain emotional reactions by (14):

1   Leading them to search out and selectively attend to certain types of events and features, a sort of cognitive hypervigilance. Thus the person involved in a train crash may listen to noises whilst on a journey and think 'What's that noise, is there something wrong?' Cognitive therapy would assist the person to substitute anxiety-reducing alternative self-statements such as: 'That noise is only the train going over points. . . . I've heard it many times before.'

2   Influencing the event and experiences through a process of evaluation. Thus the person involved in a car accident may think, 'I should have seen them coming, I should have been able to avoid them, I'm just a useless driver'. Guilt may often arise from such critical evaluation. It has been suggested that 'guilt has proved to be one of the most difficult symptoms to effectively reduce as a function of cognitive restructuring' (166). However, self-critical statements such as 'I didn't do enough – maybe I should have dived back into the water again and rescued others' can be tackled. These have to be reality tested – the reality of the situation and the range of possible reactions have to be made explicit. The therapist must help the person to build an explanation based on realities. 'The intent is to prevent the patient from over-generalising about his behavioural patterns based on actions committed during the life-threatening stress' (166). Thus, 'The water was so cold and if I had gone back in I might never have got out again. Perhaps there were more people to be rescued, but I might not be here now if I'd tried to do it myself'

is a more realistic appraisal.

3   Keeping emotionally loaded, past negative events alive and anticipated future happenings vivid. Thus the person keeps going over the events in their mind, often constructing different, more calamitous endings.

Thoughts starting with 'If only I hadn't . . . ', and 'What if . . . ?' may become rife, distorting the evaluation of future dangers. Thus, Vietnam veterans developed irrational beliefs such as 'If I get close to someone they will die and I can't stand that again', and 'Every time I care about someone, something bad happens to them' (166). A cognitive therapy approach might help a veteran to substitute more rational self-statements along the lines of:

Of course anyone I care about will eventually die, but it is relatively unlikely that they will be snatched away from me as were my buddies in Vietnam. It would be unfair to both myself and my friend [lover, spouse] to enter this relationship intending to keep them at a distance. I won't experience the rewarding parts of the relationship with such an attitude.

4   Indirectly creating events that prompt behaviour consistent with perception. Thus the person who is having difficulties in relationships with others following the trauma may think when talking to someone, 'She's asking me what it was like, but I saw her look at that man over there – I'm sure she's just like all the others, she doesn't really want to know'. This may lead to a reply along the lines of 'Look, what's the point in my telling you, you simply won't understand', a reply that only serves to reinforce others' avoidance. Cognitive therapy would assist the person to substitute a more rational alternative thought: 'I can't expect people to really understand what happened, and I can't always expect them to make allowances for the way I feel from moment to moment'.

Distorted beliefs and thinking need to be actively elicited. Therapists can employ three sorts of questions (218):

1   Evidence-based questions. These involve the detection and hypothesis testing of automatic thoughts, where the therapist enables the client to externalise thoughts and reconsider evidence. Therapists can simply ask directly about clients' thoughts. They might say: 'What were you thinking when X happened?' and then 'When you get into a situation in which you get frightened now, what goes through your mind?' If the client says 'I'm too frightened to do X, I'm hopeless', the therapist can 'adopt an inquisitive style like the television character of the detective Columbo', demonstrating puzzled confusion about the contrast between the automatic thought and other demonstrations (however limited) of coping. Once a style of hypothesis testing has been established, the client can collect data through self-monitoring, which further undermines the automatic thought.

2   Alternative-based questions. These involve the therapist helping the client to evaluate thoughts and beliefs, and to 'generate alternative

explanations for events, in addition to those he or she first adopted'. Thus the therapist might ask:

You worry that your colleagues share your belief that you are a failure because you ran away when the gunman confronted you. What makes you think that? Are there other explanations for how they have reacted to you? How do you think they would have reacted in the same situation?

3   Implication-based questions. These involve the therapist helping the client 'to examine whether his or her initial beliefs, even if true, necessarily imply everything that, at first, they seemed to imply'. Thus the therapist might say:

The gunman confronted you for two minutes. You seem to think that your place of work is too dangerous now. Is that the case? How many times has this happened to you or people you know? Is there a risk that you will allow two minutes to spoil the next twenty years by letting the gunman continue to terrorise you?

In these debates, the therapist can reflect that the client suffers a range of distortions in thinking that produce faulty logic. These include (218): (i) dichotomous, or black-and-white thinking; (ii) all or none thinking, equating 'one mistake with total failure'; (iii) overgeneralisation, one negative event confirming that everything is awful; and (iv) personalisation, where clients blame themselves rather than recognising the contribution of external factors.

Sometimes dysfunctional beliefs have to be very actively pursued by the therapist before they become clear to the client. One method for achieving this is the 'downward arrow technique' (13). This involves the therapist reducing the client's statements to their core of meaning by asking 'Suppose that were true; what would that mean for you?' The sort of progression might be: 'I can't go out'; 'I'd get scared'; 'Something might happen'; 'Me and my children would get hurt'; 'The world is so dangerous that I cannot trust anything anymore'.

One prime method for eliciting alternatives, or generating material on which alternative thoughts may be based, is 'Socratic questioning'. This has been described (218) as 'the most useful skill the clinician has'. Socratic questioning involves the therapist asking the client 'questions that lead the client to use his or her knowledge and skills in discussing and employing new concepts or procedures. Socratic questions nurture a discovery process, not merely call for the retrieval of specific facts.' Clients are led to discover and invent solutions for themselves, rather than have their minds changed or thinking corrected by the therapist.

Examples of these questions include the following (after 218):

- 'What would you do differently if you were less depressed/bothered by these thoughts?'
- 'If you could do anything at all when you are feeling fearful/depressed not to feel that way, what would it be?'

Socratic questioning may also involve exaggeration of the irrational nature of clients' cognitions, 'so that they may have an easier time mounting a rational argument or dispute against them' (292), often through a series of leading questions.

The development of an account of the traumatic event is also a therapeutic cognitive technique. From a 'constructive narrative perspective' people's lives are a narrative in which key events form particular stories. A trauma is an event whose story has to be embroidered into the wider tapestry. All forms of therapy by and large start with survivors giving the story of their traumatic event and their adjustment (or not) to it. This may be hard to do to start with, and needs repeating. Five cognitive mechanisms have been identified which survivors report using as coping methods in their account building (307). These include:

1 Comparing oneself with those who are less fortunate.
2 Selectively focusing on positive attributes of oneself in order to feel advantaged.
3 Imagining a potentially worse situation.
4 Construing benefits that might derive from the traumatic experience.
5 Setting normative standards that make one's adjustment seem normal.

If one of the goals of psychotherapy is to provide a 'means of helping clients construct a new narrative' (218), then events may be reframed by reinforcing the clients' use of these five processes, and metaphor can be employed to rework perceptions, leading clients to accounts which are congruent with their views of themselves and the world.

The metaphors used by clients in their account building may give important clues to their emotional processing (218). For example, if the client with emotional numbing describes that 'There is a wall between me and other people', the therapist can employ the client's metaphor and ask 'Who built this wall?' (after all, a wall has to be built by someone). This can be pursued further by asking

> What function do you think the builder meant the wall to serve? To keep things in, or to keep them out? Can you see over the wall? Is there a gate? Is it locked? If so, who keeps the key?

Thus, the therapist uses the client's metaphor in the Socratic dialogue. Similarly, the therapist may introduce metaphor. One of the authors was treating a mother whose elder son had been tragically killed. Worried about her younger son, she brought him to a session. On their own, and struggling to discuss the notion of bereavement with the 9-year-old, the therapist used the metaphor of a train journey to describe the process. The child's face lit up with recognition – 'Oh, in that case I think I'm near the end of the journey' he said, adding 'but I don't think mummy's train has left the station yet'. Indeed, he was so right – the mother's anxiety about him was pure projection of her own unresolved grief.

The cognitive behavioural techniques available can be summarised as the following (after 322):

1 Increasing awareness by questioning which identifies negative automatic thoughts and elicits realistic thinking.
2 Using analogies and metaphor which promotes the examination of thinking from a different perspective.
3 Encouraging personal experiments which test beliefs.
4 Reframing behaviours and events in a positive light.
5 Role reversal, where the therapist takes the role of the client and demonstrates their negative feelings, and the client takes the role of therapist to challenge these.
6 Humour.
7 Information giving.
8 Helping clients to identify their plight as a-problem-to-be-solved.
9 Modelling other people's adaptive responses.
10 Self-instructional training, where the person identifies the self-defeating, anxiety-inducing statements, and plans a series of more realistic statements which promote better coping to be used in the situation.
11 Generating alternatives to negative thinking by rehearsing the stressful situation in imagination and substituting an alternative feeling.
12 Employing distraction techniques.
13 Assessing change.

Case studies illustrate the use of these processes (317). One man was attacked with a knife whilst working as a taxi driver. His PTSD included considerable avoidance in that he was unable to go out alone, and travelled when accompanied in a car with all the doors locked, with constant hyper-vigilance. A daily thought record indicated automatic thoughts concerning the overestimation of danger. He estimated that there was an 80 per cent probability of his being assaulted if he left his home. In therapy he was asked to 'calculate the number of times he and his friends had been out alone in the three years prior to the assault' (6,913 times), and with the aid of a calculator it was computed that there was a 0.04 per cent chance of a future assault. Faced with this, the client used 'probabilistic reasoning' to counter his overestimation of danger, and adopted the premise 'My chances of being attacked are no more than other people's'. His belief in his negative automatic thought reduced to 10 per cent, and the strength of the alternative thought was rated as 90 per cent. The client, without being bidden, started to go out again with friends, and then alone. He was also sensitive to his scarring, his automatic thought being 'People with scars are assumed to be criminals . . . if anybody sees this scar, they will think I am a criminal'. He rated the strength of this belief as 85 per cent. In exploring the validity of this, the client was asked to list all the other supposed physical attributes of criminals. When he saw that the list of these did not correspond to a list of his own attributes, the strength of his belief dropped to 40 per cent. After further work, he was able to formulate an alternative response: 'Features such as acting suspiciously, having a previous criminal record, etc. are suggestive of someone being a criminal, rather than having a scar'. His belief in this thought was 100 per cent, and the strength of his previous belief now dropped to zero.

Another client who was assaulted in his own home, answering a knock at the door, had belief of 100 per cent strength that 'When there is an unfamiliar knock at the door I'm going to be attacked again'. In therapy, he calculated that he had received 14,500 knocks on the door without being assaulted, and that the risk of assault was 0.007 per cent. When he was at home after this he substituted the more rational thought that 'I've had over 14,500 unfamiliar knocks on my door and it has never been an attacker'. The strength of his original negative automatic thought dropped to 10 per cent. Further, this client blamed himself for the breakdown of his relationship after the assault. His automatic thoughts included 'I've lost everything. I'm a total failure. It's my fault I'm in such a mess. It was something I did that finished B and me', and he rated the strength of these thoughts as 90 per cent. The client was encouraged to review the evidence, and was able to reattribute causation, for example he reattributed his loss of earnings to his PTSD, rather than any inherent failing in himself. Treatment of both clients took place in ten sessions of ninety minutes' duration, and progress was maintained over six-month follow-up.

These techniques have been developed in group programmes. In one such programme (266), nineteen survivors of sexual assault were involved in twelve weekly group sessions of one and a half hours. The first session presented an information-processing formulation of PTSD, and the participants were asked to go away and write about the meaning of the event for them. Session 2 developed an ABC (Antecedent–Belief–Consequences) model, differentiating between feelings and thoughts. Then, a full account of the rape was constructed for each person over two sessions, detailing all aspects, including sensory details, emotions and thoughts. In session 5 participants were taught to identify and challenge maladaptive beliefs and in the subsequent sessions five areas of beliefs were examined, concerning safety, trust, power, esteem and intimacy. In the final sessions, subjects were asked to write about the meaning of the event again, and changes were reviewed. In comparison with a waiting list control group, the clients improved on measures of PTSD and depression, and the improvements were maintained at six-month follow-up.

A further study contrasted various procedures (87). Forty-five survivors of rape were randomly assigned to one of four treatments: stress inoculation training (incorporating relaxation training, training in coping skills to counter obsessional thinking and cognitive restructuring); prolonged exposure; supportive counselling; and a waiting list control. There were nine bi-weekly sessions of ninety minutes. Stress inoculation training was most effective (in the short term) in reducing PTSD symptoms, but prolonged exposure was also effective. Supportive counselling and being on the waiting list reduced arousal, but had no impact on intrusion or avoidance. On general symptom measures, no differences were found between the treatments. At three months, prolonged exposure showed most gains, followed by stress inoculation training, then supportive counselling.

The most effective techniques were combined in a group treatment package (88). Ten survivors of assault were offered four two-hour weekly meetings which covered education in common reactions to assault, breathing and relaxation training, and then imaginal exposure (reliving the assault), during which the therapist noted cognitive distortions about dangerousness of the world and perceived incompetence. This was followed by *in vivo* exposure which involved confronting feared but safe situations. Finally, based on the information gathered during the imaginal exposure, cognitive restructuring was carried out. Two months later there were significant reductions in PTSD symptoms, and five and a half months later there were significant reductions in depression and re-experiencing. The therapists concluded that the essential aspect of treatment was that the 'fear structure must be reactivated and new information provided which is incompatible with the structure'. The process of systematic exposure to the traumatic memory in a safe environment leads to the re-evaluation of threat cues, with the assistance of cognitive techniques, and leads to habituation.

Stress inoculation training (SIT) was used as an adjunct to some of these programmes and was shown to be effective (87), although it is not clear which aspect of the package it is that is effective. Such training involves teaching a variety of coping skills, and encouraging clients to practise these in a graded fashion. SIT is implemented in three phases (218). In the first phase the client is educated in the nature of stress and anxiety. When PTSD is specifically being addressed, the client must firstly be given an account of PTSD symptomatology, so that their experiences are normalised (as discussed in the previous chapter when examining debriefing); and secondly an account must be given of the mechanisms of trauma which is congruent with the treatment proposed, for example the model of 'shattered belief systems' if cognitive therapy is to be employed. In the second phase, the client is taught a variety of coping skills to address the physiological, behavioural and cognitive aspects of the problem emotions. Lastly, in the third phase, the client applies their new skills in imagery rehearsal, behavioural rehearsal in the session through role play, and then *in vivo* exposure. This might be used, for instance, to tackle the irrational angry outbursts which are common in PTSD. Firstly, the client would be enabled to prepare for provocation. Thus they might adopt the self-statement: 'I know when I get in their things will be all over the floor. This can make me uptight so I'll need to begin to relax myself before I go through the door.' Secondly, the client would prepare for confrontation with thoughts such as: 'OK, I'm not going to let this get to me. I'll just pick the things up myself.' Thirdly, the client would have been taught strategies to deal with the arousal that normally accompanies these situations. They would rehearse thoughts such as: 'I'm beginning to feel uptight . . . now, take a deep breath, tense the muscles, let them go, relax . . . ', Finally, they would review what had happened. If it was not handled well, instead of catastrophising, they would need to say 'I'll need to relax more before I go in next time . . . it'll get better with practice'; or if successful, they might say to themselves: 'I did well . . . I controlled my temper . . . none of the nasty aftermath of no one speaking to me . . . this really works'.

In concluding, the following points may be made about cognitive therapy:

1   Whilst exposure therapy is the first choice for clients with whom re-experiencing (or its avoidance) is a major issue, and may in itself lead to cognitive changes, these may not be therapeutically sufficient.

2   During the account-giving stage, or in the reliving of exposure treatment, the therapist must attend closely to the client's statements, listening for areas of distorted thinking. The therapist may choose to focus further on the development of the client's narrative, reworking thoughts and reframing events and reactions, as a cognitive technique in its own right.

3   An early stage of cognitive treatment focuses on education, giving the client an understanding of the range of reactions and symptoms (a framework within which to place their own reactions), and providing a model for understanding post-traumatic reactions (within which the treatment method may be justified). This will also be a further adjunct to generating an alternative narrative.

4   Negative automatic thoughts and beliefs must be actively probed for, using the information the therapist has already gleaned as a starting point. These will then need to be monitored by the client.

5   Using SIT techniques, and guided by Socratic questioning, alternative self-statements and behaviours can be generated. These can be rehearsed in therapy before being tested out in practice.

6 Cognitive therapy may be carried out in group sessions, which makes it cost effective. Eight hours of therapy (over four sessions) has been shown to be effective, but longer courses of treatment have generally been employed.

Eye movement desensitisation and reprocessing

Another treatment which has gained wide usage is eye movement desensitisation and reprocessing (EMDR) (282), a technique that was discovered entirely fortuitously. On the face of it, this procedure appears to be a type of exposure treatment with an emphasis on distraction and cognitive restructuring. Theoretically, it is suggested that survivors' information-processing mechanisms 'may be blocked by a traumatic event'. The information concerning the trauma cannot be processed and remains unintegrated. The proponents of EMDR claim that 'EMDR appears to catalyse the information processing system, making possible the appropriate metabolisation and integration of the dysfunctional information' (accelerated information processing). How the specific technique achieves this is not clear. It is a mystery enshrouded in convincing detail.

There are eight phases to treatment. Initially, there is history-taking, client preparation, and assessment, which involves identifying the components of the problem to be treated. The survivor is asked to select the image that best represents the traumatic memory, and identifies 'the negative cognition that expresses the dysfunctional, negative self-attribution' related to this. Then the survivor identifies a positive cognition which is 'more rational, realistic and empowering'. This is rated on a seven-point validity of cognition (VOC) scale, ranging from 'it feels totally false' to 'it feels totally true'. The emotion associated with the event that is to be imagined is rated on a ten-point scale of subjective units of discomfort (SUDs), from 'neutral' to 'the worst it could be'.

In the desensitisation phase, a series of rapid eye movements (saccades) are generated while concentrating on the traumatic memory. The rapid eye movements are generated by the therapist's finger moving horizontally from the extreme right to the extreme left of the client's visual field at a distance of 30–40 centimetres from the face (although diagonal, vertical and circular movements can also be used). This back and forth movement is repeated about a dozen times, each bi-directional group of eye movements being considered as one set. (Alternatively, alternate taps on the client's palms, or the therapist snapping their fingers alternately on each side of the client's head, may be used.)

After each set, the client is instructed to blank out the image or cognition, take a deep breath, and then recall the picture or words, get in touch with the feeling generated and re-evaluate the SUDs. If a new picture is recalled, then that is desensitised before returning to the old. After the distress level has dropped to zero or one, the installation phase is commenced, where the alternative cognition (or a more appropriate one that has emerged during the desensitisation phase) is installed. This is complete when the VOC reaches six or seven. The next phase comprises a body scan, where the survivor holds in their mind the imagined scene and the positive cognition, and scans their body for residual tension. Lastly, there are phases of closure and evaluation.

Permanent changes may be achieved by a single session, but we are warned (282) that 'EMDR is not a one-shot treatment', rather one whose effects need monitoring to ensure gains are retained. The following example of the use of the procedure is of a 26-year-old woman who had recently returned to the family home after an unsuccessful spell at university, and who was experiencing a serious deterioration in her relationship with her parents. She was puzzled by this as relations between them had always seemed good. At the same time she was experiencing a recurrence of a more familiar problem: low self-esteem and tearful episodes while alone with herself.

In the course of the first session she put her low self-esteem down to a year in which she was subjected to a succession of bullying episodes while at school, aged about 12. Since then she regarded herself as inferior to her peers academically, and personally unattractive. She felt a failure in the eyes of her parents and this feeling was reinforced by her more recent disappointments at college. The EMDR procedure was suggested and she agreed to try it. It was explained that she should imagine she was in a carriage on a moving train and would notice memories as though observing a scene out of the window. Sometimes this would be accompanied by strong emotions. She was not to be too concerned as the train would simply move on and a new image would replace it. A SUDs level of seven was determined for the bullying memory and this was accompanied by tearfulness and rapid breathing. After several sets of eye movements the client arrived at a much more disturbing site yielding a SUDs level of nine to ten. She described a scene in the kitchen of her old home when she was about 6 years old. Her grandmother received a friend and was serving up a cup of tea, at the same time introducing her granddaughter as 'the one who almost killed her mother when she was born'. She was referring to the fact that her mother was dangerously ill following her birth and almost died. The client had completely suppressed this scene in which she heard her grandmother lay the blame on her young shoulders. After several saccades the SUDs level reduced to four. The session then returned to the bullying episodes and again, after several further saccades, the SUDs level reduced to two. Further work on the kitchen scene then yielded a SUDs level of two. The positive cognition chosen, although against recommended procedure in that it contained a negative in the statement, was 'I am not responsible for my mother's poor health' and this yielded a validity rating of six to seven.

No further eye movement was carried out in the next (and last) session. However, the client reported that she had, on one of the intervening evenings, confronted her parents with her memory of the scene in the kitchen and explained the trauma it had caused and the subsequent effect on her over the years. In so doing, she believed she had drawn a line under it. At follow up several weeks later, she reported a positive change in her general well-being, and a gradual sense of growing self-confidence.

Another example is given by the use of the procedure with a 28-year-old Israeli woman who had suffered from a fear of the dark and other night-time fears since childhood, made worse by rocket attacks and terrorist infiltrations from the nearby Lebanon (51). Her anxiety had reached intense levels, 'making her demand that her husband check the house, windows and doors several times following the slightest sound from outside, and make him stay awake on vigil until she would fall uneasily asleep'. The memory chosen for desensitisation was that of an early incident of bombing, which led to a reported initial SUDs level of nine to ten, the accompanying bodily sensations being of a churning stomach and frozen horror. The summarising statement was 'I am terrified'. Within four sets of eye movements the SUDs level was reduced to one and the accompanying body sensation had disappeared. A new cognition of 'I am now more courageous' was introduced, initially at a VOC of three, and after three further sets of eye movements, the rating was at the maximum, seven.

> The following day the client reported that there was no paralysing fear or nervousness before going to sleep (for the first time for three months), however, she had been troubled with intense nightmares about terrorists throughout the night, waking up many times and falling asleep again to another nightmare. These nightmares lasted only for that night and the following nights had been free of fears and bad dreams. The thoughts which were so terrifying could now be entertained with only a minimum of anxiety, making her much calmer altogether. This period lasted for a week after which there was an alert following a suspected terrorist incursion. Flares lit up the sky and old fears resurfaced, although to a lesser extent than they would have done previously. During the following session these new fears and accompanying body sensations were desensitised and the desired cognition reinforced was, 'It is probably only a false alarm, and if not there is only a minute chance that anything could happen to me or my family'. During subsequent alerts with flares and distant explosions, over a period of three months . . . no further attacks of anxiety occurred.

The technique has generated a spirited debate (219). Attracted by reports of high success rates, some previously sceptical clinicians who have approached the method with a 'let's try it' attitude have become strong converts. One of the authors (MS), who is a trained EMDR therapist, found the training courses, which are faultlessly run at a remorseless pace, to have an almost irresistible evangelical zeal. The central issue is, however, whether the technique is demonstrated to work or not.

A series of thirteen controlled studies (80) all showed EMDR to have superior results, in varying degrees, to other approaches. Few of the treatments against which EMDR was tested, however, involved the focused use of the behavioural and cognitive techniques described earlier in this chapter. However, in one study (334) thirty-six subjects with PTSD were randomly assigned to treatments of (i) imaginal exposure, (ii) applied muscle relaxation, and (iii) EMDR. Treatment consisted of four sessions with daily home work over a two- to three-week period for the first two groups, and none for the EMDR group. All treatments led to significant decreases in PTSD symptoms, with a greater reduction in the EMDR group, particularly with respect to intrusive symptoms. Recent EMDR studies (80) 'with single trauma victims indicate that after three sessions eighty-four to ninety per cent of the subjects no longer meet the criteria for PTSD', for example a study of rape victims (270) where 90 per cent of participants no longer fulfilled the full criteria after treatment. However, as might be expected, negative results are reported. Thus, in one study (201) forty-five subjects with traumatic memories were assigned to (i) EMDR; (ii) non-eye-movement desensitisation (involving eye fixation on a stationary target); and (iii) a non-directive counselling session control group. Results for EMDR were not found to be significantly different from the control group and were 'possibly less efficacious than having subjects stare at a dot on the wall' (219). Overall, however, there is growing evidence that EMDR is a tool of clinical efficacy, which establishes gains rapidly.

PSYCHOTHERAPEUTIC APPROACHES

There are many different psychotherapies and psychotherapeutic techniques. Most stem from the psychoanalytic tradition in more or less direct ways. In this section we will look at the contribution of psychodynamic therapy to the treatment of post-traumatic stress. By psychodynamic therapy we are meaning therapeutic endeavours that focus on internal processes, conflicts and defences, the intra-psychic factors. The scope of such therapy in the wake of trauma is defined (188) as focusing on 'the meaning of trauma-related symptoms and behaviours and on the meaning of catastrophic life events to the person as a whole'.

Some working assumptions about intra-psychic recovery following trauma and loss have been identified (187) that are important to understanding the principles of therapy:

1   'Working through' the effects of trauma and loss is a normal process, whereby the affected person breaks down the thoughts and feelings into manageable chunks, and, over time, processes them. Processing involves: (i) the recovery of feeling-laden memories, (ii) the attribution of meaning to these memories, and (iii) the re-establishment of 'psychic continuity' with the past, that is putting the trauma in its place alongside other life experiences and beliefs. These notions should be familiar from the preceding chapters of this book.

2   This process of working through trauma is often incomplete, in that the natural resolving processes are inadequate for the task. In order to achieve a proper working through there must be a 'cohesive self', that is sufficient internal strength and resources. Certain types of severe trauma will be overwhelming in terms of the accompanying feelings, and this threatens the loss of the cohesive self.

3   Reminders of the experience, rather than giving food for working through, repeat the internal sense of threat of overwhelming feelings. Survivors develop internal barriers to protect themselves from the frightening intensity of conflicting feelings. Defences such as 'splitting and disavowal' are used to attempt to defeat the threat of further internal trauma, forming a 'trauma membrane'. Unfortunately, these split-off traumatic memories 'press for expression' in some way and set off an 'intrusion–denial' cycle which requires considerable psychological energy to manage.

4   As time passes, 'the reminders of the traumatic experience may take . . . [a] more disguised form'. The survivor loses the understanding of the connection between the disturbing emotion and the trauma itself. They know that something is very wrong, but simply do not understand it.

5   The survivor may then become suspicious of those whom they feel cannot understand the meaning of the trauma, and who pose a threat to disturbing the 'trauma membrane'. Fellow victims who understand the trauma may be safe to allow within the membrane.

Two main assumptions lie behind therapy (191). Firstly, that 'trauma and grief are best resolved by processing gradual, carefully dosed awareness of the event's significance, associated affects and conflicts'; and secondly, that there will be pressures to keep the trauma membrane intact. These will arise from within the patient and 'for the purposes of treatment this tendency is to be understood as a resistance to the work'. The therapist, however, may find it easy to collude with these pressures, owing to countertransference issues related to their own possible past trauma or loss-related feelings, or their fears about the overwhelming nature of the client's feelings.

Therapy can be seen as comprising three phases (187). The 'opening phase' begins with the victim allowing the therapist (or the therapist 'earning the right') to enter beneath the 'trauma membrane'. This is a tentative and gradual process, and can only be begun by the familiar process of asking the person to relate in as much detail as possible the trauma itself and the thoughts and feelings experienced before, during and after the events. Done in a comfortable climate, without the sense of being rushed, and with encouragement to explore in detail, rather than skim over, a depth of exploration never previously embarked upon may be achieved. Trust, once established, tends to be extremely strong. We are cautioned, however (189), that 'it is the patient who should make the reconstruction of the memory, not the doctor'. A factor that proves to be important in this phase (191) is the therapist allowing themselves to show that they are genuinely moved. This process of sharing common humanity with the survivor was emphasised earlier in this book, but carries risks, as we will note in the following chapter.

During this process the person will undoubtedly refer to painful feelings, thoughts and disturbed behaviours which they have suffered since the events, but which they do not necessarily understand as being connected. It is the therapist's task to interpret the triggers for these as being connected to the traumatic memories of the events, and the feelings associated with these.

The 'opening phase' leads to the 'working through phase'. Here, the interpretations linking triggers and feelings in the present back to the event itself lead to the identification of the 'special configuration of the traumatic event', the profile of key feelings (many of which will be highly conflicted) and their meaning in terms of the person's previous psychic development, the 'trauma-specific meaning'. The therapist may then assist the client to organise the disturbing feelings into coherent and manageable chunks.

Pace is most important. Clients may threaten not to return if asked to tell too much, too soon. 'Successful therapists maintained a steady, expectant, but non-demanding presence which facilitated gradual release of affect-laden material, as well as permission not to reveal that which the patient was not ready to convey' (191). This is highlighted in the treatment of the survivors of torture (298). The issue of trust is crucial and the therapeutic alliance would be destroyed if the therapist became seen as a persecutor, and identified with the aggressors, an outcome likely if the therapy is not paced to allow the feelings to be processed in a dose-related fashion. The experience of too much psychic pain at one time may become a torture in itself.

In considering pacing of interpretation, it is helpful to bear in mind the 'triangle of conflict' (212), which reminds us of the psychic structure associated with powerfully disturbing repressed feelings (see Figure 5.1). This triangle comprises three elements: (i) defence – the particular mechanism used to deal with the disturbing feelings; (ii) anxiety – the consciously experienced feeling which indicates the presence of powerfully disturbing emotion; and (iii) hidden feeling. The correct way of progressing through this is firstly to identify defence mechanisms, then to develop a shared understanding of the anxiety as being related to unprocessed feelings, and lastly to proceed to identify the highly conflicted and powerfully disturbing

171

hidden feelings of helplessness, rage, guilt, shame, etc. The therapist aims to create a container, a safe space where the chunks of trauma which are too painful to be managed alone can be faced without the threat of being overwhelmed. Negative transference often threatens to disrupt and shut off this process, and it is vital that this is interpreted as a reflection of feelings such as helplessness and loss of control, or frustration on the part of the survivor (187, 191).

Useful aspects of transference which appeared in the successful psychotherapies of survivors of the Beverly Hills Supper Club fire had three components (191). Firstly, there was the phenomenon of reliving the experience in therapy. 'The tendency toward repetition of trauma within the treatment situation holds a central place in the psychoanalytic psychotherapy of . . . PTSD' (189). Thus one client was walking down the corridor with his therapist when he suddenly felt that the walls were hot, and thought he could smell smoke. He fled, re-enacting having left his wife during the fire. In subsequent sessions following interpretation and examination of this, he became more stable. However, it is likely that such repetition will only be allowed when sufficient trust has developed. Secondly, there is a further transference phenomenon of the client seeing the therapist as the lost object. Indeed, we are warned (189) that 'It is the therapist's task to keep as empathically in contact with the patient in the here and now as possible, including strong feelings directed towards the place or person of the therapist'. Thirdly, there is the possibility of the client relating to the therapist as an 'auxiliary superego', as with one patient who explicitly sought permission from the therapist to move away from her dead son's children without guilt.

In the 'termination phase', the survivor begins to gain confidence in processing the painful memories, and the sense of mastery increases. The person reclaims the 'disavowed affect, gives meaning to the absurd

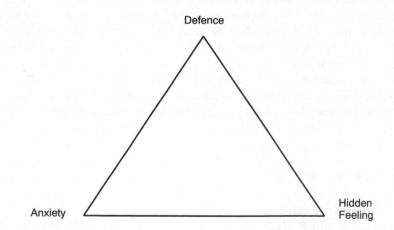

Figure 5.1 The triangle of conflict

catastrophe, and regains psychic continuity between past, present and future'. This last phase is therefore one in which the therapist helps 'the survivor find continuity in self and to disconnect from the therapy' (188). Endings are not easy, however, and many therapists view them as incomplete (298). This may represent over-optimistic attitudes on behalf of the therapist, or countertransference of survivor guilt, where the therapist feels that they have not done enough to help the client.

Many clients who experience a traumatic event have experienced earlier traumas, which may have become completely repressed. One psychoanalytic therapist (189) described a client who had been the survivor of a laboratory explosion. She described shame, and guilt that she had done something to bring on the explosion. In later discussions of the event she 'reported a specific symptom of dropping a test tube with her right hand. The symptom repeated itself, especially when she was expecting a chemical reaction to take place.' Working on the therapeutic principle that if a client repeatedly draws a therapist's attention to something, then that something represents an element of their difficulty that demands attention, the therapist suggested 'that the symptom might condense an earlier trauma. The warm exploding cylinder in her hand became then an inroad to multiple childhood incest experiences, which most often involved her being forced to masturbate her stepfather.' This exploration was only possible after the client had developed a good deal of trust, and indeed, the test tube symptom only became apparent in 'a period of relative psychological recovery'.

The issue of aggression is considered by some as being of prime importance in the process of post-traumatic decline. 'After serious trauma, the human becomes a reflection of the violence wrought upon him and remains so until there are dynamic changes in adaptive resources modifying and moderating the violent impulses via interactions with others' (319). Put simply, the survivor is involved in a terrible struggle to contain their rage and aggression, which mirrors the aggression done to them in the first place, and which has terrible feared consequences. 'Something as destructive or threatening as the original trauma is expected should one's violent impulses exceed the capacity to control them, though raging violence within was stimulated by the trauma itself.' With other defences damaged by the trauma, these aggressive impulses can only be held in check by more primitive defences such as isolation and projection, which then become symptoms of PTSD in their own right. In therapy, the feelings of aggression may be kept well hidden from the therapist, and there is the possibility that the therapist may collude with the avoidance of them. They may emerge in transference, or in countertransference when the therapist finds themselves very angry with the client, for example when they miss a session. Only by examining the realities of cause and responsibility can a balance be achieved between aggression and other more rational defences.

A study of psychotherapy with the survivors of the Beverly Hills Supper

Club fire (191) described aspects and outcome of therapy with thirty fire survivors. The therapies were brief (six to twelve) sessions, and focused on fire-related experiences. Of the thirty survivors, five never engaged in treatment, three of whom appeared to be very distressed, and two minimally. Clients with a diagnosis of PTSD, with or without major depression, were more likely to have interrupted treatments, seemingly confirming the notion that such people fear that the reactivation of memories and feelings will be overwhelming. Those with a diagnosis of depression alone were less likely to have interrupted treatments, possibly because trauma played a less important role in their difficulties. A higher rate of engagement and completed therapies was found with experienced clinicians. Patients of therapists who had been in the mortuary were more likely to complete treatment (58 per cent), than were those whose therapists did not have the experience and hence themselves had not processed personal, painful disaster-related experiences (23 per cent). Most of the completed cases had at least seven sessions. Those who completed showed more positive change than those who interrupted their treatment. Alternatively, those who interrupted their treatments did not appear to have been made worse by the experience, in that they showed no negative change afterwards. Indeed, there is evidence that both interrupted as well as completed treatments showed some further improvements over the following two years, whilst a group of non-treated patients failed to improve with time, and indeed in some respects were worse two years on.

Evidence for extent of treatment effects suggests enthusiasm should be tempered. In a study of dynamic therapy with trauma survivors, eight one-hour sessions were conducted, the first session of which involved a detailed discussion of the disaster, the remaining sessions concentrating on working 'within the limits of brief psychotherapy to help the patients deal with the effects' (316). After conclusion, measures of symptoms suggested that therapy had reduced distress levels by one-third in relation to population norms. Whilst useful, this improvement could not be described as substantial, and 'the pattern of results suggest that forty per cent of the total symptomatic gain can be achieved by simply giving the patient an appointment date'.

GROUP AND RESIDENTIAL PROGRAMMES FOR PTSD SUFFERERS

Survivor groups tend to flourish with or without professional interest. A parents' group was formed with the help of professionals after the Piper Alpha disaster, and members travelled long distances to attend. A group was formed after the Manchester air crash in 1985 to agitate for improvement in aircraft safety standards. Following the Zeebrugge disaster, the Herald

Families Association was formed, among other things, to press for the prosecution of the ferry company. Following a train crash in North Yorkshire, in which several passengers were killed, a group was formed two years after the event because no organisation would offer help. Their coming together at least partially arose out of a sense of outrage that so much was being done for survivors of other disasters and not for them. Also, these groups do not remain in isolation – associations arising from various disasters meet and offer each other support, and even combine. What these groups have in common is the desire to express identity by being together. This sense of identity is quite often centred on anger and a sense of the uniqueness of participants' experience. In a group, survivors can be witnesses for each other.

Professionally supervised 'support' groups are common after disasters. Several professionally run groups appeared following the Bradford fire in 1985. The origin of much of this work was simple expedience – it was the only practical way to see so many people with limited resources. In this context, the more informal the introduction of the idea of groupwork was, the better. Survivors were far more likely to respond to an invitation to share over a cup of tea with people who have had similar experiences, than to agree to treatment in the presence of complete strangers.

Following the Bradford fire, by far the largest group of the seriously injured were elderly men. The 'burns team' shared them out across their caseloads. During team discussions, the workers discovered that these old men were suffering in a few common areas. For example, they were plagued by survivor guilt. They were old and many of the dead were young. They believed they had behaved no better than cowards by not returning into the blaze and rescuing someone else. They had not behaved with chivalry – they were being tormented by their own ideals. The team thought that they might benefit from being in a group.

This group throws interesting light on what is meant by 'acceptable' help. They were old men set like concrete in their ways. 'It fetches tears inside' said one as he tried to explain how the fire affected him. The tears remained inside. The group had many unspoken conventions – being a man and being allowed to swallow back the tears was one of them. This was not a group in which catharsis was the aim; the men wanted to help and be helped but not to be humiliated by tears. It took the form of a small club, being friendly and supportive. Whilst at first it was a little sombre and bristly, later on people laughed. From time to time, however, they talked about some hard things. Once a quiet man told a hushed meeting about killing teenage Germans in the Italian Campaign of the Second World War. Another told how the sinking of the *Herald* hurt him more than the fire – it reminded him of how a close family member drowned off the Cornish coast years before. One of them died. The others expressed their grief but then they never mentioned the dead man's name again. At their ages any one of them could go at any time; the convention was not to talk about death, it was too immediate. They talked about their escape from the fire, but it was the unprocessed wounds of the Second World War that filled the silences most of the time. In being there with those men, the helpers mellowed in their intensity of purpose which might normally have been to push them into 'getting better' and to a level of sophistication which would have been too complicated. In the end the men assumed responsibility for the group themselves and the therapists, already demoted to making tea, faded altogether.

Similarly, crew survivors from the *Herald of Free Enterprise* met together following the disaster. After several meetings they asked the support workers to leave, because they were 'stopping them from talking about what they needed to talk about'. After a number of further meetings they asked the workers to return, because they realised that they now had even more difficulty in talking about these things. Group members wrote to survivors of the Piper Alpha disaster setting out this advice about professional participation.

Formal group approaches to treating post-traumatic stress reactions have been widely used and some are described above in relation to cognitive therapy. Group treatments have a number of advantages, some of which have already been noted in the discussion of psychological debriefing, and which can be summarised as the following:

1   Reduction of isolation and the sense of uniqueness, coupled with the provision of a sense of cohesion, support and validation, conveying a feeling of universality, and reducing feelings of stigma.
2   Confrontation by those who have experienced the trauma and 'really know', which is both more acceptable and more real.
3   Identification of common issues leads to rapid emotional processing.
4   The generation of hope and the modelling of adaptive coping.
5   Restoration of self-esteem by acting as a helper.
6   Increased adherence to home work.

Group approaches are often a key ingredient of residential programmes which have been set up for sufferers of PTSD. These sorts of initiatives have most frequently been set up for war veterans, and begun a number of years after the trauma. One such programme was the Koach Project (228), which was a residential treatment initiative for forty-one veterans of the 1982 Lebanon War. Its aims were to reduce the prevalence and severity of PTSD and other psychiatric symptoms, to improve individuals' functioning in their families and communities, and to improve their military functioning. The project was based on cognitive–behavioural principles and the concepts of milieu therapy (48), and its programme was multi-faceted, including exposure to a military setting and the anxiety-provoking stimuli that went with this; a supportive group structure; a goal-setting approach; the teaching of coping skills; physical exercise; and family involvement.

Much of the work was done in platoon groups, peer groups where those involved had shared comparable experiences. Reliving of the trauma was avoided by therapists, who directed discussion towards problem solving and the future when discussion of war experiences occurred. The groups were organised on a geographical basis so that they could continue after the residential programme had finished as mutual help groups. The 'buddy' system was also employed – all the soldiers were assigned buddies, again on the basis of geographical proximity. The buddy system was important during treatment. If a soldier left a group session, his buddy would go and get him back, and there were also instances when a soldier would help his buddy do things that he himself could not manage. As the groups became more cohesive, the system became less important, but pairs tended to remain in contact after the programme had ended.

No formal provision was made for individual therapeutic sessions, although these did, in fact, take place. In individual and group sessions, personal objectives were targeted: these were set on a daily basis, and each person had a pocket diary to record his achievements. A considerable amount of time was devoted to teaching strategies for coping with stress. Relaxation was popular, as was 'positive self-talk'. Sports and physical exercise were considered as an essential part of the project. Military training continued, and there were visits to previous war zones. Work with veterans' wives began separately, before the programme started, in group discussions. It had not been seen to be particularly important at first, but assumed more prominence as the programme progressed. A 'family day' was held three weeks into the four-week programme. This was a starting point for work in the couples' groups, which later became mutual help groups.

Although participants, both soldiers and treatment personnel, rated the experience a success, the formal evaluation did not reflect this (296). Measures of functioning and emotional distress, taken before and after the project, did not show any improvement. Some measures of emotional distress even showed a deterioration following completion of the programme. It seems possible that the veterans may have adopted the optimistic outlook of the staff involved, but that there was no improvement in their general functioning (with the exception of that related to the military environment, which might have been expected). It is possible that had attention been given to processing the traumatic experiences, more progress might have been made. Alternatively, these men had already received treatment – the failure of the techniques used does not mean that treatment is of no use, as earlier treatment may well already have improved the soldiers' functioning leading to a 'ceiling' effect.

Another residential programme has been described with Vietnam veterans (286). This programme was four months long – 'trial-and-error experience found that many veterans spend approximately four weeks developing the bonds of trust needed for effective therapy'. Treatment proceeded in four areas: (i) family therapy; (ii) group therapy; (iii) individual therapy; and (iv) milieu therapy. Medication was used as a stopgap measure for some. It was noted that the first four weeks were a period of 'holding back' – symptoms might be absent at first, but then got progressively worse, before therapeutic relationships developed and techniques began to have effect. It was further noted that 'a caution to be observed is the veteran using future-oriented issues as distractors to avoid more fundamental concerns'. Of ninety veterans passing through the programme, 71 per cent had a diagnosis of PTSD; sixty-four completed the programme, and only 14 per cent returned. Of the group who did not complete the programme, 44 per cent returned. Issues arising from the programme indicate further flaws in the Koach Project. Running for four weeks, Koach may have finished at exactly the wrong time. Secondly, the emphasis on positive coping and the future in Koach may have encouraged repression of war-related trauma.

Although no effectiveness data is available, the therapeutic ingredients of a similar project run in the UK for veterans of the Falklands conflict have been described (232). This shared the emphasis of the previous two programmes on multi-faceted treatment. The programme fell into three stages: stage 1 involved 'stirring up', or the arousal of war experiences; stage 2 involved 'taking stock', or dealing with existing problems; and stage 3 involved 'looking forward', or future developments. Treatment methods included group psychotherapy, a patient-run group, occupational therapy, sports activities and a husband and wife group. Individual sessions were also available. Initially, the veterans were attending on a daily basis, going home to their families in the evenings. The 'stirring up' stage aroused the veterans so much that it put more pressure on family life, and hence residential treatment was begun at this point, with partners attending once a week.

'Stirring up' involved the reliving of experiences. Archive film, photographs and newspaper cuttings were used in an attempt to get each veteran to tell his story of the conflict, in the group setting. The veterans also began constructing a collage, keeping diaries of their day-to-day experiences (this proved important in the early stages, but diminished as the veterans progressed) and the preparation of a life story, read out to the group three weeks into treatment. The 'taking stock' phase concentrated on current problems such as alcohol abuse, financial problems, marital dishar-mony, loss of libido, social isolation and work difficulties. These were tackled in group sessions, but sharing about sexual problems proved problematic, and was best discussed with individual therapists. The 'looking forward' phase focused on the future, and in particular whether the veterans should continue their careers with the service. The programme took place over four weeks.

In support of the somewhat more positive results of the American study, another study of veterans receiving an in-patient treatment programme (278) showed positive results extending over a follow-up period. The main effects were in the areas of self-esteem enhancement and self-awareness, interpersonal relationships and PTSD symptoms of numbing and arousal. PTSD intrusive symptomatology showed least improvement. However, in a later study of a ninety-day in-patient treatment programme, using multiple treatment modalities, whilst 48 per cent of participants showed gains in treatment, all had relapsed by one-year follow-up to pre-treatment levels of symptoms (113). Other intensive in-patient treatment programmes for veterans have showed a mixed pattern of results. One four-month programme (153) involving a variety of therapies demonstrated an increase in symptoms from admission to follow-up, although there was a decrease in violent actions and thoughts. Family and interpersonal relationships were improved at discharge, but subsequently relapsed. The veterans themselves, however, felt their morale had improved.

These studies were all conducted on veterans, years after the development of PTSD. Not only are veterans likely to have been exposed to multiple trauma, the treatment programmes were all tackling individuals who had severely chronic reactions. The paucity of gains after such extensive efforts may simply reflect the difficulties in treating severe, chronic PTSD, and are an argument in themselves for the application of crisis intervention techniques and the delivery of treatments with known effectiveness as soon as the presence of PTSD is established.

A somewhat briefer in-patient programme has been described, again studying veterans, this time of the 1991 Gulf War and other conflicts (42). In some of the cases, treatment was given much nearer in time to the actual source of the trauma itself. Treatment took place over twelve days, involving sixty-three hours of formal therapy. Phase1 involved introduction and group integration. Phase 2 involved the employment of a psychological debriefing approach with group members giving detailed accounts following the model of a taped account given by a disaster survivor. Phase 3 included didactic teaching about stress and its management, PTSD, and drugs commonly used and abused by PTSD sufferers. Muscular relaxation was taught and practised on a daily basis. Phase 4 was one of problem solving, which focused on coping strategies, and goals were identified. In the fifth and final phase, family members were involved. Although the study was not controlled, considerable improvement was noted, and after a one-year follow-up 85 per cent of participants no longer qualified for a diagnosis of PTSD. The use of medication during follow-up did not appear to be beneficial.

PSYCHOTROPIC MEDICATION IN THE TREATMENT OF PTSD

Psychotropic medication cannot be seen as a primary treatment for PTSD. Whilst, as the evidence below indicates, drug therapy can ease certain symptom groups, it does not lead to remission. Indeed, it would be surprising, given the range of symptoms and emotional, cognitive and behavioural changes, if a medication could achieve this.

The characteristics of a suitable medication for someone who suffers from PTSD include the following (284):

1 It leads to significant improvement in a symptom.
2 It does not lead to tolerance (loss of therapeutic effect) and have marked withdrawal effects.
3 It does not lead to abuse and cannot be used to commit suicide (particular issues in combat veterans).
4 It causes few, bearable side effects.
5 It does not require blood tests.
6 It 'does not cut a person off from the world or from himself'.

Three areas of medication have been explored:

1 *Anti-depressants*. Mono amine oxidase inhibitors (MAOIs) are the oldest group of anti-depressants. The MAOI phenelzine has been shown to reduce intrusive and avoidance symptoms by 50 per cent (171). However, there can be problematic side effects with this drug. Tri-cyclic anti-depressants (TCAs) such as amitriptyline and imipramine have been shown to have some beneficial effects on hyperarousal, intrusive recollections, flashbacks and nightmares, but had less effect on avoidant symptoms and emotional numbing. One TCA, desipramine, had no effects. Where TCAs had a therapeutic effect, this was modest, and in cases where symptoms were not of severe intensity. Effects increased with duration of treatment, which had to be for a minimum of two months (61).

The latest generation of anti-depressants is the selective serotonin reuptake inhibitors (SSRIs). The most well known of these currently is fluoxetine (prozac), but there are also sertraline and paroxetine. Fluoxetine has a demonstrated effect on symptoms of PTSD (331) particularly in non-chronic sufferers, having most impact on arousal and numbing symptoms, and helps avoidance. One therapist described how fluoxetine when used with veterans allowed them 'more time to think before they act, particularly in anger' (284). Put another way, 'fluoxetine has been shown to be able to significantly decrease people's propensity to interpret sensory stimuli as a recurrence of the trauma and to increase their capacity to use cognitive functions to interpret affectively laden issues' (63). Obviously, if a marked depression is present, an anti-depressant is a treatment of choice. Fluoxetine improved depressive symptoms in both the non-chronic and chronic patients referred to above, but whilst it improved emotional numbing in non-chronic patients, it did not have this effect with chronic cases of PTSD.

2 *Anxiolytics.* As anxiety is a prominent feature of PTSD, it might be hoped that these well-established drugs might be of benefit to PTSD sufferers. Benzodiazepines, for instance, are of interest because they are known to reduce arousal levels. However, when benzodiazepines were used with trauma survivors with high levels of initial distress, treated within several days, no benefit could be demonstrated (99). Some positive effects have been noted for a few benzodiazepines (alprazolam and clonazepam), but the side effects and possibilities for withdrawal problems may outweigh their usefulness. There is little or no evidence concerning anxiolytics that work in a different way to the benzodiazepines, such as buspirone. Similarly, there is little evidence on the effects of hypnotics such as temazepam on specific PTSD-related sleep problems.

Although not strictly speaking anxiolytics, the beta-adrenergic blockers, such as propanolol, reduce sympathetic nervous system arousal. Propanolol has been found to be effective in a range of PTSD symptoms (180), including explosiveness, nightmares, intrusive recollection, sleep problems, hyperalertness and startle symptoms. The effect on aggression may be particularly useful in cases where this is a marked problem. Clonidine, an adrenergic antagonist, may also have some use.

3 *Other medications.* The anti-convulsant carbemazepine has been shown to have beneficial effects in chronic PTSD (347) with intrusive and hyperarousal components, and this medication is often used to treat those with aggressive behaviour. Lithium may also be helpful (284).

In conclusion, it has been suggested that if a patient has an established PTSD, then the doctor treating them should initially try an SSRI or a TCA, with a willingness to select a second drug (either an anti-convulsant, a mood stabiliser or a benzodiazepine), dependent on symptoms. With acute symptoms, drugs that decrease arousal may be the treatment of choice (63). However, drug therapy is unlikely to be given alone in a specialist treatment setting, and there is known to be a positive interaction between medication and psychological therapy in 75 per cent of cases (23).

SUMMARY – THERAPEUTIC INGREDIENTS OF EFFECTIVE TREATMENT

Effective treatment of PTSD will comprise the summed effects of the following:

1 Non-specific effects:

(a) The survivor's decision to enter treatment, which is reflective of commitment.

(b) The quality of the therapeutic relationship, which is largely governed by the therapist having an appropriate attitude to the survivor's experiences, appearing trustworthy, competent and caring.

2 Appropriate skilled assessment to decide which treatments are appropriate.

3 Technique-specific effects:

(a) Use of prolonged exposure.

(b) Use of cognitive restructuring techniques.

(c) Use of techniques of stress inoculation training, including education.

(d) Use of additional techniques such as EMDR, medication, etc.

The time-scale over which these may be effective, and the extent of effect, will be governed by the skill and experience of the therapist and the complexity and severity of the client's problems.

BEREAVEMENT COUNSELLING AND THERAPY OF ABNORMAL GRIEF

Trauma and grief

In Chapter 1, we noted that trauma and grief were two separate, albeit linked, entities. Furthermore, trauma is primary. It arises immediately, before the process of bereavement is established, and may interfere with, or completely block, its resolution. This is due to the presence of, collectively or individually, re-experience phenomena, post-traumatic rumination, post-traumatic avoidance, and emotional numbing. For the helper, there is one single guiding principle: if grief is to be successfully resolved, *the traumatic element must be dealt with first*.

Post-traumatic rumination is often related to the circumstances surrounding the death: the known facts (which may often be limited), concerning causation or what the loved one was doing; the absence of a body or the presence of a body which was never viewed; and the other issues touched upon in Chapter 1. Proper organisation of services, both in terms of attitude on the part of the authorities and through the medium of 'advocacy', can actively reduce the scope of such rumination, by ensuring that the bereaved have access to as many 'facts' as possible. As a woman bereaved by the Lockerbie disaster wrote (56):

I kept wondering how much John and his fellow passengers had known and had suffered as the plane exploded at 31,000 feet. By not calling a spade a spade, I was pushed further into despair and isolation because I wasn't given permission to ... ask my questions.

The problems, and solutions, may be illustrated by the issue of viewing bodies. Up to 50 per cent of the bereaved regret not viewing the bodies of their loved ones, and 33 per cent feel prevented in doing so (134). There is therefore much room for improving good practice, especially as those who view have less intrusive, ruminative phenomena. The allocation of time and good quality input from a support worker to the decision-making process whether to view or not is all that is required to avoid a negative outcome. Such workers are not always included in the mortuary process after disaster, and those who advise not to view are often those who are least suited to enable the bereaved to come to a decision, from either the standpoint of time available or expertise.

What principles can policy and practice be based on? Firstly, no one should be encouraged to view based on the blind enthusiasm for the process on the part of the helper. There will always be some individual who will suffer as a result of viewing. What must be ensured is that people who wish to do so are not prevented. Six steps in the process can be elaborated (128):

1   All the bereaved must be offered the opportunity to view.
2   Those who choose to do so should be enabled to go through their reasons for wanting to see the body, as well as their fears. It is in this process that the helper may assist the bereaved in giving weight to different parts of the equation of 'To view – Not to view'.
3   Next, the helper should view the body themselves and be able to give preliminary feedback on its state. It may be at this point that those who might regret viewing later may make the decision not to. It must also be recognised that some relatives may simply want to know that a certain type of damage has not occurred, and may be happy with this knowledge alone. One Zeebrugge family had formed the belief that their loved one's chest had been eaten away. Perusal of photographs by the helper showed this was not the case. The relatives did not ask whether the body was damaged in any other way, and the helper did not volunteer the information that it was indeed otherwise decayed in a rather unpleasant way.
4   Then, the bereaved and the helper should view the body together. It should be borne in mind that the bereaved may be very sensitive to what they think may be disapproval, and a little cough when the person reaches towards the deceased may be seen as discouragement of something unacceptable. Positive encouragement may be given (352), such as:

'Please hold his hand if you want to'.
'Feel free to talk if you have things to say.'
'I am sure you want to say goodbye.'

5   Afterwards there should be a debriefing, in which the relative is allowed
     to talk about the experience, or to pose any questions about the reason
     for the state of the body (e.g. signs of damage from a post-mortem).
6   Lastly, in case of decisions regretted later, photographs of the deceased
     should always be available, for later viewing.

Chapter 1 gave examples of the use of material from inquests, including
statements made by others, to build formulations of how the loved one died.
Whilst review of the loved one's death would form part of the initial process
of any bereavement counselling, it is rare in the case of expected death
through illness that a formulation has to be built, or information sought in
this way. Only with as solid a formulation as possible can speculation about
the death be contained as much as possible. If it is not contained, then rumination will block grieving from properly commencing.

Rumination and imagery, either real or imagined, perhaps actually of the
loved one's death, if the person was present, or the supposed way they died,
if they were not, may be treated by the use of the exposure techniques
described earlier in this chapter. One client entered treatment many months
after the death of her daughter in a fire in the block of flats where she lived.
Proper fire escape procedures were not available owing to negligence on the
part of the contractor. The client had become excessively preoccupied with
the events surrounding the death. Therapy had begun with encouraging her
to write down her preoccupations, but she found it difficult to do this. As
she was able to name her thoughts in sessions, the use of a taped account
was agreed. In the session the client described in detail waking up that
morning, hearing the knock on the door, seeing the policeman, thinking
'Why are they here?', hearing the news and feeling confusion and terror. The
account then developed to the point where the client went to stand outside
the burnt-out building, and was looking up at it, experiencing confusion,
terror, disbelief and despair. Later, in a second session of taping, the client
verbalised for the first time ever the second area of preoccupation, which
involved detailed fantasy imagery concerning the way her daughter may
have died. She described how she thought her daughter had struggled
towards the fire escape. She described her imaginings of how her daughter's
body had been consumed by fire, and her supposed terror. (These imaginings continued to preoccupy her despite the evidence from the inquest that
her daughter had died as a result of smoke inhalation, not burns.)

Unfortunately, treatment in this case was not of great benefit. The central
problem was that the client eventually revealed that she was unable to carry
out home work with the tape. It was simply too painful, and her avoidance

was too pronounced. After this became clear, the treatment approach was discontinued. Whilst the technique holds good, the importance of careful assessment and monitoring of use is crucial. In this case, the anger that the mother felt was a powerful block to progress, although after the treatment she described some general improvement and better social integration.

EMDR has also been used with reactions related to traumatic death. In a case study of a woman whose husband was shot when he investigated a possible intrusion in their house overnight, the following images and thoughts were dealt with in a set of five treatment sessions (294). In the first session the image used was that of the man lying dead on the floor and his widow's guilt for not going to his side. It took sixty minutes before she reported feeling that it was acceptable for her to have remained in the bedroom. In the second session the image used concerned the man's pain as he lay dying. She was able to accept that he had died in pain, and was frightened, but this now no longer distressed her in the same way. Thoughts dealt with in this session concerned guilt for not having taken precautions to prevent the break-in, which she was able to reframe as naïvety. In the third session, feelings of vulnerability appeared and within the session the woman was able to see herself rather as vulnerable, but not helpless. The last two sessions focused on her engagement with life, and she was left able to recall her husband with positive memories and feelings.

Grief counselling

In Chapter 1, two descriptions of bereavement were given: one passive, describing it as comprising a series of components; and one active, describing it as being a process of 'working through', and having four tasks (349):

1   Accepting the reality of the loss.
2   Experiencing the pain of grief.
3   Adjusting to an environment in which the loved one is no longer present.
4   Withdrawing from the deceased and reinvesting emotional energy in new activities and relationships.

Grief counselling is intimately tied to these goals – its aims are (349):

1   To increase the sense of reality of the loss.
2   To help the person deal with both expressed and underlying feelings.
3   To help the person overcome the various blocks to readjustment.
4   To encourage the person to make a 'healthy emotional withdrawal' from the deceased and to feel comfortable reinvesting that emotion in another relationship.

In achieving this, grief counselling has a number of core principles, as follows (after 349).

Help the bereaved make the loss real

The best way to make the loss a reality is to get the person to describe it in as much detail as possible. This not only is the beginning of the therapeutic road for the bereaved – it also signals something crucial about the nature of counselling. It indicates that the counsellor is not going to collude with the bereaved person's natural tendency to shy away from this reality.

There are two stages to making the loss real. The first involves exploring the events surrounding the death itself. If the person had died after an illness, the story would have begun with a description of the illness – how it was discovered, what was its course, etc. In the case of sudden violent death, the story begins with the last parting, the circumstances (how, when and where), how the person learnt about it, what happened and what the person felt in the initial hours and days following the death, what the funeral was like, and what the person has experienced since.

This is not unlike the debriefing process in its emphasis on establishing the facts, thoughts and feelings about the event. Often, what is described to the counsellor is not a retelling at all, but the telling of the whole story for the first time. It is frequently the case that the bereaved has never told the whole sad catalogue of events before, simply because they have never been asked. The social reality is that it is simply too painful for family and friends to hear. It is not unusual for the bereaved to say to the counsellor: 'You know, this is the first time that I have ever put the whole thing together/put that into words before'.

The second part of making the loss a reality is for the bereaved to talk about the dead person, to describe the relationship and its history, to identify not only a loss, but what has been lost. When visiting those bereaved by disaster, it is not unusual to find that a special collection of photographs of the deceased is displayed prominently. The counsellor will not of course know what the deceased looked like, and the process of confronting the reality may begin by simply asking 'Is this X?' Often during the first session the person will ask, 'Do you want to see some more pictures?', and this may prove a useful tool to beginning the process of discussing the lost relationship.

Help the person identify and express feelings

The identification and expression of feelings which may hitherto have been avoided is a central part of the counselling process. The feelings with which difficulty is often experienced include anger, guilt, anxiety and helplessness, with particular emphasis on the first two.

Anger is probably the most difficult feeling of grief to express. If it is expressed, it is rarely experienced as anger towards the deceased, who is, of course, often the true target. It is often 'not productive to attack the anger issue directly' (59). People will generally only be able to disclose more negative things about the dead person when they feel they have established the positive things. The counsellor can enable the person to build a balance if they firstly ask 'What do you miss about X?', and only when a good list of positives has been established, focus on the other side by asking 'What don't you miss about X?' In some cases, however,

> all the person has is negative feelings and it is important to help him or her to get in contact with the corresponding positive feelings that exist, even though these may be few in number. Holding only negative feelings may be a way of avoiding sadness that would become conscious upon admission of any significant loss.

A similar process may be used to deal with feelings of guilt. The bereaved may as equally be prone to survivor guilt as those who survived the impact itself. Again, therapeutically, it is important to reality-test, and establish a balance. In a death that was expected, and the person feels guilt, it is possible to establish the balance by exploring 'What is it that you feel you didn't do?', and then counterbalancing by asking 'Now, what did you do?' Typically the bereaved will be able to identify many things that they had not identified previously. However, those bereaved by disaster may be denied this luxury – the feeling of helplessness, which may be intimately related to the guilt, may be paramount. For them, the key area to explore will be conflicts related to the parting, and decisions that put the person in the position where they met their death.

Catharsis, or the intense experience and outpouring of feelings, is important, but it must not be assumed that catharsis is a goal in its own right. The person must be encouraged to identify what the feelings are related to, or what the conflict is that they are attached to. This is what emotional processing is about – the working through not simply of feelings, but their significance. 'Merely crying . . . is not enough. The bereaved need help in identifying the meaning of the tears, and this meaning will change . . . as the grief work progresses' (287).

Provide a safe place

The counselling relationship and sessions create a place where it is safe to grieve. By encouraging the expression of feelings, the counsellor is communicating the message 'it is safe to express these feelings – they will not overwhelm me, and they will not overwhelm you – they are desperately painful, but they are endurable'. The counselling session therefore becomes a container bounded by the strength of the relationship, which can hold the emotion as it is released, rather than needing to 'put the lid' on it. The counsellor who feels in any way uncomfortable with extremes of feeling will undoubtedly communicate this with the message 'I cannot bear it', which may leave the bereaved person with the sense that nowhere is safe to express their pain.

Grief needs time. It needs time within the session, and the relationship needs to be available over time. In Chapter 4 we outlined the need to need to time-limit sessions, and whilst this is true, it is also true that time must be given for feelings stirred up in sessions to become containable by the person by the time the session ends. An intense feeling cannot be abruptly terminated – it must be allowed to abate of its own accord, this extinction being part of the emotional processing.

The process of working through takes time. This is not to say that 'time heals'. Time does nothing by itself except provide the person with the opportunity to work actively at processing their feelings. However, there are landmarks over time: a wedding anniversary, a birthday, the first Christmas without the person, or the anniversary of the death, which will have a special significance, and the counsellor may need to provide more time for the person at such periods.

Normalise behaviour

We have stressed repeatedly throughout this book the important therapeutic effect of the person understanding that what they are experiencing is not an isolated phenomenon, but that it is also experienced by others in similar situations. This is very much a need in working with the bereaved. A good example is the experience of the pseudo-hallucination of thinking that you hear, feel the presence of, or even see the dead person. Whilst to some this may be comforting, others may feel that they are going mad. To know that this is normal may be powerfully reassuring.

Respect and challenge defences

Defences may be benign and protective, or malignant and destructive – either way, they must be respected. Denial will, at times, be a necessary reaction to protect the person from what feels like unendurable pain. Counsellors will see denial wax and wane, and this slipping in and out of greater and lesser acceptance of the death is not an abnormal process that the counsellor should 'break down' – it is a naturally protective process. Other defences, however, are highly damaging, such as excessive smoking and drinking. This was noted extensively in those affected by the Zeebrugge disaster (110).

Coping styles in bereavement will of course often reflect previous coping styles in general. As we have noted earlier in this chapter, whilst discussing psychotherapy, it is important that the person understands their defences before understanding the painful feelings that are being defended against. For the counsellor the task is to 'highlight these coping styles and help the client to evaluate their effectiveness' (349).

Often within families there are a multiplicity of coping styles. One person's style of 'getting on with things' may be deeply resented by another who is openly, or even excessively, demonstrating their grief. Communication about these different perceptions and feelings is often poor. Such a pattern is described in an account of a couple bereaved by the Zeebrugge disaster (58). The Browns had lost two sons in their late twenties, and were visited by a counsellor, who described Mrs Brown's reactions thus: 'As soon as I arrived and she started to tell me about her loss, she cried a great deal; my impression of her was that she believed that she could not stop crying'. Mr Brown, however, presented a different picture: 'I found he seemed to have very few friends and stayed very much on his own – his whole life consisted of going to work and back again, with very little else but his garden to sustain him'.

The couple had beliefs about the expression of feelings that were in opposition.

> Mr Brown believed that if a member of his family cried or contemplated suicide, it would prevent the spirits of the dead people passing through the various stages to get to heaven. He was able to tell me that at the age of eleven, he would sit listening to his parents saying in a strongly religious way that you do not interrupt the person's way to the afterlife by showing feelings. The best way would be to accept their passing, and this indeed was how Mr Brown was behaving. Mrs Brown, on the other hand, believed that if a person did not cry or show how much he cared, it proved that he did not feel anything.

The couple's communication was damaged – they were 'not talking to each other, but at each other. Mr Brown would withdraw, and Mrs Brown would attack him verbally with her belief about him not showing his feelings.' Tackling this problem necessitated working with them conjointly.

> I invited them to say each other's names and spend some time listening to each other as they explained their positions again. This was done to a point whereby they did listen and at least were able to gain some level of acceptance of each other. They then both decided they wanted to continue counselling.

Other sorts of family communication difficulties are seen between children and a parent following the other parent's death – the surviving parent will not talk to the child for fear of upsetting the child (and, presumably, themselves), and the child similarly does not speak of the death for fear of upsetting the parent. The use of techniques which improve communication, such as reviewing the events leading up to the death, encouraging the children to talk about the dead parent, and their feelings of grief are of long term benefit. In a study of bereaved children, those who had received this help had less difficulties. Stimulating feelings did no harm – children who cried had fewer difficulties than those who did not (22).

Encourage withdrawal from the deceased

The bereaved may need to be encouraged to withdraw their feelings from preoccupation with the deceased, and invest them in active participation in the world in the 'here and now'. The problems that they have in decision making may at one level simply reflect lack of knowledge about what to do ('my husband was the only person who knew how to deal with the central heating/understood the finances/drove the car . . . '), but at another level this reflects a flight from the real world which contains the reality of the absence of the deceased. Enabling decision making is therefore therapeutic by creating a confrontation with and mastery of the real world. Alternatively, the bereaved often tend to hasty decision making, for instance about moving house, which similarly reflects a flight from the reality of the death by avoidance of things that were associated with the deceased. It is thus necessary to encourage close analysis of certain types of decision making.

One of the most important things to facilitate is the reinvestment of emotional energy in new things, be they new activities or even new relationships. The bereaved often feel that by doing this they are in some way losing faith with the dead. Encouraging a gentle engagement with the world allows the discovery of value, however limited, in things not associated with the deceased.

Identify pathology and refer

Grief counselling is intended to facilitate grieving and restore and support a normal process. Sometimes this is not enough, and more specialised interventions are needed. However, grief counselling is not incompatible with other interventions such as medication. There are no grounds whatsoever for believing that anti-depressant medication impedes counselling.

Therapy for abnormal grief

Therapies for abnormal grief can be described under two headings, psychotherapeutic approaches and guided mourning techniques. Neither has been described in any detail in the treatment of those who have been bereaved by mass disaster.

Psychotherapeutic approaches

Psychotherapeutic approaches are in many ways an extension of the principles of bereavement counselling, applied by those with a formal training in psychotherapeutic techniques in general. There will, however, be particular features that may need to be focused upon:

1 Where dependence on the deceased and guilt are present, there may be a special need to concentrate repeatedly and in great detail on the relationship with the dead person.
2 Where absence of feeling is marked, the fear of what may happen if feelings are released will need to be interpreted and worked through.
3 Where intense anger is present, there will be a need to consider the role of displacement, where the anger is experienced as directed against a particular other rather than as towards the deceased. This may be a particular feature of dependent relationships.
4 In cases of extreme guilt, it will be necessary to seek for hostile fantasies towards the dead person.
5 In cases of chronic grief, there will be a need to explore the special meaning of the lost relationship.

Such psychotherapeutic interventions may still be short term, and focused entirely on the lost relationship. However, for some people it may be absolutely necessary to examine the origins of, say, the fear of releasing intense feelings, which may have its roots in the person's primary relationships and development. Often, the dependency on a spouse may represent the presence of conflict which is related to the distant past of childhood, and which had achieved some resolution to a greater or lesser degree in the marriage. The balance achieved is destroyed by the partner's death, pushing the bereaved back into the earlier conflict. A further issue which may make the therapy one of a more long term nature is where the current loss reactivates a much earlier loss, which then needs working through in its own right.

Guided mourning

Guided mourning is a series of techniques which provide a structure for working through the feelings and thoughts of the grief process in which the person has become stuck (253, 182, 217, 124). It is of particular value when avoidance of the reality of the death and an obsession with the lost person are prominent. Guided mourning has two components: firstly, the stimulation of the emotions of grief and the prevention of the person's avoidance of them, thus allowing the emotions to extinguish; and secondly, the reworking of conflicts associated with the loss. People for whom the approach is unsuitable include those who have a history of psychosis or multiple psychiatric problems, those who are socially isolated, and those who present suicide risks, who should receive the treatment on a residential basis. It is also not an approach that would be considered until some time after the loss, for example twelve to twenty-four months, unless special considerations warranted it.

As with exposure therapy, it is necessary to explain the nature of the treatment in great detail to the person. Important points include the following:

1　Explanation of the rationale for the treatment, that it will be painful, and that things will get worse before they get better.
2　The person must contract not to break off the therapy within a given time span, estimated at a maximum of two months.
3　The person must contract not to commit suicide.
4　The person may show any emotion to any extent, but must not hit the therapist or break objects.
5　The nature of the client and therapist as a working alliance should be stressed.

In making these points, it may be necessary to use a written contract. Partners (should they not be the subject of the grief) and close relatives must be briefed about the nature of the treatment, and prepared for possible reactions. If there is little or no environmental support, it may be wise not to begin therapy on an out-patient basis.

The physical setting for therapy is important – the person should be sitting in a comfortable chair away from the light, with intrusions in the form of telephone calls blocked. A box of tissues should, as ever, be placed by the person as it acts as an implicit invitation to cry. It may well be better to conduct the therapy in the client's own home, which may make the stimulation of feelings easier. The planning of sessions is important, and what happens in between may be as important as what happens in the session. Therapy should be intensive, two to three times a week, but this may depend on what happens in the session, and more time may need to be allowed in between for working through. One and a half hours should be allowed for a session with some leeway.

Therapy begins in a predictable way, with the recounting of the story of the loss. Usually the client cries and will apologise and attempt to go on, so the therapist must say: 'No, leave the story, cry . . . '. The initial outburst is important and the therapist must avoid colluding with the bereaved person's avoidance of pain by indicating that the session is a place where the client can and must cry. From the story, the therapist will be able to make hypotheses about important events and conflicts. The clues will be in the parts of the story which elicit intense pain, and the parts of the story which are skipped over hurriedly – these will contain important material to which conflicts are attached. With respect to the latter the therapist must ask 'Can you tell me a bit more about that?' At the end of the first session the therapist has a picture of the circumstances of the death and the specific emotions attached to it, which will indicate where in the process of grieving the person is stuck. The client will hopefully be left with the impression that strong emotions are containable, and that release engenders relief.

The initial phase of therapy concentrates on the stimulation of emotion. To achieve this, 'linking objects' (336) may be used. These may be either objects which have had special connections with the deceased but which are avoided, or objects which are treasured, looked at and touched regularly, almost as extensions of the deceased. They may be objects such as photos, clothes, letters, music, food or furniture, or may be places, activities, people or even thoughts. The therapist may have to search hard for an object, and there may also be a number of different emotions linked to the one object. Therapy can begin with the confrontation with the standard object of an important photograph of the deceased, more individual linking objects being used later. This creates a sense of the immediacy of the deceased, and makes avoidance of the reality of their absence difficult. Verbal statements may be used to emphasise this reality, working in a hierarchical way from the things which are simply missed, to 'I will never do X, Y and Z with you again', to 'I will never see you again', and finally to 'You are dead [name], and I will never see you again'. Painful emotions are stimulated again and again until they can no longer be elicited or are reduced to untroublesome proportions. Response prevention (213) may be an important part of therapy, particularly where there are overt rituals such as kissing the dead person's photograph. The person has to attempt to prevent themselves from performing the action.

It is important to watch for side-roads and pseudo-problems, especially when they are used to switch at the height of an emotional response. The person must be brought back to the particular situation. Occasionally the therapist may choose a tack which generates no response, and here it is best simply to drop the line of approach – the situation being worked on may not be important, or may be so important that denial is still uppermost. Denial will break down, and pushing may damage the therapeutic alliance.

Once the emotional blocks have been breached, conflicts, such as those of guilt or unfinished business, will become apparent, or take on a central role. These conflicts can be worked on using the 'third chair' technique in which the person externalises and identifies the conflict by establishing a dialogue with the deceased. In the case described below, Mr Clark approached the relinquishing of his grief by asking permission from his dead son to stop grieving. The externalisation of his guilt was only possible, however, after he had been able to experience and release fully the depth of his feelings; and only as the process of catharsis and externalisation carried him towards relinquishing, was the resolution of his guilt possible.

In using the third chair, the deceased can be explained to, asked forgiveness of, and unfinished business may be completed, with the survivor able to speak out loud all the things they were never able to say to the dead person. It is preferable to use this technique rather than the therapist role-playing the dead person, and hence risking powerful transferences which may upset the balance of the therapeutic alliance.

It is advisable to indicate to the person at the end of the session what progress has been made, and to set home work exercises, similar to those in the session to be carried out at home. The most difficult step will be towards the end, in terms of relinquishing the dead person. The bereaved may well be frightened of losing memories of the dead person for ever. Acts of relinquishing are helpful, ranging from a spoken formula to an active deed, such as a symbolic burial.

These processes are illustrated by the case of Mr Clark, who had become depressed and was drinking heavily two years after the death of his eldest son, Frank. The relationship had been a difficult one, but in the preceding years they had become very close. On the way back from having a drink together, Frank's motor cycle, unknown to Mr Clark, crashed into a parked vehicle, and the lad choked to death on his own vomit. On assessment, the components of denial (retention of some of Frank's ashes); desolate pining (hours spent alone in tears yearning for him); aggression (towards passers-by who had failed to help him); and guilt (for not following Frank home), appeared enhanced.

The initial sessions used a particularly important photograph of Frank placed on a seat in front of him to stimulate Mr Clark's feelings. At first he was asked to list all the things he would miss about him, and then he was asked to repeat these things, saying that he would never do these things again, until he was able to say 'I will never see you again', and 'You are dead, Frank, and I will never see you again'. The third session was held in a car on the site of Frank's death, a place which Mr Clark had previously avoided. After this session the spot lost its painful meaning for him and he was able to pass it without sadness.

In the next two sessions the 'third chair' was used to deal with questions of whether Frank's death had been painful, and whether he too was angry at those who had failed to help him. As these issues were put to rest, Mr Clark decided he now felt able to scatter the rest of Frank's ashes. The night before this he burnt the carton in which the ashes had been contained, unbidden, and as he watched his son's name burn he began to feel 'lighter'. The next day he scattered the ashes into a country lake where he and Frank used to fish, and as he did so, he spontaneously said 'Goodbye, son', and burst into tears. As the crying abated he said 'It's like some big, black cloud has been lifted from me'. Therapy had lasted seven sessions.

Preliminary studies of the use of this therapy show between 40 (253) and 90 (182) per cent of clients as highly improved, with up to 18 per cent (253) unchanged and none made worse. What constitutes the characteristics of those who do not respond to this approach is, however, unclear.

6

DISASTER WORKERS

Those involved with disaster fall into two groups: service receivers and service providers. These two groups may be further categorised on the dimension of direct or indirect involvement (see Table 6.1). Service providers, the rescuers and helpers, are often the forgotten survivors of disaster.

Until recently, disaster workers have been neglected both by researchers and their own employers for a variety of possible reasons. These include popular stereotypes of helpers as being strong and resourceful (a perspective often cherished by members of the emergency services) as opposed to survivors who might be viewed as helpless and lacking resources (285). Emergency service personnel often hide emotion, some describing (186) how their uniforms provide protection from the experience of distress (at least whilst they are wearing them). Helpers are simply not supposed to be at risk whereas the needs of direct survivors are much more obvious.

Studies of helpers, both in the emergency services and in the mental health field, indicate that this neglect is unjustified. This chapter will review

Table 6.1 Classification of disaster victims

	Direct exposure to impact/site	*Indirect exposure to impact/site*
Service Receivers	Impact survivors	Other bereaved (relatives and friends)
	Bereaved impact survivors	Immediate affected community
		Wider community (e.g. those in similar situations/affected by media coverage)
Service Providers	Rescue and emergency service personnel	Psychosocial helpers
	Investigation and identification personnel	Supporters to service providers
		The wider organisation

key studies on the known effects on rescue, emergency service and identification personnel, as well as those offering psychological support, of becoming involved in a major incident. Strategies for ameliorating this stress will be outlined.

PSYCHOLOGICAL AFTEREFFECTS OF EMERGENCY SERVICE WORK

After disaster, both the living must be rescued and the dead recovered. News coverage of earthquakes often shows the joy of rescuers when, after striving for days, a live survivor is uncovered. Sometimes, however, when all have perished, the sole task is the harrowing one of recovering and identifying the human remains. Traumatic stimuli abound in disaster situations – a number of badly damaged human bodies may be distressing for even the hardiest emergency worker and the deaths of children present particular difficulty.

For rescue and emergency service personnel, three distinct event stressors have been identified: personal loss or injury; mission failure; and traumatic stimuli (3). Personal loss or injury may be of a variety of types. Rescuers often work in dangerous conditions and are sometimes injured or even killed. Fears may develop about health after exposure to toxic substances. The sense of loss may be about being unable to do what was expected, owing to the nature of events, or more personally, owing to fatigue. Such personnel generally have high expectations about their own performance. If rescue attempts end in failure, there can be extreme disappointment and intense feelings of personal failure and unworthiness. This may be enhanced if there is a high media profile for the tragedy, or a public enquiry reveals that better decisions might have been made.

In one study (75), fire-fighters were asked to list what sorts of incidents disturbed them most. These comprised, in descending order of perceived stress:

1   Dead or injured children (cited by 98 per cent).
2   High rise fires with threat to life involved.
3   Multi-casualty incidents.
4   Death.
5   Threat of personal mutilation or death.

Interestingly, the aspect which bothered them most about their job was administrative aspects of the organisation. Similarly, in a study of British ambulance personnel (150), four factors of job stress were identified:

1   Organisation/management aspects.
2   New, unfamiliar and difficult duties.

3   Work overload.
4   Interpersonal relations, including dealing with injured children and death of patients.

In another study of ambulance personnel which detected high stress levels (314), it was noted that 'ambulance workers complained of pressure of work, of the emotional and physical demands of being on call, of changing shift work patterns, of a poor relationship between management and crews and of not being valued for their skills'. These studies suggest that in such organisations the greatest area of stress is to be found in everyday organisational issues. Post-traumatic stress is therefore an addition to a burden which may well, at last, bring some workers to their knees.

Members of the emergency services do not have to be involved in a major disaster to experience post-traumatic stress. A study of police officers involved in the more severe critical incidents of everyday police work found psychological symptom levels as high, if not higher, than those of officers involved in major disaster (72). Critical incident stress is therefore a definite, if relatively small but acute, area of stress. There is clear evidence that a significant percentage of rescue, emergency service and identification personnel experience stress in the short term, and that perhaps 10 per cent are affected over longer periods of time (269).

Operation 'Overdue'

In November 1979 a DC10 airliner on a non-stop tourist flight crashed on the slopes of Mount Erebus in Antarctica. All 257 passengers and crew were killed. The body recovery was undertaken by scientists, police and Federated Mountain Club climbers from New Zealand. Human remains were bagged, and flown to an ice-strip where they were repacked and returned to New Zealand where police, dentists and embalmers completed the task of identification. Within ten weeks all were identified save for 16 per cent of victims who were buried in a communal grave.

One hundred and eighty of those who had participated in these terrible tasks were followed up at three and twenty months (306). Stressors differed depending on where the person had worked.

> Those on Mount Erebus found their frozen body recovery work arduous, visually offensive and somewhat hazardous underfoot. Those on the ice-strip had to cope in short intensive bursts with heavy, thawing, slithering loads of juicy flesh ... those in the mortuary found the ... work in overcrowded, overheated and malodorous conditions tiring, and some of the most experienced felt that the unrelenting procession of bodies deprived them of the

regular breaks which might otherwise have helped them to cope with their pent-up feelings.

Several workers reported persistent intrusive images of disfigurements, body contortions and fixed facial expressions, or dreams in which they were in aircraft collisions, trapped in claustrophobic situations akin to the mortuary, or experienced role reversal with the corpses. Only seven workers suffered severe enough reactions to warrant intervention with these symptoms.

Initially, just over 80 per cent reported changes in sleep, 76 per cent reported changes in appetite, 50 per cent reported changes in feelings, 40 per cent reported changes in talking, and 33 per cent reported changes in social activities. In some, these changes were sustained over a period of four weeks, but had reverted at twenty months. At this point only 8 per cent expressed a need to talk over their experiences, and 15 per cent had flashbacks; 80 per cent felt they had overcome any problems satisfactorily, and a few felt they had benefited from the experience, one of whom was 'very moved to find that by talking to his father about the debriefing he had inadvertently unlocked his father's experiences from handling bodies in concentration camps in World War II'.

Just under a third of the workers had spontaneously used imagery to help them cope with their tasks: 43 per cent had regarded bodies as some kind of object, 30 per cent had seen them as either frozen or roasted meat, 13 per cent as plane cargo, 7 per cent as waxworks and 7 per cent as scientific specimens. Thus they were able to 'create and maintain an emotional distance from their work until such time as they were able to readjust their feelings'. There were significantly fewer of those who used this imagery in the high stress group than those who did not.

Stress levels as measured by questionnaire fluctuated over time: 35 per cent were in the high stress group immediately on finishing their work and just over 20 per cent remained there at three months, although some had entered this group for the first time, showing for some a worsening of symptoms as they got further from the events; 23 per cent of workers were still in this group after twenty months. Those who were older and who had more experience of victim recovery work were those who fared best.

The Bradford fire

The rescue and emergency services are disciplined organisations whose 'training directs them to focus upon their external performance, and to deny and suppress their feelings' (305). It is difficult for such personnel to ask for help. However, in 1978, after the San Diego mid-air collision, thirty of the 380 police who dealt with the recovery of the 144 deceased accepted the offer of psychological counselling for serious sleep disturbances, nightmares, loss of appetite and sex drive, anxiety, anger and hostility.

Police officers 'carry with them the myth that they should be able to take anything in their stride' (161). They often distance themselves from the horror of their tasks with humour.

> A charred human-shaped mass with a smoking hole in the thorax demonstrates the folly of playing on electrified railways. The police officers on the scene commented: 'Wow, that's how I like my steak!' . . . 'Yes, and we could put some taters in there to roast with it'.

New recruits quickly learn from senior officers 'to bottle up their fears, sorrows and revulsion and to replace these at least publicly with a show of bravado and practical competence'. Officers are often more concerned with 'getting it right' and not making mistakes than they are about their feelings. Showing feelings is equated with weakness which is equated with incompetence.

After the UK's 1985 Bradford football stadium fire disaster, senior police officers, disturbed that a week or so after the fire officers involved showed no signs of adjusting to their experiences, set up a confidential screening and counselling programme (71): 399 officers were sent a screening questionnaire, and 59 per cent returned it, of whom 15 per cent were 'likely cases' for psychiatric problems and 9 per cent 'likely serious cases'.

Just over half (57 per cent) of the 'likely cases' group opted for counselling, and 65 per cent of the 'likely serious cases' group did so, totalling thirty-three officers in all. The twenty-two who did not opt for counselling did so because of confidentiality issues, and their problems being unconnected with the disaster. Following assessment, officers had two or three treatment sessions, comprising problem-solving cognitive therapy. Three weeks after these had ended they were reassessed, and all but two now fell in the 'likely non-case' group. At nine months, one still showed evidence of disturbance.

Of the group who received treatment, 35 per cent met all four (DSM-III) criteria for a diagnosis of PTSD, and 21 per cent met three of the four criteria. More generally, five different types of psychological difficulties could be detected: performance guilt, reconstruction anxiety, generalised irritability, focused resentment and motivational changes.

Performance guilt

Performance guilt was experienced in connection with rescue activities. The fire had developed so rapidly that decisions about what to do, and where to tell people to go, could easily with hindsight be seen as being wrong. 'The guilt feelings seemed to be most intense in cases where bystanders had inadvertently "confirmed" an officer's imagined failings by their offhand comments'. Officers would go over events, thinking 'If only I'd realised how it was going to develop, then I would have . . . '.

The memories of seeing spectators burning to death in areas where they were trying to effect a rescue; dying unbeknown in areas which were thought to have been cleared; or running down sealed corridors against instructions, to their deaths, were more powerful than any comments from family, friends or work colleagues to the effect that they could have done all they could.

Reconstruction anxiety

Reconstruction anxiety involved the creation of frightening alternative scenarios, concerning what might have happened. These constructions were so vivid that for some it was difficult to distinguish between them and reality. Many officers experienced this for only a short period after the events, whilst for others it became a more persistent problem.

Generalised irritability

One of the most common and persistent changes, irritability, showed itself both at home and at work, in relation to events which often had no connection with the fire. It made the officers feel bad, and in many cases had negative effects on relationships, eroding social support systems at a time when the officers needed them most.

Focused resentment

Bitter resentment was directed at the behaviour of certain journalists, the obstructiveness of young spectators, the football club itself and the management of the compensation fund. 'Among other things, this set them up for furious and near violent exchanges if other people failed to agree with them.'

Motivational changes

Some officers felt that many aspects of their job no longer felt important to them, and 'found great difficulty in bringing themselves to "perform" as required', this extending to the home for a few. It seemed as though the frailty of human existence, which had been so clearly demonstrated, had affected their philosophies of life so that other things appeared inconsequential.

Body recovery duty after three British disasters

Body recovery from the destroyed Piper Alpha oil platform was able to be carefully planned and managed, and the police officers who carried out these duties were followed up some three months later (4). Their psychological symptom scores on questionnaires were surprisingly low. Although post-traumatic imagery was present, there was no increase in psychiatric morbidity, and no increase in days off due to sickness following these duties, emphasising the difference between distress and 'caseness'. Coping methods included humour, talking with colleagues and thinking about the positive benefits of the work. In contrast with how they felt about normal duties, team members felt they were kept well informed, had a sense of purpose and felt useful. They found management and ethos in contrast to routine police work, and valued good team spirit. Preparation for the task was found to be valuable.

The Heathrow Police Victim Recovery and Identification team, which comprises twenty-eight specialised and trained police volunteers, worked during the 1988 Lockerbie disaster, and assisted with body recovery at the sinking of the *Marchioness* pleasure boat in the Thames in 1989. Questionnaires concerning thoughts, feelings and symptoms arising from these incidents were administered in conditions of strict confidentiality (313). The scores of the policemen on measures of general symptoms were largely within the normal range and their scores on a measure of trauma were 'only slightly higher than the normal comparison'. The probable psychological distress rate was 16 per cent (with 3 per cent in the moderate to severe category). Stress levels were not correlated with age, number of incidents attended or years in service. Comments:

> revealed an extroverted well-knit team with many jokes and friendly banter between the officers. At the same time . . . they kept a respectful silence when one officer said that he felt that the degree of support from spouses was crucial, and that he had been 'written off' for five weeks after Lockerbie.

During operations, the voluntary nature of the work had been stressed, strict discipline was slackened, and the distance between the commanding officer and the men was reduced. A group identity had been maintained. It was concluded that despite the fact that whilst clearly the officers had experienced some stress related to their body recovery duties, this stress could be 'considerably reduced by the selection of stable and extroverted individuals, who are given training in carrying out their task, managed in a humane, concerned manner, and monitored thereafter as a further expression of concern for their welfare'.

The psychological well-being of the wider group of police officers at Lockerbie was also monitored (224). The officers were divided into three groups: those on patrol duties, those on search duties and those who worked in the mortuary. Those on patrol duty had the lowest levels of physical symptoms, whilst those on search duties had an intermediate level of such symptoms, also thinking about their work more than the patrol group. A glimpse of the sort of stress this task involved is indicated in the comments of one officer:

> I experienced a feeling of hopelessness due to the fact that all the boys seemed to be doing was 'hoovering' or cleaning up the countryside around Lockerbie. I felt an inability to do anything worthwhile. You knew everyone was dead and there was no chance of rescuing anyone and the persons responsible . . . would be almost impossible to identify.

There were also specific things which were predictably distressing – one officer could not get the image of finding a child's Christmas present with the label on it saying 'not to be opened until Christmas'. Another (300) found a child's body in a tree with a teddy bear below. He could only think of the child holding the bear throughout their fall from the aircraft, in the context of his own children.

Those who worked in the mortuary had more physical symptoms and thought about their work more than the other two groups. They also had an increased level of sickness after they returned to normal duties. (However, none of the three groups differed on a measure of psychological symptoms. The researchers opined that it may be more acceptable in the police culture to acknowledge physical symptoms than psychological symptoms.) Some officers were rotated through the mortuary, others had more permanent duties there, giving high and low exposure groups to this work. Counter-intuitively, the high exposure group had significantly less physical symptoms, and thought about their work less. The officers described how

> being in the mortuary for longer provided an opportunity to understand the process of the forensic examinations and to become intellectually absorbed in the enquiries. There was more of a sense of a contribution to solving the crime and of making some sense of their own role in the event.

Those who were in the mortuary for short periods of time did more 'labouring work' and had little opportunity to make sense of the experience.

MINIMISING STRESS IN EMERGENCY SERVICE DISASTER WORK

Selection

The start of the process of attempting to mitigate emergency service stress may ideally be to select individuals who are naturally resistant by virtue of certain characteristics. Unfortunately, our knowledge in this area is sketchy.

The volunteer police officers involved in the Heathrow recovery and identification team (313) were found to have significantly lower measures of neuroticism, and somewhat higher levels of extroversion (as measured by the Eysenck Personality Questionnaire) than the general population. It was this that led the researchers to conclude that stress would be reduced by the selection of 'stable and extroverted individuals'.

In a study of volunteer emergency workers and fire-fighters in Australia (225), workers appeared to be average on personality variables, including hardiness (see below), and defensive style. It was concluded that 'while certain personality measures may reflect a general diasthesis toward poorer coping, they may be less useful than a specific work variable for predicting who is at risk of occupationally induced stress'.

Training

In a study of Norwegian soldiers who had to rescue other soldiers from an avalanche (152), these 'spontaneous rescuers showed similar levels of symptoms to victims buried in the avalanche'. The training and discipline of the military background therefore offered no protection against stress. This might well be borne in mind by authorities who draft in large groups of soldiers to deal with disaster situations, as was done at Lockerbie.

Moving up the scale of preparedness, in a bus disaster in Norway in 1988, which involved the deaths of twelve children and four adults, the reactions of voluntary helpers such as the Red Cross were compared with those of professional helpers (77). Whilst both groups experienced similar reactions, those of the volunteers were more intense, although the long term negative impact at eighteen months was low. The implication is that increasing training and experience, making as much of the unpredictable as predictable as possible, is protective.

The reactions of a group of specially trained volunteer disaster workers were contrasted with a group of fire-fighters, both being involved in earthquake search and rescue (241). The fire-fighters had considerable experience of routine rescue work, but had no special training for disaster situations: 'The volunteer group's training focused on increasing awareness of the personal and psychological consequences of disaster work and on creating realistic performance expectations'. Training reduced the likelihood of the demands of the disaster being perceived as stressors, and lessened reports of psychological symptomatology. Thus, even further up the scale of preparation, it must not be assumed that experience of routine emergency work gives adequate protection against stress in disasters. Further specific training is needed to augment this, as demonstrated with the Heathrow body recovery team (313).

Training and experience regulate the workers' appraisal of the events, affecting their expectations of what is to be encountered. 'The closer these expectations are to the reality of the situation, the higher the levels of predictability and perceived control, thus reducing helplessness and uncertainty' (314). As discussed in the model of trauma presented in Chapter 1, psychological reactions are seen (241) as a 'function of the extent to which routine schemata (the mental models or representations defined by expected operational activities and supports) allow a worker to make sense of the atypical events and reactions that typify the disaster experience'. These sorts of routine operational schemata can be very situation specific. Training therefore has to focus on a variety of disaster contexts and generalise understanding, 'promoting predictability, control and adaptability'. The training offered to the volunteer group referred to above (241) involved a review of film and video material concerning disaster 'to increase awareness of the nature of the disaster operating environment and its inherent constraints', and attempts were made to increase

> physical and psychological resilience using outdoor survival training, training in simulated disaster work, and using information from the disaster site to define roles and tasks prior to arrival on site. Preparation for the interpersonal context of disaster work was enhanced by developing leader capability for disaster work and developing support networks within a team context.

Personal coping strategies can also be enhanced. Imagery was used spontaneously by workers involved in 'Operation Overdue' (306) to mitigate against distressing sights. This can be deliberately enhanced. In the Norwegian bus crash which killed twelve children (76), almost all of the on-scene rescuers and health care professionals used strategies of emotional distancing, and used activity to restrict reflection. They suppressed emotions and actively avoided thinking about the ramifications of the event. 'I had to attain a detached stance. Not think that they were children or human beings with families', one worker remarked. They used pleasant mental images to avoid reflection. They refrained from receiving too much distressing visual stimulation. 'I did not look at the dead children, as I knew this would interfere with my primary task', another worker commented. Only a few reported using humour, in contrast with studies reported above. Again, these are strategies which can be refined and directed, as long as later opportunities are given for appropriate psychological processing.

Organisation and management

The studies cited above indicate that the organisation must be aware that certain management styles and practices will minimise stress further. These include:

1 Keeping welfare in mind. Throughout the operation, senior officers must keep their officers' welfare at the forefront of their minds alongside the maintenance of the operation itself. Such officers must be prepared to acknowledge stress/distress in themselves before they can expect their subordinates to do so.

2 Maintaining voluntary status. If a team is made up of volunteers then members must be allowed to discontinue if they wish, without implied criticism.

3 Reduction of bureaucracy. Unnecessary bureaucracy is seen by workers as getting in the way of an already difficult task.

4 Reduction of strict discipline. The bending of rules (e.g. body recovery teams taking a nip of spirits with their tea) promotes a more relaxed atmosphere.

5 Reduction of distance between officers and subordinates. The more officers become closer to their team and the task, the greater will be the sense of comradeship and understanding.

6 Maintenance of group ethos. A sense of team is strengthened by meeting as a group, dining together, etc.

7 Provision of information. Regular briefings about the progress of the operation as a whole, and how individual tasks fit into the overall operation, promote a sense of understanding and purpose, especially if the task appears mundane.

8 Keeping to one task. Following one task through allows a sense of understanding and commitment to develop, especially if it is particularly difficult or unpleasant.

9 Close liaison with other agency teams. Before any emergency occurs, liaison should have been set up with other services' teams, to reduce on-scene rivalry. Such meetings must be maintained during the operation.

10 Debriefing. Operational debriefing must be carried out, and psychological debriefing offered.

11 Praise and recognition by senior officers is crucial to maintain a sense of worth.

12 Management follow-up. Individual officers should have the opportunity for personal review to ensure continued adjustment.

Detecting stress on-scene

Intervention must be available at the scene in case acute reactions develop which may impair an individual's ability to continue working effectively. The person who might do this may be a mental health professional who is familiar with emergency work, or an officer not involved with line management at the scene. Their role is that of observer and advisor, identifying those personnel who may need a break or change in duty and advising those in command accordingly. A process of 'gearing down' is helpful, where stressed individuals may be moved from the centre of the incident to the periphery, and, if appropriate, to rest. During this process some ventilation of feelings and reactions may be achieved.

A military psychologist was attached to the Belgian Gendarmerie Disaster Victim Identification (DVI) team recovering bodies from the *Herald of Free Enterprise*, with the aim that if any psychological disturbance arose amongst the team members, who although experienced had never faced such a mass body recovery, it would be detected as soon as possible. The stressed individual would then be kept as close to the building where the identification was proceeding for reintegration into the task as soon as possible, employing principles of proximity, immediacy and expectancy. They would be treated as a police officer rather than as a patient and not removed to a hospital or first-aid post and hence pathologised. The psychologist wore work clothes identical to the team members: boots, a white disposable overall and a cap, gloves and mask.

An example of a typical intervention is provided by the following conversation with a man who had left the building without reason on the second day of the identification process (250).

PSY: Aren't you feeling well?

X: No, it's too much.

PSY: What is going on?

X: Damn it, a child, a four year old . . . . Oh, God . . .

PSY: Where are you working?

X: Internal autopsy.

PSY: That's bad, but you left your post.

X: (*Irritated*) That's not true – P has replaced me until they've finished with that child.

PSY: Will you go back afterwards?

X: Of course. What do you think I am? Do you have children?

PSY: No.

X: Then your psychology can't understand this. Now, damn it, you can go and tell the commander I'm a coward. I've got three children about that age.

PSY: You've got my word as an officer that no one will know anything about this talk.

X: You'd better be right. Can you go and see whether they've finished with that child?

PSY: (*Returning*) The child is done, there's an adult on the table again. What do you think?

X: I'll do as I said I would.

For the rest of the day this individual kept a suspicious eye on the psychologist, but that evening in the mess they had a long discussion and two months later the psychologist had supper with him at his home. There were approximately ten interventions of this type for 150 personnel, and none required any follow-up treatment.

It is clear that such interventions may be regarded with suspicion by emergency personnel. Although in the example given above, all personnel had been advised of the presence of a psychologist in advance, few had apparently taken this in, and for one man it increased his fear rather than reduced it. 'OK, I knew this wouldn't be pleasant, but that it would be so bad that even psychologists are necessary . . . ', he remarked. Personnel may fear that they are being spied on. The psychologist had the initials 'PSY' on the front of his overall and the leader of the Dutch DVI observation squad, observing that he had no identification on his back, wrote 'SPY' on the rear of his overall, unknown to him. It emerged in debriefing that the fact that the psychologist occasionally wrote in a log was experienced by the men as spying for commanders and a danger to their careers. Any weakness may be seen, it is often feared, as unsuitability and unfitness for promotion. This outlines the importance of the integration of such debriefing personnel into the team so that familiarity and trust will develop.

Aftercare

1   *Defusing*. This activity should occur within a few hours of the incident. Again, it may be led by a mental health professional, but more frequently by a commander. It can be 'spontaneous as those who had been involved . . . gather around after cleaning equipment and preparing their units for the next call' (222).

   The aim of defusing is to create a supportive and positive atmosphere in which initial concerns and reactions can be voiced. Destructive criticism has the potential to develop and this must be blocked. Acceptance should be encouraged, and excessive sick humour contained. Although such meetings can arise spontaneously, it is probably best that they become an accepted part of routine, and that everyone's attendance be mandatory.

   > About one hour is usually enough to go through the process. During this time, the team members and leaders should check on each other's well-being and provide support and friendship to those who seem to be hardest hit by the incident (222).

2   *Debriefing*. This process can be followed by a formal psychological debriefing as described earlier. It has been suggested that attending to negative emotions in debriefing may undermine the positive experience of the work being found to be professionally rewarding (222). This, however, ignores the fact that many officers do not find it rewarding,

and view debriefing positively (269). What is likely is that debriefing which is grafted onto procedures specially because of the disaster, rather than being a regular part of an overall approach to stress in general within the organisation, will be treated with more suspicion, and be less effective. This counters the risk that debriefing after a disaster may further cement together an elite, who will have difficulty in reintegrating.

3   *Further intervention.* Providing psychological support for emergency service personnel often runs into powerful resistance from both staff and their managers. There is a fear of opening 'Pandora's Box'. To allow officers to explore their vulnerability or to express distress might open the floodgates and inaugurate a culture dramatically the reverse of the normal macho image. Many believe repression is the best course to encourage so that staff can get on with their jobs. Whilst these cultural norms prevail, it is difficult to introduce an effective provision of staff care. As long as it is perceived as a sign of weakness of character for a person to seek help emotionally then the staff counsellor will always be a last and secret resort. However, 'Hope' also emerged from Pandora's Box – the Bradford fire study (71) showed that focused treatment was very effective in restoring officers to effective status quickly. As suggested above, such organisations need an overall approach to stress, within which debriefing following traumatic events will be situated. As part of this procedure, the 'buddy' system may usefully be employed (242).

PSYCHOLOGICAL EFFECTS OF PSYCHOSOCIAL DISASTER SUPPORT WORK

The rescue worker experiences the confrontation with death in the form of broken bodies – the psychological helper experiences it in a prolonged exposure to intense emotion and extensive grief. With psychosocial disaster support work, there is a lack of clear and shared role definitions at a time of heightened demand. When helpers offering psychological support were compared with emergency personnel (260), no significant differences were found on any variables including impact on life function, anxiety, depression and sleep problems. However, depressed feelings were more likely to arise in off-site workers, who also suffered high levels of helplessness and frustration. Three sources of stress for helpers in disasters have been described (259):

1   The close encounter with death, which reminds helpers of their own vulnerability.
2   Sharing the anguish of victims and families, and the close empathic identification that often results.
3   Role ambiguity and conflict.

The vicarious confrontation with death and terror may lead to an awareness in the helper of their own mortality, or may awaken memories of earlier losses. Most frequently, it stirs anticipatory fears about losses yet to come, notably the helper's close relationships, especially children. 'The worker grieves for those who died, for his community, and for himself and the losses he will one day suffer' (259).

Identification with the survivors may be a powerful and possibly problematic process. As has been described, after the Zeebrugge disaster, two teams worked with the passengers and the crew. A polarisation developed, manifesting itself in many subtle ways, but notably at the inquests. When the jury brought in a verdict of 'unlawful killing', those who worked with the passengers felt a sense of excitement, justice and vindication – those who worked with the crew, who had now been officially and publicly identified as being at fault, became defensive and protective of their clients.

Under the pressure of crisis intervention work (92):

> physical exhaustion inevitably takes its toll, along with the added ingredients of emotional stress and trauma. It becomes necessary for workers to wear many hats, so to speak, by engaging in numerous activities which transcend the specific areas of expertise and training for which they have been oriented.

After the Beverly Hills Supper Club fire (190), it was noted how 'a frequent cycle seemed to plague those of us working in outreach: resistance, zeal, over-extension, frustration and anger'.

The immediate response of potential helpers is 'We must do something'. One of the notable features of disaster aftermath is the landslide of offers of help – people want, almost need, to help. Those who become involved often experience elation, and indeed, the immediate post-impact phase requires the engagement of high levels of energy and involvement. This 'high' is both rewarding and practical – it helps solve problems. However, this may develop into 'counterdisaster syndrome'. Frequently the helper becomes over-involved, and may even experience the narcissistic belief that they are the only person who can, or really knows how to, help the victims. This will lead to overwork which not only is unproductive and inefficient, but may be counter-productive in terms of the guilt and resentment that arises in fellow workers.

A sense of helplessness is also common, where helpers feel unequal to the enormity of the task either through lack of preparedness, training or other personal resources. This may lead to prolonged and guilty recrimination after the event, where the helper reflects on the supposed inadequacy of their own performance. Alternatively, a sense of anger may develop, focusing either on those who were at fault in causing the disaster, or on those in the various helping organisations who have blocked and frustrated efforts to help.

A volunteer multi-disciplinary mental health team comprising nineteen members working with survivors of the 1983 Australian Ash Wednesday bush fires was studied in terms of stress levels following the end of their on-site involvement (16). Over four weeks they talked with about 450 individuals and families and acted in consultation to a number of local groups, such as counselling and guidance services, teachers and women's groups.

The initial reactions of the mental health workers to the disaster site were strong. One noted how 'I was shocked, very sad, speechless initially, very upset'. Two-thirds of the workers indicated that they experienced the following emotions to a severe or moderate degree: shock/bewilderment; dependency/need for team support; confusion/uncertainty; depression/sadness; and helplessness. Anxiety/distress, euphoria/excitement and anger/rage were rarely reported at this point. Two-thirds indicated severe or moderate fatigue, and one-third disturbance of sleep patterns and increased muscle tension. With time, emotional and physical reactions decreased although depression/sadness and dependency/need for team support were still of moderate intensity in over half the team, as was severe or moderate fatigue. In addition, nine indicated that they had become ill during their disaster work (usually colds and influenza), five had motor vehicle accidents, three domestic accidents, and eight felt their eating, smoking and/or drinking habits had changed. Over a third reported dreams or thoughts of themselves in the fire situation, and a similar number described personal traumas being reawoken. One person 'kept thinking of my experience in the war, especially travelling home and wondering if our family home had been bombed'. Despite the fact that eight found the experience depressing, and most found it frustrating and stressful, almost all found the experience to be emotionally valuable to a considerable or moderate extent, and fourteen out of seventeen reported that it had given them new insights into their conceptual thinking about their work.

Two studies provide particular insight into the mechanisms of stress of providing psychosocial aftercare.

The Gander air disaster – stress in army family assistance officers

Following the 1985 Gander air disaster, in which 248 soldiers who all came from the Fort Campbell community perished, 131 army family assistance officers (FAOs), who worked with the families of victims, were studied (11). The FAO is typically a young officer living in the same geographic region as the bereaved, the general guidance given in the task being to 'assist the family in any way possible', in either a practical or emotional sense. Whilst this role generally ends after the funeral, in the Gander disaster the long body recovery and identification process made the role a protracted one – five and a half months on average. As it had been found in a study of rescue workers after the Dallas/Fort Worth Delta Airline crash (168) that those who worked primarily with families of victims displayed more symptoms than any other group, the FAOs were followed over a period of a year in terms of intensity and duration of helping activities. Psychiatric symptoms, major illness indicators and psychological well-being; social/personality factors, namely social support from family, friends and superiors; as well as 'hardiness' or 'dispositional resilience', were studied.

Hardiness is described as consisting of three closely related elements: (i) commitment, a sense of meaning given to one's existence, including self, others and work; (ii) control, a sense of autonomy and ability to influence one's own destiny; and (iii) challenge, a zest for life that leads one to perceive change as an exciting opportunity for growth, rather than a threat to security or survival. There is good evidence that hardiness is an important dimension in influencing how people process and cope with stressful life events (234).

Most FAOs felt unprepared to deal with the profound grief they encountered, particularly at their first meetings with the bereaved, where the sorrow and anger expressed left them feeling sad, helpless and disturbed. They found the initial two-week period of disruption and disorder particularly trying, especially in relation to obtaining accurate information and other communication problems. Further difficult aspects included the long body identification process (which was a particular cause of the feeling of helplessness); and the identification of the worker with the victim and family, with the FAOs coming to see themselves in the place of the dead person.

The symptoms most commonly reported at six months were: headaches (40 per cent), feeling nervous or tense (33 per cent), insomnia (31 per cent), general aches and pains (29 per cent), common cold (25 per cent), depressed mood (21 per cent), and tired/lacking energy (20 per cent). At one year, however, twice as many symptoms were reported. A delayed expression of the stressful effects seemed to have occurred, possibly reflecting anniversary reactions as the assessment was made at the twelve-month point.

The more exposure FAOs had to the bereaved, the more their psychological well-being diminished. The effect was worst for those who were low in both hardiness and social supports, whilst those high in both maintained relatively high levels of well-being. For those high in just one or the other a more complex pattern emerged in terms of illness levels. The group reporting highest illness levels at low exposure are those low in hardiness, but high in social support. One explanation might be that social support for those low in hardiness has the unfortunate effect of encouraging illness behaviour. However, illness decreased as exposure increased for this group. It seems possible that low levels of exposure may generate more conflict for such individuals as whilst others reinforce the importance of their work they are in fact doing little. As exposure increases and they do more actual FAO work, the conflict diminishes.

Role issues were identified as problematic by the FAOs. Their role was wide and hence unclear, not to mention unfamiliar. Time allocation problems arose owing to normal job demands, leading to role conflict. The support of superior officers here was an important resource. Hardiness, as a personality characteristic, may have had protective effects through an ability to adjust more rapidly to confusion, and to see this as a challenge rather than a threat. It may also have helped the FAOs to see the activity as highly meaningful, enabling them to be more committed. They may also have been able to make optimistic retrospective appraisals of their achievements, benefiting from their experiences rather than being damaged by them.

Two major British disasters – stress in social workers

In a study of social workers involved in disaster support work with survivors of the UK's Piper Alpha and Clapham train crash disasters (129) two major sources of stress were identified both in the post-impact period and in the long term: contact with clients' distress, and role-related difficulties. During the first month of disaster support work the initial contact with clients was also listed as stressful; over the long term, conflict with the worker's normal job or colleagues was frequently mentioned. In addition to the ongoing stress, specific issues such as lack of the body of the deceased, attendance at memorials, and the inquiries created high points of stress during both the short and long term.

Identification

Identification with survivors' experiences was a major stressor, affecting almost the whole group in one way or another: 99 per cent had found themselves imagining how they would have coped if they had been a survivor themselves, with 63 per cent imagining themselves as bereaved and 36 per cent as directly involved in the disaster; 88 per cent found themselves ruminating on the survivors' experiences, mainly in terms of their reactions, and thinking 'how would I have coped?'; 63 per cent found that this reminded them of earlier unhappy memories, mostly related to personal bereavement but also to other loss-related situations such as divorce.

Eighty-five per cent of workers reported feeling helpless in the face of survivors' experiences. This largely involved feelings of impotence to take the clients' pain away or was related to being asked 'impossible' questions. On symptom measures, the high identification group had a tendency to greater cognitive disturbance such as unpleasant intrusive thoughts.

Role conflict and organisational issues

Role problems were a major source of stress: 87 per cent reported confusion about what was expected of them in their role as a disaster support worker. For 51 per cent this concerned role ambiguity issues such as unclear or unrealistic expectations on the part of the client, lack of professional boundaries, uncertainty about focus (whether therapeutic or practical help was required) and uncertainty about level of contact. This stemmed from organisational factors such as management expectations and lack of information, or lack of training and experience. Just over half reported overworking. High levels of role problems were associated with high general psychological symptom scores and low psychological well-being scores.

Sixty-seven per cent felt that avoidable circumstances had prevented them from carrying out their work as they would have liked. For 39 per cent this stemmed from conflicts with their ordinary jobs; for 14 per cent it concerned lack of time or resources; and for 14 per cent it concerned management pressure and lack of information. The disaster work created problems in normal jobs for just over half of the group; 48 per cent had difficulties with time demands and reprioritisation of tasks, but other problems included loss of interest in usual work, doubts about reintegration into it, and team issues such as colleagues viewing disaster support work as an avoidance of more 'genuine' work responsibilities.

Lastly, 40 per cent felt that their contribution had not been acknowledged by other professionals and 21 per cent reported difficulties with other agencies. Problems included interprofessional rivalry, unwillingness to share information or co-operate with clients' requests, poor feedback, or clients' resentment towards the social worker through previous involvement of another agency.

Personal impact

In terms of the personal impact of stress, as indicated by reported changes in social life, use of drugs, involvement in accidents or visits to their GP, 64 per cent reported no difference or a change in a positive direction. Only 10 per cent felt that the disaster support work created any problems in their personal lives. These, rarely rated as severe, entailed the demands made by out-of-hours work and consequent concern or resentment from the worker's partner, and reflected a cluster of symptoms of negative affect including irritability, detachment and depression.

In terms of more positive long-lasting changes, 61 per cent felt their attitude to life had changed; 34 per cent described a reprioritisation of values, a sense of gratitude for what they had, a new appreciation of life, or a determination to live for the moment; 85 per cent felt they had benefited from the experience, half seeing the work as useful experience and others noting increased confidence and job satisfaction; 99 per cent believed that their clients appreciated the help they had offered. From a negative standpoint, 27 per cent reported (often together) a heightened sense of their own and loved ones' mortality and vulnerability, or a lack of control or uncertainty over their lives.

Coping strategies

Coping strategies included both personal and professional measures. Personal strategies were varied and included hobbies, sport, sharing the experience, cutting oneself off from the experience and socialising. Whilst religious or spiritual beliefs were rated as important by 44 per cent, only three workers used prayer as a method of coping. The majority were able to share the experience with their families, but half felt unable to share with friends.

By far the most frequently used professional strategy was that of sharing with colleagues (used by all but one worker). The majority received informal peer support and peer supervision, but 40 per cent reported that they did not receive formal individual supervision (although most received formal group supervision from someone within the organisation). The quality of support was generally rated as reasonable or good.

Extent of stress

Levels of psychological symptoms were consistently higher than population norms for the measures used, and the scores of 60 per cent of social workers fell in a 'high stress' group, as compared with between 20 and 30 per cent of the rescue and identification workers involved in 'Operation Overdue' (306), the same measure having been used in both studies.

Social workers who were low in hardiness and those who reported more role conflict had higher symptom levels and more negative psychological well-being. Degree of identification with clients, perceived quality of social support and social work experience all had some effects, largely on workers' cognitive processes, rather than emotions such as anxiety or depression. Greater identification and lower quality of social support both had adverse effects on workers' mental abilities, creating problems with memory, concentration and making decisions. Perceived poor quality of social support led to increased preoccupation with the events. Experiencing social supports as helpful was related to reduced experience of role conflict. Those with greater experience had higher anxiety levels. This counter-intuitive finding, albeit one echoed in the literature on rescue workers (225), may reflect more responsibility being allocated to such workers, or alternatively, as such workers are older, they may be more sensitive to mortality issues, and because of their greater experience of loss, may empathically identify with the bereaved more readily.

215

The effect of length of time of working with the disaster was investigated by comparing the Clapham train crash team (four months post-disaster) with the Piper Alpha team (nine months post-disaster). The only effect was that the latter group who were further in time from the immediate post-impact period had greater positive well-being levels. These workers appeared, to some extent, to have adjusted to some of the stresses of disaster support work. Exposure, in terms of the extent of contact with clients, did not have any significant effect, although the high exposure group had consistently higher symptom scores.

The life event measures revealed that a surprisingly high number of workers had experienced close personal bereavements in the year prior to the disaster, and significant differences were found between bereaved and non-bereaved workers, with the bereaved showing adverse effects on cognitive processes and more preoccupation with events.

Moderation of stress

In terms of the importance of the various potential moderating variables, it was found that the personal coping style of hardiness was the single most important moderator of both symptoms and well-being. The second most important moderator was ongoing life stress in the shape of immediately preceding life events. The two elements specific to the disaster support work which proved important moderators were role conflict (which moderated symptoms) and identification (which moderated well-being). The demands of disaster support work may therefore be broadly categorised into 'professional/external' and 'personal/internal'.

1   *Professional/external – role/organisational problems.* This feature of disaster support work may distinguish those offering psychological support from others. Unlike the tasks of emergency personnel, those of support workers are often poorly defined, and it may be that this diffuse role is a core problem. Not only does the individual worker have great difficulty in making the task less diffuse, but the parent organisation's lack of familiarity with the disaster situation means that it has no experience with which to aid the worker. The preparatory activities described in Chapter 3 of this book should go some way to alleviating this problem, and the benefits of training as observed for rescue workers earlier in this chapter will apply.

There are two sources of role-related stress (47): role conflict and role ambiguity. The former occurs when demands exceed time available or effort expended, when incompatible demands are faced and when there is individual/organisation conflict, for example difficulty in meeting the competing demands of the disaster work and normal jobs. This problem featured prominently for teams working on Merseyside in the aftermath

216

of the Hillsborough disaster (230). Role ambiguity results from lack of information necessary for adequate performance of role, or lack of established professional boundaries.

2   *Personal/internal – identification.* Survivor contact may be stressful in both quantitative (exposure level) and qualitative (degree of identification) terms. With respect to quantity, larger caseloads have been associated with higher levels of identification, but larger caseloads have no significant effect in their own right (129).

Since 'hardier' social workers appeared less likely to identify with clients, the effects of identification may be mediated by individual differences in coping style. Identification is a double-edged sword. Without being able to empathise and identify, the worker may not be able to engage the survivor. Indeed, it has been suggested that 'the capacity for sustained empathy is pivotal for the recovery process' (345). It is an illuminating process – it can focus the attention of the helper on areas of pain and anguish which are not immediately obvious. On the negative side, it may increase helpers' susceptibility to the impact of their clients' distress and create problems with disengagement. Again, it has been suggested that in the treatment of PTSD, countertransference reactions 'are perhaps the primary cause of treatment failure' (345). Identification is a normal, unavoidable process, but it is rarely a therapeutic tool consciously selected and confidently displayed. Contact with the client and their experience provokes it, and the worker suffers it. Once it has taken place, the worker must accept their own pain as a legitimate part of the process of being a helper, and deal with it in supervision.

The nature of identification may be very individual. The authors conducted a series of sessions with two parents whose entire family of five children had been killed in a house fire. The first interview, which took the form of the recounting of the events, was sad, but not overly distressing. At the start of the second interview, the mother drew from her bag photographs of all the five children and set them out on the table. She then set out the five death certificates, one under each picture. Again this was sad, but it was what happened next that was particularly disturbing. The mother brought out two charred children's drawings, which had been pinned up in the kitchen, the seat of the fire. One of the authors was at once moved to tears – all he could see was identical drawings by his identically aged daughter in his own kitchen at home. He declared why he was upset immediately, the emotion resolved, and the client was able to see that a depth of empathy had been achieved without being dismayed that the therapist was disabled by the enormity of her loss. If the therapist had not been able to resolve this, then the state of 'empathic strain' (345) would have been reached.

Identification is so intense because the worker realises that disaster could befall anyone, anytime, anywhere. After a few weeks' exposure to

survivors, the worker may be acutely in touch with the possibility that
they could, for instance, be killed in their car returning from the interview, or that someone could be trying to contact them at that very
moment to inform them that a child or partner has been killed. The
worker may look at the client and see themselves – the 'mirror' effect. But
there is another level of reflection – the identification with the hopelessness of the client. Prostrate in the face of insurmountable difficulty, the
helper may also be filled with hopelessness. This may lead to overinvolvement. One worker accepted an invitation to attend birthday parties of the
children of a survivor. Another became a drinking companion to a client.
In each case, in the face of hopelessness, all the worker had left to substitute for professional inadequacy was a personal relationship.

This has also been referred to as 'parallel process' (279) – 'the themes
and issues evident in clients, both individually and collectively, can be
paralleled in individual counsellors or interactions among members of a
crisis intervention team' (303). It also is part of the therapeutic arena of
countertransference as more broadly defined. Strictly speaking, 'parallel
process is a mirroring of the current relationship in the here and now
while countertransference is an "as if" phenomenon – the therapist . . .
is reacting to the client . . . "as if" he were some figure in his past' (303).
However, 'clearly, empathy, identification, and countertransference are
inter-related processes' (345). Indeed, a continuum of identification
exists, extending from more to less personal. The example given above
of the disaster worker realising that as disaster can happen to anyone
they might easily be killed on the way home is at the less personal end of
the continuum – the worker has recognised something about 'the human
condition', albeit with sudden personal force. The example of the
author's reactions to the children's drawings moves along the continuum
towards the increasingly personal – he was identifying to a specific loved
one. Distress evoked by the client about a loss in the therapist's past
moves further along the continuum until the point of countertransference 'proper' may be reached – the therapist reacts unconsciously
towards the client as if they were a significant figure related to that loss.

Alternatively, the process may be seen as based on two types of countertransference reactions (CTRs). Objective CTRs are expectable
emotions and cognitive reactions experienced by the therapist towards
the client's story and towards them as a person, whereas subjective
CTRs are reactions based on the therapist's personal conflicts. Further,
two directions of response to CTR can be identified. Type II CTR is
that described above, the mode of overidentification. Type I CTR is the
mode of avoidance, in which the therapist withdraws and represses
empathy, intellectualising and distancing themselves from the client
(345). An interesting example of this latter process is given by a small
disaster support team. One member left to have a baby, which tragically

was still-born. On the day she came back into the office, all the team members bar one took the day off. It was not that they did not care, rather that they could not bear to acknowledge that disaster could affect them too.

A model of disaster support work stress

The response of psychological helpers appears to be determined by an inter-action between at least the following factors:

1 Constitutional factors such as coping style (hardiness).
2 Non-disaster-related environmental factors such as prior life events.
3 Environmental factors related to disaster support work, such as role issues and impact of client contact.

As the most sensitive measures of symptoms in the study of social work teams in the aftermath of disaster (129) were those that reflected cognitive problems, it seems probable that just as in the case of emergency service workers discussed above (and indeed just as for the survivors themselves), cognitive factors may be crucial in determining helpers' responses. The three factors above act together to influence cognitive appraisal, and whether cognitive schemata about work – its value, purpose and utility – are confirmed or invalidated may be central in determining levels of stress. Figure 6.1 presents a model of this process.

Hardier individuals are thought to appraise situational stress more favourably, and apply more adaptive coping strategies. They may literally be able to adapt their work-related cognitive schemata. They may have enhanced commitment to the work, and be better able to manage and adapt to the diffuse role. Further, the hardy individual's increased sense of control over their own destiny may be the element that modulates identification with survivors. They may be more able to keep a sense of separateness.

MINIMISING STRESS IN DISASTER SUPPORT WORK

Many of the same mechanisms described earlier in this chapter to mitigate stress in rescue workers will equally benefit those involved in psychosocial care.

Selection

The first step is the selection of appropriate staff. In the disasters that

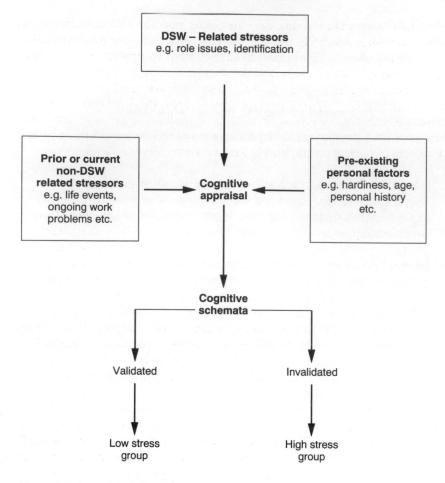

Figure 6.1 A model of disaster support work stress

occurred in the UK in the 1980s, no preparation had been made and the selection of staff was performed on an *ad hoc* basis, with little other than intuition to guide the process of deciding who would make a good disaster support worker, and who would not. In the very immediate post-impact phase, selection was a luxury that time simply did not allow – it was a case of welcoming on board whichever workers responded to their perception that they may be needed. Poor selection decisions were naturally made. After one of the disasters of the late 1980s, a social worker was selected for some intensive work in the very immediate aftermath because they had suffered a spouse bereavement in the previous year, and hence 'would understand better'. This led, not to greater understanding, but suffering. In the years that have followed these experiences, disaster support teams have been selected, trained and put in place. However, in the post-impact period following a large-scale incident, it is inevitable that many untrained workers will be drawn in to assist. The needs of these workers will be considered below.

The literature already reviewed would lead to the conclusion that managers should select workers high in hardiness, with a strong sense of commitment, challenge and control; and with low levels of recent life changes, particularly those related to bereavement. But other than giving a paper and pencil test, how can hardiness be assessed in an interview? One disaster team manager made the following comments on selection (126), attempting to build a team some six weeks after the disaster:

> I had little idea what I was looking for – to tell the truth I was desperate for a team at all. Looking back on what I discussed with candidates, I think I was looking for the following: (i) People who had a strong sense of work identity, not necessarily as a particular type of professional, but at the interface of personal strength/therapeutic ethos/appropriate identity as a helper. Theoretical perspective, I felt, was largely irrelevant. (ii) A strong sense of independence. (iii) Experience of loss-related work.

What was being sought for was an indication of personal strength, granting ability to bear the onslaught of pain; a therapeutic ethos, giving ability to allow the expression of the pain, and see it as valuable; yet at the same time searching for evidence of the worker having an appropriate identity as a helper, an ability to see themselves as separate from the client's distress, and able to maintain a boundary. A strong sense of independence is particularly necessary to tolerate the loneliness of outreach work. Thus during the work following the Zeebrugge disaster, counsellors found themselves 'on the road' for perhaps four days before returning to base. Experience of loss-related work was seen as valuable, and as possibly the nearest most relevant trauma that workers might have experience of. Overall, some of these issues may well be seen as reflections of hardiness, and, clearly, it is quite possible to operationalise questions about hardiness in an interview setting.

Assessing personal motivation, and what attracts people to work with extremes of human emotion, is not easy. Social workers beginning to be involved in the aftermath of a major British disaster gave the following reasons for their interest (126):

1   Being a glutton for punishment.
2   Being attracted to intensity.
3   The desire to help.
4   Unusual work, taking one out of a rut.
5   Excitement.
6   A sense of having something to offer.
7   The possibility of furthering one's career.

Motivations are therefore many and varied, being both selfless and selfish, and disaster workers will need most of them to power themselves through the work. But should a manager be concerned about a worker's apparent attraction to working with intense human emotion? The answer lies in the extent to which the attraction is voyeuristic, related to the worker's vicarious management of their own fears and anxieties about extreme, loss-related feelings. It is probably not possible to know in advance whether this is likely to be the case, however. The manager can only be aware of the issue and watch the worker's level of involvement. Yet strong involvement is not necessarily pathological – disaster support work demands more personal involvement than any other sort of work. It is overinvolvement, as discussed above, which heralds the paired sinkage of worker and client.

The issue of personal losses can be taken at either a simple or a complex level. Organisations such as CRUSE, the organisation for the bereaved, recommend, for instance, that a two-year gap should elapse between a major bereavement and attending one of their training courses. The research cited above would lend some support to this view. Alternatively, an attempt may be made to judge how the worker's loss has been worked through. How this is done within the confines both in terms of time and expectation of a selection interview, as well as an equal opportunity policy, remains a problem.

Training

Training disaster workers obviously cannot prepare them for all eventualities. Yet training is crucial for exactly the same reasons as were discussed above for rescue workers: to promote predictability, control and adaptability. In training, the following key issues must be covered:

1   Workers must begin by addressing the material of disaster personally. They must consider how it would be if such events happened to them, or their families. They must do this immediately to ground themselves, before considering anything else, in the issue of identification.
2   Training must next consider the issues of the difficulty in asking for help. Again, workers can do no better than to address this by considering what services they or their families would want, and how they would wish to be approached. This should be considered before any formal attention is given to outreach methods.
3   Workers then need to absorb information about the nature of post-traumatic stress reactions, and bereavement by sudden violent death. This is their map of the territory they will explore with their clients.
4   Training must address the principles of outreach and debriefing. It can cover initial letters, telephone calls and initial meetings. It can cover debriefing, and how key therapeutic strategies can be woven into a series of therapeutic sessions. It must focus on when to refer on.

5   Lastly, training must identify the issues of disaster work stress, and
    focus on personal coping strategies.

Management

Any disaster support team must have a manager, and in order to maximise
the efficiency of the team during its life, management must have the
following qualities:

1   *Sense of boundaries.* The manager must have a strong sense of personal
    boundaries. As we have noted, the dividing line between strong involve-
    ment and counterdisaster syndrome may be thin. Team members may
    work non-stop, refusing to hand over to others or leave. Such behaviour
    will be counterproductive because not only will it become inefficient,
    but it can cause resentment in other workers who are not similarly
    affected. The manager has to ensure, by their own example and by
    instruction, that this does not occur, for instance simply by instructing
    staff to go home. The temptation for the poor manager will be to take
    advantage of this pattern of behaviour, because it simply means less
    work to be allocated.
2   *Constant commitment.* Managers must have constant commitment. They
    must have a profound belief that the work of the team is essential,
    almost that it is the most important thing in the world. This is necessary
    as a counterweight to the natural doubts that will arise for disaster
    support workers as to whether they are doing something that is worth-
    while, effective or appropriate.
3   *Control and overcontrol.* Managers must not be overanxious or overcon-
    trolling. They must not fall prey to the infectious belief that their own
    personal view of how the work should be carried out is God-given.
    Because of the intensity of the work, if workers feel that their different
    skills are not being used, and that they are being forced into a rigid
    model of work, they will soon feel devalued. Disaster support workers
    are, however, prone to fall into a trap of elitism, which mirrors the
    'victim self-consciousness' of their clients, and a worker who leaves may
    be dismissed with the comment 'Oh, they just weren't suited for this sort
    of work'.
       Lastly, whilst it is important to make team decisions about aspects of
    service delivery, disaster support workers are apt to be touched by the
    same difficulties in making decisions and forward planning as are their
    clients, and hence the manager must be firm about prioritisation, even
    though they fear that decisions may be unpopular.
4   *Acceptance of distress.* Members of the helping professions can be very
    cruel. Just as emergency service workers may fear that by showing
    distress they may be branded as weak, so helping professionals may be

similarly unkind to their colleagues when they voice their distress, saying 'X simply can't take it' – a view which serves to reinforce the speaker's omnipotence and distance them further from their own anxieties. The role of management here is crucial. Whilst managers must be prepared to engage with the most difficult situations themselves, they must not be invincible. The leader must be able to 'fail', to experience helplessness and to demonstrate by personal example that it is acceptable to show distress, and that it is not a sign of weakness.

That this is not easy to achieve in practice was demonstrated in the response to the staff care service set up by the British Association of Social Workers after the Hillsborough disaster (114). Whilst team leaders clearly demonstrated 'a heightened sense of responsibility for their workers', it seemed as if they felt that 'they weren't doing their job properly if one of their staff needed help from an outsider'. One worker described his leader mentioning someone from another team who had sought help and shouting, whilst banging on the table, 'That is not going to happen in this team'. Over the two years, the external counsellor involved in this project saw twenty-one workers 'for formal, individual counselling sessions, which were directly connected with helping those affected by the Hillsborough disaster. The work ranged from one-off sessions to long-term help for a year.' Two-thirds of the staff in the longest running team were seen.

5   *Respect for individual defences.* Individual workers' defences must be respected, just as clients' defences must be respected. It must not be assumed that if workers do not all share their feelings in the same way that they are lesser beings. A sense of the value of sharing distress may become a destructive cult within a disaster team, in which 'those who share most openly are best'. Black humour, just as used by the emergency services, is common in disaster support workers, and should not be despised or discounted. It is again another aspect of the 'mirroring' by which workers, just like survivors themselves, develop humour about themselves and the tragic but absurd events which brought about their misfortune. In counterbalance to the seriousness of the everyday work, a sense of fun and positive self-care, even pampering, is important to develop.

6   *Positive feedback.* Disaster workers are very prone to feeling discounted and unrecognised within their own organisations. It is therefore essential that they are given positive feedback. One way of achieving this is through validation outside the organisation, by encouraging workers to present to groups of professionals about their work.

7   *Lastly, the manager must actively manage workers' caseloads.* It is important that a caseload is evenly balanced between survivors and bereaved, and different types of bereavement. One worker who took it upon himself to see a number of parents who lost children found himself in

receipt of very strong feelings, both positive and negative, from the families. He became very concerned about his own children's safety in everyday situations, preoccupied when walking down the road with them that a car might mount the pavement.

Chronologically, one of the first tasks for the manager will be the provision of care for crisis workers. Many workers without preparatory training are drafted in to help in the initial days post-disaster. The role of the worker in the immediate crisis is necessarily different to that of the longer term. Helping professionals will work intensely, for long hours, over a short period of time. Their tasks may be practical, rather than therapeutic, and they will certainly be new to them. One social worker in a training session several weeks after a major British disaster spoke of her night spent standing with relatives in front of a notice board where updated casualty lists were being posted. It was a profoundly painful experience for her – 'I felt so helpless – there was simply nothing I could do – I was as helpless as them', she said. It is no wonder that workers often develop intense bonds with families in such moments of crisis, and one of the reasons that those who are involved right from the moment of crisis are often more effective in their work with clients in the long term (191).

Such crisis workers will largely be stood down. Some workers will not see this as a dilemma – they feel they have done a particular and valuable job, and may feel guilty about continued absence from their regular job. Others will feel an intense sense of dismissal and exclusion. Some have been very badly treated indeed – in one disaster they were replaced at short notice by a long term team. Not only were they not debriefed, but their natural interest in what was to happen to 'their clients' after the hand-over was ignored. In a meeting with an outside consultant, they expressed real hurt and anger. Another group of workers who had provided early and exhausting cover to disaster survivors were asked if they could be available if required on a more long term basis. They were to hear nothing further. When such workers are 'retired', they will need certain support. This will include:

(a) Debriefing.
(b) Updating with future developments, in terms of the disaster itself, the clients, and the development of the service offered to them.
(c) Awareness of the opportunities for further support.
(d) Inclusion in further events of a supportive/training nature to increase the sense that they have a valuable perspective to share.

Supervision

Ongoing supervision is essential, and the role of social support for workers is established as being a major buffer to stress (11). Supervision will need to cover a number of areas:

1 *Individual casework.* Individual casework is best supervised within the team. In some ways supervision is the wrong description, because it implies greater knowledge/experience supervising lesser, and in this area of work all are generally learning together. The most appropriate model may be individual peer intervision, with group supervision, with or without an external clinical consultant, where team members present aspects of their work to each other. Case supervision is crucial, not least because of the clear evidence of the stress caused by identification.

One area that should be closely monitored in supervision is the need to refer on to others if the team's resources cannot meet the needs of a particular client. Just because a team is identified as 'the disaster workers', it does not mean that such a group has a monopoly of clients or all the answers to their problems. Disaster support workers have the potential to become 'rescuers', a position born out of helplessness, possessive of their clients, and may devalue other agencies who are not so close to the events because they 'cannot understand', or would use 'the wrong sorts of models', such as a psychiatric approach.

2 *Team process.* The team also needs to look at its own functioning, for working with the powerful feelings of clients may lead to powerful projections of disturbing feelings within the team. Rivalry, jealousy and anger all have the potential to run riot in a disaster team. Anger, in particular, may be a powerful feeling diffusing across from the client group, and this in turn may be projected upwards onto managers. Someone external to the team is essential in assisting in the understanding of this.

3 *The personal/professional boundary.* Whilst the workplace is not the place for therapeutic personal exploration (anyone who wishes this should be directed to therapeutic resources outside the agency), the powerful personal feelings raised by disaster work must be recognised. Identification, and the feelings this process gives rise to, must be acknowledged and shared, but if they result in a need for therapeutic assistance, then the organisation must be prepared to make provision outside for such support.

One area of personal support that workers often need to discuss is the effect that disaster work may have on the worker's family. The time-demanding nature of the work may lead spouses and children to feel deserted, excluded and deprived. The worker may in turn feel that the family is making no effort to understand, yet again mirroring the experiences of many survivors.

Debriefing and leaving the work

After its period of work, it is essential that the disaster support team is able to leave, or cease its work, successfully. The formal psychological debriefing model may have a role to play here, yet has its limitations. It may be a useful starting point to assist the crisis workers who will only work in the post-impact phase, whose problems were addressed above. One of the problems is that such workers will have faced multiple stressors – there is no one incident to debrief from. This was acknowledged in the debriefing of Red Cross workers after the 1989 San Francisco earthquake disaster, where a 'multiple stressor debriefing model' was used (8). This simply meant that in the initial stages opportunity was given for the workers to 'discuss several incidents which affected them', and that a special part of the debriefing was directed at identifying coping strategies.

In debriefing such workers, within the model of debriefing discussed in Chapter 4, a number of specific areas should be focused on, and a good initial starting point is to address the following sorts of questions:

- 'Where were you when you heard about X?'
- 'How were you approached about becoming involved?'
- 'What did you initially encounter? What were the most difficult things?'

Thoughts and reactions to these will naturally arise and be addressed. It will then be necessary to focus on:

- 'How did things change?'
- 'What tasks did you have to adopt as time went by?'

Because of the nature of the stressors already known to be important, it will be necessary to ask:

- 'What were your reactions to the tasks you had to do?'
- 'What were your reactions to the way it was organised and the support you received?'

In concluding, it is important to address the issues:

- 'What have you learnt about yourself from this?'
- 'What have you learnt about the way that such things should be handled?'

It is evident from these two last questions that debriefing, in its widest sense, has two foci in facilitating ending in this work, one emotional and one intellectual. In terms of the emotional task, endings are what such a team will have been working with, and now members have to achieve a 'good enough' ending for themselves, to ensure that they take minimal amounts of unresolved conflict away into new settings. Four areas need attention in the ending process:

1 *The work.* Team members have to leave a particular type of work, which will have been very distinct from that which they have done before. In finishing, workers have to be able to see importance in other types of work, and take up a new incarnation or resume a previous one. Again, this mirrors their clients who have to take up new tasks in life.

2 *The role.* Team members may also have to leave behind particular roles – 'grief therapist', 'trauma counsellor', or however they have seen themselves and whatever identity they have given themselves to assist their passage through their work. Again, this mirrors the task of the clients, who have to leave behind the roles of 'survivor' or 'bereaved'.

3 *The clients.* Stronger bonds are formed in disaster work than any other, owing to the stronger sense of partnership, or shared journey between helper and client. It may be very difficult to say 'goodbye' to those with whom so much has been shared. It has to be ensured that the worker's departure is not another 'bad ending' for the client, yet at the same time the worker must leave, not only because such contacts have to end, but because the negotiation of the ending is a positive therapeutic task for the client. The worker must always bear in mind the fact that there must be an ending, so that they may guard against fostering dependency, and must be enabled to accept that their goals were limited, that they could not achieve everything that need to be done, indeed, that it was not their job to achieve 'everything'. The worker must leave accepting that they were 'good enough', or that certain failures were inevitable.

4 *The team.* If a team does not have a continuing existence, disaster workers have to leave their colleagues, those with whom they have 'passed through the fire'.

These four aspects can again only be facilitated by an outsider. The team working with passenger survivors and bereaved from the Zeebrugge disaster engaged a therapist with considerable experience in the area of loss to help them with the process of disengagement, in a series of four group meetings, moving through the above tasks in an orderly progression.

Another vital area of debriefing is the intellectual task, requiring spending time reviewing the work from both a clinical and an organisational standpoint to identify what has been learnt, and to record this in a way that the experience can be passed on to others. This approximates to the 'formulation' of the survivor, the need to understand and make sense of the experience. The worker must finish the task feeling that something valuable has been learnt and can be passed on, so that the painfully gained lessons are not simply lost.

Finally, of course, all the other rituals of leaving such as parties are essential – survivors and bereaved are not the only ones who find memorials important. After their leaving lunch, a number of the members of the Zeebrugge team found it important to go down to the seashore, almost to say goodbye to the sea which had been the unwitting cause of so much suffering, and which had changed their own lives so emphatically.

REFERENCES

1   Adshead, G., Canterbury, R. and Rose, S. (1995) 'Current provision and recommendations for the management of psycho-social morbidity following disaster in England', *Disaster Prevention and Management* 4: 5–12.

2   Aichley, R.C. (1975) 'Dimensions of widowhood in later life', *The Gerontologist* 15: 176–178.

3   Alberta Professions and Occupations Bureau (1989) *Critical Incident Stress Debriefing*, Alberta: Occupations Bureau.

4   Alexander, D.A. and Wells, A. (1991) 'Reactions of police officers to body handling after a major disaster', *British Journal of Psychiatry* 159: 547–555.

5   Allen, A.J. (1991) *Disasters: Planning for a caring response*, HMSO: Department of Health.

6   Allen, M.J. *et al.* (1989) 'Coping with the early stages of the M1 disaster: at the scene and on arrival at hospital', *British Medical Journal* 298: 651–654.

7   American Psychiatric Association (1994) *Diagnostic and statistical manual of mental disorders* (4th edition), Washington, DC: APA.

8   Armstrong, K., O'Callaghan, W. and Marmar, C.R. (1991) 'Debriefing Red Cross disaster personnel: the multiple stressor debriefing model', *Journal of Traumatic Stress* 4: 581–594.

9   Artiss, K.L. (1963) 'Human behaviour under stress: from combat to social psychiatry', *Military Medicine* 128: 1011–1015.

10 Bartone, P. (1988) 'Mourning, ritual and recovery after an airline tragedy', Paper presented at the annual meeting of the Eastern Psychological Association, Buffalo, NY.

11 Bartone, P., Ursano, R.J., Wright, K.M. and Ingraham, L.H. (1989) 'The impact of a military air disaster on the health of family assistance workers', *Journal of Nervous and Mental Disease* 177: 317–328.

12 Baum, A., Fleming, R. and Davidson, L.M. (1983) 'Natural disaster and technological catastrophe', *Environment and Behaviour* 3: 333–354.

13 Beck, A.T., Kovacs, M. and Weisman, A. (1979) 'Assessment of suicidal ideation: the scale for suicidal ideation', *Journal of Consulting and Clinical Psychology* 47: 343–352.

14 Beck, A.T., Emery, G. and Greenberg, R.L. (1985) *Anxiety disorders and phobias: A cognitive perspective*, New York: Basic Books.

REFERENCES

15 Belter, R.W. and Shannon, M.P. (1993) 'Impact of natural disasters on children and families', in C.F Saylor (ed.) *Children and Disasters*, New York: Plenum Press.

16 Berah, E., Jones, H. and Valent, P. (1984) 'The experience of a mental health team involved in the early phase of a disaster', *Australia and New Zealand Journal of Psychiatry* 18: 354–358.

17 Berardo, F.M. (1970) 'Survivorship and social isolation: the case of the aged widower', *The Family Co-ordinator*, 11–25 January.

18 Bernstein, D.A. and Borkovec, T.D. (1977) *Progressive relaxation training. A manual for the helping professions*, Champaign, IL: Research Press.

19 Berren, M.R., Santiago, J.M., Beigel, A. and Timmons, S.A. (1989) 'A classification scheme for disasters', in R.Gist and L. Lubin (eds) *Psychosocial aspects of disaster*, New York: Wiley.

20 Bisson, J.I. and Deahl, M.P. (1994) 'Psychological debriefing and prevention of post-traumatic stress', *British Journal of Psychiatry* 165: 717–720.

21 Bisson, J.I., Jenkins, P.L. and Bannister, C. 'A randomised controlled trial of psychological debriefing for victims of acute burn trauma', *Psychosomatic Medicine* (in press).

22 Black, D. and Urbanowicz, M.A. (1987) 'Family intervention with bereaved children', *Journal of Child Psychology and Psychiatry* 28: 467–476.

23 Bleich, A., Siegel, B., Garb, R. and Lehrer, R. (1986) 'PTSD following combat exposure: clinical features and psychopharmacological treatment', *British Journal of Psychiatry* 149: 365–369.

24 Boman, B. (1979) 'Behavioural observations on the Granville train disaster and the significance of stress for psychiatry', *Social Science and Medicine* 13: 463–471.

25 Bordow, S. and Porritt, D. (1979) 'An experimental evaluation of crisis intervention', *Psychological Bulletin* 84: 1189–1217.

26 Bowen, G.R. and Lambert, J.A. (1986) 'Systematic desensitisation therapy with post-traumatic stress disorder', in C. R. Figley (ed.) *Trauma and its wake*, Vol. 2, New York: Brunner Mazel.

27 Bremner, J.D. *et al.* (1993) 'Childhood physical abuse and combat-related post-traumatic stress disorder in Vietnam veterans', *American Journal of Psychiatry* 150: 235–239.

28 Brett, E.A. and Ostroff, R. (1985) 'Imagery and post-traumatic stress disorder: an overview', *American Journal of Psychiatry* 142: 417–424.

29 Brewin, C.R., MaCarthy, B. and Furnham, A. (1989) 'Social support in the face of adversity: the role of cognitive appraisal', *Journal of Research in Personality* 23: 354–372.

30 Broadbent, D. (1971) *Decision and stress*, New York: Academic Press.

31 Brom, D., Kleber, R.J. and Hofman, M.C. (1993) 'Victims of traffic accidents: incidence and prevention of post-traumatic stress disorder', *Journal of Clinical Psychology* 49: 131–139.

32 Bromet, E.J. (1989) 'The nature and effects of technological failures', in R. Gist and L. Lubin (eds) *Psychosocial Aspects of Disaster*, New York: Wiley.

231

33 Bromet, E.J. and Dunn, L. (1981) 'Mental health of mothers nine months after the Three Mile Island accident', *The Urban and Social Change Review* 14: 12–15.

34 Bromet, E.J., Schulberg, H.C. and Dunn, L.O. (1982) 'Reactions of psychiatric patients to the Three Mile Island nuclear accident', *Archives of General Psychiatry* 39: 725–730.

35 Brooks, N. and McKinlay, W. (1992) 'Mental health consequences of the Lockerbie disaster', *Journal of Traumatic Stress* 5: 527–544.

36 Brown, G.W. and Harris, T. (1978) *Social origins of depression: a study of psychiatric disorder in women*, London: Tavistock.

37 Bryant, R. and Harvey, A.G. (1996) 'Initial post-traumatic stress responses following motor vehicle accidents', *Journal of Traumatic Stress* 9: 223–234.

38 Bryant, R.A. and Harvey, A.G. (1996) 'Visual imagery in post-traumatic stress disorder', *Journal of Traumatic Stress* 9: 613–620.

39 Bunn, T.A. and Clarke, A.M. (1979) 'Crisis intervention: an experimental study of the effects of a brief period of counselling on the anxiety of relatives of seriously injured or ill hospital patients', *British Journal of Medical Psychology* 52: 191–195.

40 Burstein, A. (1985) 'Post-traumatic flashbacks, dream disturbances, and mental imagery', *Journal of Clinical Psychiatry* 46: 374–378.

41 Burstein, A. (1989) 'Post-traumatic stress disorder in victims of motor vehicle accidents', *Hospital and Community Psychiatry* 40: 295–297.

42 Busuttil, W., Turnbull, G.J., Neal, L.A., Rollins, J., West, A.G., Blanch, N. and Herepath, R.(1995) 'Incorporating psychological debriefing techniques within a brief group psychotherapy programme for the treatment of post-traumatic stress disorder', *British Journal of Psychiatry* 167: 495–502.

43 Capewell, E. (1994) 'Responding to children in trauma: a systems approach for schools', *Bereavement Care* 13: 2–7.

44 Caplan, G. (1964) *Principles of preventive psychiatry*, New York: Basic Books.

45 Carlier, I.V.E., Lamberts, R.D., Van Uchelen, A.J. and Gersons, B.P.R. 'Effectiveness of psychological debriefings: a controlled study of police officers', *The Lancet* (in press).

46 Charlton, P.F.C. and Thompson, J.A. (1996) 'Ways of coping with psychological distress after trauma', *British Journal of Clinical Psychology* 35: 517–530.

47 Cherniss, C. (1980) *Staff burnout: Job stress in the human services*, London: Sage.

48 Clark, D.H. (1977) 'The therapeutic community', *British Journal of Psychiatry* 131: 553–564.

49 Clayton, P.J., Halikas, A. and Maurice, W.L. (1972) 'The depression of widowhood', *British Journal of Psychiatry* 120: 71–77.

50 Cobb, S. and Lindemann, E. (1943) 'Neuropsychiatric observations on the Coconut Grove fire', *Annals of Surgery* 117: 814–824.

51 Cohen, A. and Lahad, M. (1993) 'Eye movement desensitisation', in M. Lahad and A. Cohen (eds) *Community Stress Prevention*, Vol. 2, Kyriat Shmona, Israel: Community Stress Prevention Centre.

52 Collins, J.J. and Bailey, S.L. (1990) 'Traumatic stress disorder and violent behaviour', *Journal of Traumatic Stress* 3: 203–220.

REFERENCES

53   Cowan, M.E. and Murphy, S.A. (1985) 'Identification of post-disaster bereavement risk predictors', *Nursing Research* 34: 71–75.

54   Creamer, M., Burgess, P., Buckingham, W. and Pattison, P. (1989) *The psychological aftermath of the Queen Street shootings*, Dept of Psychology, University of Melbourne.

55   Creamer, M., Burgess, P. and Pattison, P. (1992) 'Reaction to trauma: a cognitive processing model', *Journal of Abnormal Psychology* 101: 452–459.

56   Crummock, V. (1996) 'Journey of a young widow', in K.J. Doka (ed.) *Living with Grief after Sudden Loss*, Bristol, PA: Taylor & Francis.

57   Cummings, E. (1969) *The Multigenerational Family*, Michigan: Univerity of Michigan Press.

58   Cunningham, V. (1988) *Herald disaster: From the shop floor*, Unpublished manuscript.

59   Daly, R.J. (1983) 'Samuel Pepys and post-traumatic stress disorder', *British Journal of Psychiatry* 143: 64–68.

60   Danielli, Y. (1985) 'The treatment and prevention of long-term effects and intergenerational transmission of victimization: a lesson from holocaust survivors and their children', in C.R. Figley (ed.) *Trauma and its Wake*, Vol .1, New York: Brunner Mazel.

61   Davidson, J. (1992) 'Drug therapy of post-traumatic stress disorder', *British Journal of Psychiatry* 160: 309–314.

62   Davidson, J., Swartz, M., Storck, M., Ranga Rama Krishnan and Hammett, E. (1985) 'A diagnostic and family study of post-traumatic stress disorder', *American Journal of Psychiatry* 142: 90–93.

63   Davidson, J.R.T. and van der Kolk, B.A. (1996) 'The psychopharmacological treatment of post-traumatic stress disorder', in B.A van der Kolk, A.C. McFarlane and L. Weisaeth, (eds) *Traumatic stress: the effects of overwhelming experience on mind, body and society*, New York: Guilford Press.

64   Davis, R.C. and Friedman, L.N. (1985) 'The emotional aftermath of crime and terrorism', in C.R. Figley (ed.) *Trauma and its Wake*, Vol. 1, New York: Brunner Mazel.

65   Deahl, M., Gillam, A.B., Searle, M.M. and Srinavasan, M. (1994) 'Psychological sequelae following the Gulf war: factors associated with subsequent morbidity and the effectiveness of psychological debriefing', *British Journal of Psychiatry* 165: 60–65.

66   de Beuklar, D. (1989) 'Experiences of the social intervention service', Paper presented at conference on the Zeebrugge disaster, Brussels.

67   DeFazio, V. (1975) 'The Vietnam era veteran', *Journal of Contemporary Psychotherapy* 7: 9–15.

68   de Loos, W. (1989) 'Blood pressure and cortisol in traumatic stress reactions', Paper presented at the 4th International Conference on Psychological Stress and Adjustment in Time of War and Peace, Tel-Aviv, Israel.

69   Dimsdale, J.E. (1974) 'The coping behaviour of Nazi concentration camp survivors', *American Journal of Psychiatry* 131: 792–797.

70   Dohrenwend, B.P., Dohrenwend, B.S., Kasl, S. and Warheit, G. (1979) *Report of the public health and safety task force on behavioural effects to the President's*

commission on the accident at Three Mile Island, Washington, DC: US Government Printing Office.

71 Duckworth, D. (1986) 'Psychological problems arising from disaster work', *Stress Medicine* 2: 315–323.

72 Duckworth, D.H. (1991) 'Everyday psychological trauma in the police service', *Disaster Management* 3: 224–227.

73 Duke, D. (1980) 'A study of the effects of bereavement in a sample of those bereaved in the area covered by Horton parish, South Shields', M.Phil. thesis, Newcastle Polytechnic.

74 Dunning, C. (1988) 'Intervention strategies for emergency workers', in M. Lystad (ed.) *Mental health response to mass emergencies*, New York: Brunner Mazel.

75 Dyregrov, A. (1989) 'Caring for helpers in disaster situations: psychological debriefing', *Disaster Management* 2: 25–30.

76 Dyregrov, A. and Mitchell, J.T. (1992) 'Work with traumatised children: psychological effects and coping strategies', *Journal of Traumatic Stress* 5: 5–18.

77 Dyregrov, A., Kristoffersen, J.I. and Gjestad, R. (1996) 'Voluntary and professional disaster-workers: similarities and differences in reactions', *Journal of Traumatic Stress* 9: 541–556.

78 Eitinger, L. (1962) 'Concentration camp survivors in the post-war world', *American Journal of Orthopsychiatry* 32: 367.

79 Ellis, A. (1962) *Reason and Emotion in Psychotherapy*, New York: Lyle Stuart.

80 EMDR Institute (1997) *Controlled Studies*, inst@emdr.com.

81 Erikson, K. (1979) *In the Wake of the Flood*, London: George Allen & Unwin.

82 Fairbank, J.A. and Nicholson, R.A. (1978) 'Theoretical and empirical issues in the treatment of PTSD in Vietnam veterans', *Journal of Clinical Psychology* 43: 44–55.

83 Figley, C.R. (1988) 'Toward a field of traumatic stress', *Journal of Traumatic Stress* 1: 3–16.

84 Flannery, R.B., Fulton, P., Tausch, J. and Deloffi, A. Y. (1991) 'A program to help staff cope with psychological sequelae of assaults by patients', *Hospital and Community Psychiatry* 42: 935–938.

85 Fleming, R., Baum, A., Gisriel, M.M. and Gatchel, R.A. (1982) 'Mediating influences of social support on stress at Three Mile Island', *Journal of Human Stress* 14–22.

86 Foa, E.B., Steketee, G. and Rothbaum, B.O. (1989) 'Behavioural/cognitive conceptualizations of post-traumatic stress disorder', *Behaviour Therapy* 20: 155–176.

87 Foa, E.B., Rothbaum, B.O., Riggs, D.S. and Murdock, T.B. (1991) 'Treatment of post-traumatic stress disorder in rape victims: a comparison between cognitive-behavioural procedures and counselling', *Journal of Consulting and Clinical Psychology* 59: 715–723.

88 Foa, E.B., Herst-Ikeda, D. and Perry, K.J. (1995) 'Evaluation of a brief cognitive-behavioural programme for the prevention of chronic PTSD in recent assault victims', *Journal of Consulting and Clinical Psychology* 63: 948–955.

REFERENCES

89   Foa, E.B., Molnar, C. and Cashman, L. (1995) 'Change in rape narratives during exposure therapy for post-traumatic stress disorder', *Journal of Traumatic Stress* 8: 675–690.

90   Frank, E. and Stewart, B.D. (1983) 'Physical aggression: treating the victims', in P.J. Clayton and J.E. Barrett (eds) *Treatment of depression: Old controversies and new approaches*, New York: Raven Press.

91   Frank, E., Anderson, B., Stewart, B.D., Dancu, C., Hughes, C. and West, D. (1988) 'Efficacy of cognitive behaviour therapy and systematic desensitisation in the treatment of rape trauma', *Behaviour Therapy* 19: 403 420.

92   Frederick, C.J. (1977) 'Current thinking about crisis or psychological intervention in United States disasters', *Mass Emergencies* 2: 43–50.

93   Frederick, C. (1980) 'Effects of natural vs. human induced violence upon victims', *Evaluation and Change*, Special issue, 71–75.

94   Frederick, C.J. (1987) 'Psychic trauma in victims of crime and terrorism', in G. R. Van den Bos and B.K. Bryant (eds) *Cataclysms, Crises and Catastrophes*, Master Lecture Series, American Psychiatric Association, 6: 55–108.

95   Freedy, J.R., Saladin, M.E., Kilpatrick, D.G., Resnick, H.S. and Saunders, B.E. (1994) 'Understanding acute psychological distress following natural disaster', *Journal of Traumatic Stress* 7: 257–274.

96   Freud, S. (1910) 'The origin of psychoanalysis', in J. Rickman (ed.) *A general selection from the works of Freud*, London: Hogarth.

97   Friedman, K., Bischoff, H., Davis, R.C. and Person, A. (1982) *Victims and Helpers: Reactions to Crime*, New York: Victim Services Agency.

98   Fulton, R. and Owen, G. (1977) *Adjustment to loss through death: a sociological analysis*, University of Minnesota: Center for Death Education and Research.

99   Gelpin, E., Bonne, D., Peri, T., Brandes, D. and Shalev, A.T. (1996) 'Treatment of recent trauma survivors with benzodiazepines: a prospective study', *Journal of Clinical Psychiatry* 57: 390–394.

100   Gibbs, M.S. (1989) 'Factors in the victim that mediate between disaster and psychopathology: a review', *Journal of Traumatic Stress* 2: 489–514.

101   Giel, R. (1990) 'Psychosocial processes in disasters', *International Journal of Mental Health* 19: 7–20.

102   Gifford, R.K. and Tyler, M.P. (1990) 'Consulting in grief leadership: A practical guide', *Disaster Management* 2: 218–224.

103   Gleser, G.C., Green, B.L. and Winget, C. (1981) *Prolonged Psychological Effects of Disaster: A study of Buffalo Creek*, New York: Academic Press.

104   Gorer, G. (1965) *Death, Grief and Mourning in Contemporary Britain*, London: Cresset.

105   Green, B.L. (1994) 'Long-term consequences of disasters', Paper presented at the NATO conference on Stress, Coping and Disaster, Bornas, France.

106   Green, B.L. (1994) 'Traumatic stress and disaster: mental health effects and factors influencing adaptation', in F. Liehmac and C. Nadelson (eds) *International Review of Psychiatry*, Vol. 2, Washington, DC: American Psychiatric Press.

107   Green, B.L., Grace, M.C., Lindy, J.D., Titchener, J. and Lindy J.G. (1983) 'Levels of functional impairment following a civilian disaster: the Beverly Hills supper club fire', *Journal of Consulting and Clinical Psychology* 51: 573–580.

108   Green, B.L., Lindy, J.D. and Grace, M.C. (1985) 'Post-traumatic stress disorder: towards DSM-IV', *Journal of Nervous and Mental Disease* 173: 406–411.

109   Griffiths, J.A. and Watts, R. (1992) *The Kempsey and Grafton bus crashes: The aftermath*, University of New England, Australia: Instructional Design Solutions.

110   Gunn, J. (1989) 'The Zeebrugge disaster', Paper presented at EEC symposium on PTSD, London.

111   Hacker-Hughes, J.G.H. and Thompson, J. (1994) 'Post traumatic stress disorder: an evaluation of behavioural and cognitive behavioural interventions and treatments', *Clinical Psychology and Psychotherapy* 1: 125–142.

112   Haga, E. (1985) 'The wet grave, sudden death and the bereaved', *Nord. Psykiatr. Tidsskr.* 39: 23–28.

113   Hammarberg, M. and Silver, S.M. (1994) 'Outcome of treatment for post-traumatic stress disorder in a primary care unit serving Vietnam veterans', *Journal of Traumatic Stress* 7: 195–216.

114   Harper, J. (1993) 'Reaching out: running a staff care service in the aftermath of disaster', in T. Newburn (ed.) *Working with disaster*, Harlow: Longman.

115   Hartman, C.R. and Burgess, A.W. (1985) 'Illness-related PTSD: a cognitive behavioural model of intervention with heart attack victims', in C.R. Figley (ed.) *Trauma and its Wake*, Vol. 1, New York: Brunner Mazel.

116   Henderson, A.S. and Bostock, T. (1977) 'Coping behaviour after shipwreck', *British Journal of Psychiatry* 131: 15–20.

117   Herlofsen, P. (1988) 'Psychosocial intervention after a military disaster', Paper presented at the 4th International Conference on Psychological Stress and Adjustment in Time of War and Peace, Tel-Aviv, Israel.

118   Herman, J.L. (1992) 'Complex PTSD: a syndrome in survivors of prolonged and repeated trauma', *Journal of Traumatic Stress* 5: 377–391.

119   Hiley-Young, B. *et al.* (1994) *Post-traumatic syndrome and disorder*, Palo Alto, CA: National Center for PTSD.

120   Hobbs, M. Personal communication.

121   Hobbs, M., Mayou, R., Harrison, B. and Worlock, P. (1996) 'A randomised controlled trial of psychological debriefing for victims of road traffic accidents', *British Medical Journal* 313: 1438–1439.

122   Hodge, J.R. (1971) 'The whiplash neurosis', *Psychosomatics* 12: 245–249.

123   Hodgkinson, P. Unpublished data.

124   Hodgkinson, P.E. (1982) 'Abnormal grief: the problem of therapy', *British Journal of Medical Psychology* 55: 29–34.

125   Hodgkinson, P. (1988) 'Psychological after-effects of transportation disaster', *Medicine, Science and the Law* 28: 304–308.

126   Hodgkinson, P.E. (1988) 'Managing a disaster team', Paper presented at the First European Conference on Traumatic Stress Studies, Lincoln, UK.

127   Hodgkinson, P.E. (1990) 'The Zeebrugge disaster III: psychosocial care in the UK', *Disaster Management* 2: 131–134.

128   Hodgkinson, P. (1995) 'Viewing the bodies following disaster: does it help?', *Bereavement Care* 14: 2–4.

REFERENCES

129   Hodgkinson, P.E. and Shepherd, M.A. (1994) 'The impact of disaster support work', *Journal of Traumatic Stress* 7: 587–600.

130   Hodgkinson, P.E. and Stewart, M. (1988) 'Missing, presumed dead', *Disaster Management* 1: 11–14.

131   Hodgkinson, P.E. and Stewart, M. (1992) 'The psychological trauma in mass burns casualties', *Disaster Management* 4: 221–223.

132   Hodgkinson, P.E. and Stewart, M. (1993) 'Trauma, crisis intervention and psychological debriefing', *Industrial and Environmental Crisis Quarterly* 7: 145–154.

133   Hodgkinson, P., Parkes, C.M. and Braund, H. (1990) 'The Zeebrugge disaster: psychological adjustment in the first year', Unpublished paper.

134   Hodgkinson, P.E., Joseph, S., Yule, W. and Williams, R. (1993) 'Viewing human remains following disaster: helpful or harmful?', *Medicine, Science and the Law* 33: 197–202.

135   Hodgkinson, P.E., Joseph, S., Yule, W. and Williams, R. (1995) 'Measuring grief after sudden violent death: Zeebrugge bereaved at thirty months', *Personality and Individual Differences* 18: 805–808.

136   Hoiberg, A. and McCaughey, B.G. (1984) 'The traumatic after-effects of a collision at sea', *American Journal of Psychiatry* 141: 70–73.

137   Holmes, T.H. and Rahe, R.H. (1967) 'The social readjustment rating scale', *Journal of Psychosomatic Research* 1: 213–218.

138   Hood, A.N. (1909) 'Personal experiences in the great earthquake', *Living Age* 261: 355–365.

139   Horowitz, M.J. (1975) 'Intrusive and repetitive thoughts after stress', *Archives of General Psychiatry* 32: 1457–1463.

140   Horowitz, M.J. (1978) *Stress response syndromes*, New York: Jason Aronson.

141   Horowitz, M.J. (1986) *Stress response syndromes*, 2nd edition, New York: Jason Aronson.

142   Horowitz, M.J. (1986) *Image formation and cognition*, New York: Appleton-Century-Crofts.

143   Horowitz, M.J., Wilner, M., Kaltreider, N. and Alvarez, W. (1980) 'Signs and symptoms of post-traumatic stress disorder', *Archives of General Psychiatry* 37: 85–92.

144   Hough, R.L., Vega, W.A., Valle, R., Kolody, B., Griswald de Castillo, R. and Tarke, H. (1990) 'Mental health consequences of the San Ysidro McDonald's massacre', *Journal of Traumatic Stress* 3: 71–92.

145   Husaini, B.A. and Negg, J.A. (1980) 'Characteristics of life events and psychiatric impairment in rural communities', *Journal of Nervous and Mental Disease* 168: 159–166.

146   Hytten, K. and Hasle, A. (1989) 'Fire fighters: a study of stress and coping', *Acta Psychiatrica Scandinavia* 80: 50–55.

147   Hytten, K. and Herlofsen, P. (1989) 'Accident simulation as a new therapy technique for post-traumatic stress disorder', *Acta Psychiatrica Scandinavia* 80: 79–83.

148   Ingraham, L.H. (1988) 'Grief leadership in work groups', Paper presented at the Fourth Annual Uniformed Services University of the Health Sciences Conference on Military Medicine, Bethesda, MD.

149   Inman, D.J., Silver, S.M. and Doghrami, K. (1990) 'Sleep disturbance in post-traumatic stress disorder: a comparison with non-PTSD insomnia', *Journal of Traumatic Stress* 3: 429–438.

150   James, A. (1988) 'Perceptions of stress in British ambulance personnel', *Work and Stress* 2: 319–326.

151   Janoff-Bulman, R. (1985) 'The aftermath of victimisation: rebuilding shattered assumptions', in C.R. Figley (ed.) *Trauma and its Wake*, Vol. 1, New York: Brunner Mazel.

152   Johnsen, B.H., Eid, J., Lovstad, T. and Michelsen, L.T. (1997) 'Post-traumatic stress disorder and substance abuse: use of research in a clinical setting', *Journal of Traumatic Stress* 10: 133–140.

153   Johnson, D.R., Rosenheck, R., Fontana, A., Lubin, H., Charney, D. and Southwick, S. (1996) 'Outcome of intensive in-patient treatment for combat related post-traumatic stress disorder', *American Journal of Psychiatry* 153: 771–777.

154   Jones, D.R. (1982) 'Emotional reactions to military aircraft accidents', *Aviation, Space and Environmental Medicine* 53: 595–598.

155   Jones, R. (1978) *The new psychology of dreaming*, Harmondsworth: Penguin.

156   Joseph, S., Yule, W., Williams, R. and Hodgkinson, P. (1993) 'The *Herald of Free Enterprise* disaster: measuring post-traumatic symptoms 30 months on', *British Journal of Clinical Psychology* 32: 327–331.

157   Joseph, S., Yule, W., Williams, R. and Hodgkinson, P. (1993) 'Guilt and distress 30 months after the capsize of the *Herald of Free Enterprise*', *Personality and Individual Differences* 14: 271–273.

158   Joseph, S., Yule, W., Williams, R. and Hodgkinson, P. (1994) 'Correlates of post-traumatic stress at 30 months: the *Herald of Free Enterprise* disaster', *Behaviour Research and Therapy* 32: 521–524.

159   Joseph, S., Williams, R. and Yule, W. (1995) 'Psychosocial perspectives on post-traumatic stress', *Clinical Psychology Review* 15: 515–544.

160   Joseph, S., Dalgliesh, T., Thrasher, S., Yule, W., Williams, R. and Hodgkinson, P. (1996) 'Chronic emotional processing in survivors of the *Herald of Free Enterprise* disaster: the relationship of intrusion and avoidance at 3 years to distress at 5 years', *Behaviour Research and Therapy* 34: 357–360.

161   Joyce, D. (1989) 'Why do police officers laugh at death?', *The Psychologist* 2: 379–380.

162   Kanzler, E., Shaffer, D., Wasserman, G. and Davies, M. (1990) 'Early childhood bereavement', *Journal of the American Academy of Child and Adolescent Psychiatry* 29: 413–520.

163   Kasl, S.V., Chisholm, R.F. and Eskenazi, B. (1981) 'The impact of the accident at the Three Mile Island on the behavior and well-being of nuclear workers: II', *American Journal of Public Health* 71: 484–495.

164   Kastenbaum, R. (1969) 'Death and bereavement in later life', in A.H. Kutscher (ed.) *Death and Bereavement*, Springfield, IL: Thomas.

165   Keane, T.M. and Kaloupek, D.G. (1982) 'Imaginal flooding in the treatment of a post-traumatic stress disorder', *Journal of Consulting and Clinical Psychology* 50: 138–140.

REFERENCES

166 Keane, T.M., Fairbank, J.A., Caddell, J.M., Zimering, R.T. and Bender, M.E. (1985) 'A behavioural approach to assessing and treating post-traumatic stress disorder in Vietnam veterans', in C.R. Figley (ed.) *Trauma and its Wake*, Vol. 1, New York: Brunner Mazel.

167 Keane, T.M., Fairbank, J.A., Caddell, J.M. and Zimering, R.T. (1989) 'Implosive (flooding) therapy reduces symptoms of PTSD in Vietnam combat veterans', *Behavioural Therapy* 20: 245–260.

168 Keating, J.P. *et al.* (1987) 'Post-disaster stress in emergency responders', Paper presented at APA meeting, Chicago.

169 Klingman, A. (1987) 'A school-based emergency crisis intervention in a mass school disaster', *Professional Psychology: Research and Practice* 18: 604–612.

170 Kolb, L.C, Burris, B. and Griffiths, S. (1984) 'Propanolol and clonidine in the treatment of chronic post-traumatic stress of war', in B.A. van der Kolk (ed.) *Post-traumatic Stress Disorder: Psychological and Biological Sequelae*, Washington, DC: American Psychiatric Press.

171 Kosten, T.R. (1992) 'Alexithymia as a predictor of treatment response in PTSD', *Journal of Traumatic Stress* 5: 563–573.

172 Krell, G.I. (1974) 'Support services aid relatives of victims', *Hospitals JAHA* 48: 56–59.

173 Kubany, E.S. (1994) 'A cognitive model of guilt typology in combat-related PTSD', *Journal of Traumatic Stress* 7: 3–20.

174 Kuch, K., Swinson, R.P. and Kirby, M. (1985) 'Post-traumatic stress disorder after car accidents', *Canadian Journal of Psychiatry* 30: 426–427.

175 Lacey, G.N. (1972) 'Observations on Aberfan', *Journal of Psychosomatic Research* 16: 257–260.

176 Lahad, M. 'Bibliotherapy as an instrument for assessing and coping with stress: six-piece story making (6-PSM) and BASIC Ph', Unpublished manuscript.

177 Lahad, M., Ankor, C. and Cohen, A. (1993) 'Stress intervention programme with adolescents', in M. Lahad and A. Cohen (eds) *Community Stress Prevention*, Vol. 2, Kiryat Shmona: Community Stress Prevention Centre.

178 Lalonde, S., Borrill, J., Jones, E. and Wood, C. (1988) 'Community responses to a near disaster', Unpublished paper, Psychology Dept, North Lincolnshire Health Authority.

179 Lammens, J. and Hodgkinson, P.E. (1990) 'The Zeebrugge disaster I: triage, treatment, and aftercare', *Disaster Management* 2: 123–127.

180 Lebedun, M.. and Wilson, K.E. (1989) 'Planning and integrating disaster response', in R. Gist and L. Lubin (eds) *Psychosocial Aspects of Disaster*, New York: Wiley.

181 Leopold, R.L. and Dillon, H. (1963) 'Psychoanatomy of a disaster: a long-term study of post-traumatic neuroses in survivors of a marine explosion', *American Journal of Psychiatry* 119: 913–921.

182 Lieberman, S. (1978) 'Nineteen cases of morbid grief', *British Journal of Psychiatry* 132: 159–163.

183 Lifton, R.J. (1971) *History and Human Survival*, New York: Vintage Books.

184 Lifton, R.J. (1983) 'Responses of survivors to man-made catastrophes', *Bereavement Care* 2: 2–6.

239

185   Lindemann, E. (1944) 'Symptomatology and management of acute grief', *American Journal of Psychiatry* 101: 141–148.

186   Lindstrom, B. and Lundin, T. (1982) 'Stress reactions among rescue and health care personnel after a major hotel fire', *Nord. Psykiatr. Tidsskr.* 36: Supplement 6.

187   Lindy, J.D. (1986) 'An outline for the psychoanalytic psychotherapy of post-traumatic stress disorder', in C.R. Figley (ed.) *Trauma and its Wake*, Vol. 2, New York: Brunner Mazel.

188   Lindy, J.D. (1993) 'Focal psychoanalytic psychotherapy of post-traumatic stress disorder', in J.P. Wilson and B. Raphael (eds) *International Handbook of Traumatic Stress Syndromes*, New York: Plenum Press.

189   Lindy, J.D. (1996) 'Psychoanalytic psychotherapy of post-traumatic stress disorder', in B.A. van der Kolk, A.C. McFarlane and L. Weisaeth (eds) *Traumatic stress: the effects of overwhelming experience on mind, body and society*, New York: Guilford Press.

190   Lindy, J.D. and Green, B.L. (1981) 'Survivors: outreach to a reluctant population', *American Journal of Orthopsychiatry* 51: 468–478.

191   Lindy, J.D., Green, B.L., Grace, M. and Titchener, J. (1983) 'Psychotherapy with survivors of the Beverly Hills supper club fire', *American Journal of Psychotherapy* 37: 593–610.

192   Lopez-Ibor, J.J., Soria, J., Canas, F. and Rodriguez-Gamazo, M. (1985) 'Psychopathological aspects of the toxic oil syndrome catastrophe', *British Journal of Psychiatry* 147: 352–365.

193   Loughrey, G.C, Bell, P., Kee, M., Roddy, R.J. and Curran, P.S. (1988) 'Post-traumatic stress disorder and civil violence in Northern Ireland', *British Journal of Psychiatry* 153: 554–560.

194   Lowenthal, M.F. and Berkman, P.L. (1967) 'Suicide in the widowed', *American Journal of Epidemiology* 81: 23–34.

195   Lundin, T. (1979) *On crisis theory – reactions to sudden and unexpected death*, Proceedings of the 10th International Conference for Suicide Prevention and Crisis Intervention, Ottawa, Canada.

196   Lundin, T. (1984) 'Disaster reactions: a study on survivors' reactions following a major fire disaster', Unpublished paper.

197   Lundin, T. (1984) 'Long-term outcome of bereavement', *British Journal of Psychiatry* 145: 424–428.

198   Lundin, T. (1984) 'Morbidity following sudden and unexpected bereavement', *British Journal of Psychiatry* 144: 84–88.

199   Lundin, T. (1987) 'The stress of unexpected bereavement', *Stress Medicine* 3: 109–114.

200   Lundin, T and Otto, U. 'Acute post-traumatic stress reactions to an industrial gas leakage disaster', Unpublished paper.

201   Lytle, R. (1992) 'An investigation of eye movement desensitisation reprocessing: failure to replicate Shapiro's claims', Unpublished manuscript, Dept of Psychology, Pennsylvania State University.

202   McCaughey, B.G. (1986) 'The psychological symptomatology of a US naval disaster', *Military Medicine* 151: 162–165.

REFERENCES

203 McFarlane, A.C. (1987) 'Life events and psychiatric disorder: the role of a natural disaster', *British Journal of Psychiatry* 151: 362–367.

204 McFarlane, A.C. (1988) 'The phenomenology of post-traumatic stress disorders following a natural disaster', *Journal of Nervous and Mental Disease* 176: 22–29.

205 McFarlane, A.C. (1988) 'The aetiology of post-traumatic stress disorders following a natural disaster', *British Journal of Psychiatry* 152: 116–121.

206 McFarlane, A.C. (1989) 'The aetiology of post-traumatic morbidity: predisposing, precipitating and perpetuating factors', *British Journal of Psychiatry* 154: 221–228.

207 McFarlane, A.C. (1992) 'Avoidance and intrusion in post-traumatic stress disorder', *Journal of Nervous and Mental Disease* 180: 439–445.

208 Machin, L. (1982) 'In the last analysis', *Community Care*, 20 May: 14–15.

209 MacLeod, D. (1991) 'Psychological debriefing: rationale and application', *Practice* 5: 103–110.

210 McLeod, W. (1975) 'Merphos poisoning or mass panic?', *Australia and New Zealand Journal of Psychiatry* 9: 225–230.

211 Maddison, D.C. and Walker, W.L. (1967) 'Factors affecting the outcome of conjugal bereavement', *British Journal of Psychiatry* 113: 1057–1067.

212 Malan, D.H. (1979) *Individual Psychotherapy and the Science of Psychodynamics*, London: Butterworths.

213 Marks, I.M., Hodgson, R. and Rachman, S.J. (1981) 'Treatment of chronic obsessive-compulsive neurosis by in-vivo exposure', *British Journal of Psychiatry* 127: 349–364.

214 Martin, H.L. (1970) 'Parents' and children's reactions to burns and scalds in children', *British Journal of Medical Psychology* 43: 183–191.

215 Martin, H.L., Lawries, J.H. and Wilkinson, A.W. (1968) 'The family of the fatally burned child', *The Lancet* i: 628–629.

216 Mason, D. (1989) Paper presented at disaster management conference, Wolverhampton, UK.

217 Mawson, D., Marks, I.M., Ramm, L. and Stern, R.M. (1981) 'Guided mourning for morbid grief: a controlled study', *British Journal of Psychiatry* 138: 185–193.

218 Meichenbaum, D. (1994) *A clinical handbook/practical therapist manual for assessing and treating adults with post-traumatic stress disorder*, Waterloo, Ontario: Institute Press.

219 Metter, J. and Michelson, L.K. (1993) 'Theoretical, clinical, research, and ethical constraints of the EMDR technique', *Journal of Traumatic Stress* 6: 413–415.

220 Middleton, W. (1995) 'Bereavement phenomenology and the processes of resolution', MD thesis, University of Queensland.

221 Miller, E. (1940) *Neuroses in war*, London: Macmillan.

222 Mitchell, J.T. (1983) 'When disaster strikes: the critical incident debriefing process', *Journal of the Emergency Medical Services* 8: 36–39.

223 Mitchell, J.T. (1988) 'The history, status and future of critical incident stress debriefings', *Journal of the Emergency Medical Services* 8: 36–39.

REFERENCES

224 Mitchell, M., McLay, D., Boddy, J. and Cechi, L. (1991) 'The police response to the Lockerbie disaster', *Disaster Management* 3: 198–205.

225 Moran, C. and Britton, N.R. (1994) 'Emergency work experience and reactions to traumatic incidents', *Journal of Traumatic Stress* 7: 575–586.

226 Morris, M. (1982) *If I should die before I wake*, New York: Dell.

227 Nader, K.O. (1997) 'Childhood traumatic loss: the interaction of trauma and grief', in C.R. Figley, B.E. Bride and N. Mazza (eds) *Death and trauma*, Washington, DC: Taylor & Francis.

228 Nardi, C. (1985) *Koach project: Aims and objectives*, Medical Corps, Israel Defence Forces.

229 Nevin, C. (1996) 'Who lives? Who dies?', *The Guardian*, 26 November.

230 Newburn, T. (1991) 'Organisational pressures and role stresses in the lives of the Hillsborough social work teams', *Disaster Management* 3: 187–192.

231 Nixon, J. and Pearn, J. (1977) 'Emotional sequelae of parents and siblings following the drowning or near-drowning of a child', *Australia and New Zealand Journal of Psychiatry* 11: 265–268.

232 O'Connell, M. Unpublished manuscript.

233 Olumide, S. (1990) 'The unexpected death of children through disaster', *Bereavement Care* 9: 8–10.

234 Orr, E. and Westman, M. (1989) 'Does hardiness moderate stress, and how? A review', in M. Rosenbaum (ed.) *Resourcefulness: On Coping Skills, Self Control and Adaptive Behaviour*, New York: Springer.

235 Parker, N. (1977) 'Accident litigants and neurotic symptoms', *Medical Journal of Australia* 2: 318–322.

236 Parkes, C.M. Unpublished paper.

237 Parkes, C.M. (1972) *Bereavement: studies of grief in adult life*, Harmondsworth: Penguin.

238 Parkes, C.M. (1985) 'Bereavement', *British Journal of Psychiatry* 146: 11–17.

239 Parkes, C.M. (1993) 'Psychiatric problems following bereavement by murder or manslaughter', *Bereavement Care* 12: 2–6.

240 Parkes, C.M. and Weiss, R.S. (1983) *Recovery from bereavement*, New York: Basic Books.

241 Paton, D. (1996) 'Training disaster workers: promoting wellbeing and operational effectiveness', *Disaster Prevention and Management* 5: 11–18.

242 Paton, D. (1997) 'Post-event support for disaster workers: integrating recovery resources and the recovery environment', *Disaster Management and Prevention* 6: 43–49.

243 Perlberg, M. (1979) 'Trauma at Tenerife: the psychic aftershocks of a jet disaster', *Human Behaviour* 8: 49–50.

244 Perlin, S. and Schmidt, A. (1975) 'Psychiatry', in S. Perlin (ed.) *A Handbook for the Study of Suicide*, New York: Oxford University Press.

245 Pitman, R.K., Altman, B., Greenwald, E., Longpre, R.E., Macklin, M.L., Poire, R.E. and Steketee, G.S. (1991) 'Psychiatric complications during flooding therapy for post-traumatic stress disorder', *Journal of Clinical Psychiatry* 52: 17–20.

246 Polak, P.R., Egan, D., Vandebergh, R. and Williams, W.V. (1975) 'Prevention in mental health: a controlled study', *American Journal of Psychiatry* 132: 146–149.

247 Punchard, E. (1989) *Piper Alpha – A survivor's story*, London: Star Books.

248 Pynoos, R.S. (1992) 'Grief and trauma in children and adolescents', *Bereavement Care* 11: 2–10.

249 Pynoos, R.S., Frederick, C., Nader, K., Arroyo, W., Steinberg, A., Eth, S., Nunez, F. and Fairbanks, L. (1987) 'Life threat and post-traumatic stress in school-age children', *Archives of General Psychiatry* 44: 1057–1063.

250 Quintyn, L., De Winne, J. and Hodgkinson, P.E. (1990) 'The Zeebrugge disaster III: the disaster victim identification team – procedures and psychological support', *Disaster Management* 2: 128–130.

251 Rachman, S. (1980) 'Emotional processing', *Behaviour Research and Therapy* 18: 51–60.

252 Rando, T.A. (1996) 'Complications in mourning traumatic death', in K.J Doka (ed.) *Living with grief after sudden loss*, Bristol, PA: Taylor & Francis.

253 Ramsay, R. (1977) 'Behavioural approaches to bereavement', *Behaviour Research and Therapy* 15: 131–135.

254 Ramsay, R. and de Groot, W. (1977) 'A further look at bereavement', Paper presented at the European Association for Behaviour Therapy Conference, Uppsala.

255 Raphael, B. (1977) 'Preventative intervention with the recently bereaved', *Archives of General Psychiatry* 34: 1450–1454.

256 Raphael, B. (1978) 'Mourning and the prevention of melancholia', *British Journal of Medical Psychology* 51: 303–310.

257 Raphael, B. (1979–1980) 'A primary prevention action programme: psychiatric intervention following a major rail disaster', *Omega* 10: 211–225.

258 Raphael, B. (1983) *The anatomy of bereavement*, New York: Basic Books.

259 Raphael, B. (1986), *When disaster strikes*, London: Hutchinson.

260 Raphael, B., Singh, B., Bradbury, B. and Lambert, F. (1984) 'Who helps the helpers? The effects of a disaster on the rescue workers', *Omega* 14: 9–20.

261 Rawlins, T. (1985) 'Survivors', *Nursing Times*, 27 November: 12–14.

262 Redmond, L.M. (1996) 'Sudden violent death', in K.J. Doka (ed.) *Living with Grief after Sudden Loss*, Bristol, PA: Taylor & Francis.

263 Regester, M. (1989) *Crisis Management*, London: Business Books.

264 Renzenbrink, I. (1989) 'After the shootings: disaster recovery in Melbourne, Australia', *Bereavement Care* 8: 31–33.

265 Resnick, H.S., Kilpatrick, D.G., Dansky, B.S., Saunders, B.E. and Best, C.C. (1993) 'Prevalence of civilian trauma and post-traumatic stress disorder in a representative sample of women', *Journal of Consulting and Clinical Psychology* 61: 984–991.

266 Resnick, P.A. and Schnicke, M.K. (1992) 'Cognitive processing therapy for sexual assault victims', *Journal of Consulting and Clinical Psychology* 60: 748–756.

267 Richards, D.A. and Rose, J.S. (1991) 'Exposure therapy for post-traumatic stress disorder. Four case studies', *British Journal of Psychiatry* 158: 836–840.

268 Richards, D.J., Lovell, K. and Marks, I.M. (1994) 'Post-traumatic stress disorder: evaluation of a behavioural treatment programme', *Journal of Traumatic Stress* 7: 669–680.

269 Robinson, R.C. and Mitchell, J.T. (1993) 'Evaluation of psychological debriefings', *Journal of Traumatic Stress* 6: 367–382.

270 Rothbaum, B.O. (1997) 'A controlled study of eye movement desensitisation and reprocessing for post-traumatic stress disordered sexual assault victims', *Bulletin of the Menninger Clinic* (in press).

271 Rothbaum, B.O. and Foa, E.B. (1992) 'Exposure therapy for rape victims with post-traumatic stress disorder', *The Behaviour Therapist* 15: 219–222.

272 Rothbaum, B.O. and Foa, E.B. (1996) 'Cognitive-behavioural therapy for post-traumatic stress disorder', in B.A. van der Kolk, A.C. McFarlane and L. Weisaeth (eds) *Traumatic Stress: The Effects of Overwhelming Experience on Mind, Body and Society*, New York: Guilford Press.

273 Rutter, M. (1966) 'Bereaved children', in *Children of sick parents*, Maudsley Monographs 16, London: Oxford University Press.

274 Salmon, T.W. (1919) 'The war neuroses and their lesson', *New York State Journal of Medicine* 59: 993–994.

275 Savage, W. (1978) 'Perinatal loss and the medical team', *Midwife, Health Visitor and Community Nurse*, September: 292–295.

276 Schindler, F.E. (1980) 'Treatment by systematic desensitisation of a recurring nightmare of a real life trauma', *Journal of Behaviour Therapy and Experimental Psychiatry* 11: 53–54.

277 Schneidman, E.S. (1969) 'Suicide, lethality and the psychological autopsy', *International Psychiatry Clinics* 6: 225–250.

278 Scurfield, R.M., Kenderdine, S.K. and Pollard, R.J. (1990) 'Inpatient treatment for war-related post-traumatic stress disorder: initial findings on a longer-term outcome study', *Journal of Traumatic Stress* 3: 185–202.

279 Searles, H.F. (1955) 'The informational value of the supervisor's emotional experiences', *Psychiatry* Vol. 18.

280 Seligman, M.E.P. (1975) *Helplessness: On Depression, Development and Death*, San Francisco: Freeman.

281 Shapiro, D. and Kunkler, J. (1990) *Psychological support for hospital staff initiated by clinical psychologists in the aftermath of the Hillsborough disaster*, Sheffield, England: Sheffield Health Authority Mental Health Services Unit.

282 Shapiro, F. (1995) *Eye Movement Desensitisation and Reprocessing: Basic Principles, Protocols and Procedures*, New York: Guilford Press.

283 Shay, J. (1991) 'Learning about combat stress from Homer's *Iliad*', *Journal of Traumatic Stress* 4: 561–580.

284 Shay, J. (1997) 'About medications for combat PTSD', jshay@world.std.com.

285 Short, P. (1979) 'Victims and helpers', in R. Heathcote and B. Tong (eds) *Natural Hazards in Australia*, Canberra: Australian Academy of Science.

286 Silver, S.M. (1986) 'An inpatient program for PTSD: context as treatment', in C. R. Figley (ed.) *Trauma and its Wake*, Vol. 2, New York: Brunner Mazel.

287 Simos, B.G. (1979) *A Time to Grieve*, New York: Family Service Association.

288 Simpson, M.A. (1997) 'Traumatic bereavements and death-related PTSD', in C.R. Figley, B.E. Bride and N. Mazza (eds) *Death and Trauma*, Washington, DC: Taylor & Francis.

289 Sims, A.C.P., White, A.C. and Murphy, T. (1979) 'Aftermath neurosis: psychological sequelae of the Birmingham bombings in victims not seriously injured', *Medicine, Science and the Law* 19: 78–81.

290 Singh, B. and Raphael, B. (1981) 'Post-disaster morbidity of the bereaved', *Journal of Nervous and Mental Disease* 169: 203–212.

291 Smith, J.R. (1986) 'Sealing over and integration: modes of resolution in the post-traumatic stress recovery process', in C. R. Figley (ed.) *Trauma and its Wake*, Vol. 2, New York: Brunner Mazel.

292 Smyth, L.D. (1994) *Clinician's manual for the cognitive-behavioural treatment of PTSD*, Maryland: RTR Publishing.

293 Solomon, M.J. and Thompson, J. (1995) 'Anger and blame in three technological disasters', *Stress Medicine* 11: 199–206.

294 Solomon, R.M. and Shapiro, F. (1997) 'Eye movement desensitisation and reprocessing: a therapeutic tool for trauma and grief', in C.R Figley, B.E. Bride and N. Mazza (eds) *Death and Trauma*, Washington, DC: Taylor & Francis.

295 Solomon, S.D., Smith, E.M., Robins, L.N. and Fishbach, R.L. (1987) 'Social involvement as a mediator of disaster-induced stress', *Journal of Applied Social Psychology* 17: 1092–1112.

296 Solomon, Z. (1989) Unpublished manuscript.

297 Solomon, Z. and Benbenishty, R. (1986) 'The role of proximity, immediacy and expectancy in frontline treatment of combat stress reaction among Israelis in the Lebanon war', *American Journal of Psychiatry* 143: 613–617.

298 Somnier, F.E. and Genefke, I.K. (1986) 'Psychotherapy for victims of torture', *British Journal of Psychiatry* 146: 323–329.

299 Stallings, R.A. and Quarantelli, E.L. (1985) 'Emergent citizen groups and emergency management', *Public Administration Review* 45: 93–100.

300 Stewart, M. Contemporary notes.

301 Stewart, M. and Hodgkinson, P.E. (1989) 'Disaster and the media', *Disaster Management* 1: 15–17.

302 Taiminen, T.J. and Tuominen, T. (1996) 'Psychological responses to a marine disaster during the recoil phase: experiences from the *Estonia* shipwreck', *British Journal of Medical Psychology* 69: 147–154.

303 Talbot, A. (1990) 'The importance of parallel process in debriefing crisis counsellors', *Journal of Traumatic Stress* 3: 265–278.

304 Tarsh, M.J. and Royston, C. (1985) 'A follow-up study of accident neurosis', *British Journal of Psychiatry* 146: 18–25.

305 Taylor, A. (1983) 'Hidden victims and the human side of disasters', *UNDRO News,* March/April: 6–12.

306 Taylor, A. and Frazer, A. (1982) 'The stress of post-disaster body handling and victim identification work', *Journal of Human Stress* 8: 4–12.

307 Taylor, S.E., Wood, J. and Lichtman, R. (1983) 'It could be worse: selective evaluation as a response to victimisation', *Journal of Social Issues* 39: 719–740.

308 Taylor, V. (1977) 'Good news about disaster', *Psychology Today,* October: 93–126.

309 Terr, L.C. (1981) 'Psychic trauma in children: observations following the Chowchilla school-bus kidnapping', *American Journal of Psychiatry* 138: 14–19.

310 Terr, L.C. (1983) 'Chowchilla revisited: the effects of psychic trauma four years after a school-bus kidnapping', *American Journal of Psychiatry* 140: 1543–1550.

311 Thoits, P.A. (1982) 'Conceptual, methodological, and theoretical problems in studying social support as a buffer against life stress', *Journal of Health and Social Behaviour* 23: 145–159.

312 Thompson, J. (1985) *Psychological aspects of nuclear war*, Leicester: British Psychological Society.

313 Thompson, J. (1993) 'Psychological impact of body recovery duties', *Journal of the Royal Society of Medicine* 86: 628–629.

314 Thompson, J. and Suzuki, I. (1991) 'Stress in ambulance workers', *Disaster Management* 3: 193–197.

315 Thompson, J.A., Charlton, P.F.C., Kerry, R., Lee, D. and Turner, S.W. (1995) 'An open trial of exposure therapy based on deconditioning for post-traumatic stress disorder', *British Journal of Clinical Psychology* 34: 407–416.

316 Thompson, J., Chung, M.C., Jackson, G. and Rosser, R. (1995) 'A comparative trial of psychotherapy in the treatment of post-trauma stress reactions', *Clinical Psychology and Psychotherapy* 2: 168–176.

317 Thrasher, S.M., Lovell, K., Noshirvani, H. and Livanou, H. (1996) 'Cognitive restructuring in the treatment of post-traumatic stress disorder – two single cases', *Clinical Psychology and Psychotherapy* 3: 137–148.

318 Tierney, K.J. (1989) 'The social and community contexts of disaster', in R. Gist and L. Lubin (eds) *Psychosocial Aspects of Disaster*, New York: Wiley.

319 Titchener, J.L. (1986) 'Post-traumatic decline: a consequence of unresolved destructive drives', in C. R. Figley (ed.) *Trauma and its Wake*, Vol. 2, New York: Brunner Mazel.

320 Toubiana, Y., Milgram, N. and Noy, S. (1985) 'A therapeutic community in a forward army field hospital: treatment, education and expectancy', in N. A. Milgram (ed.) *Stress and Coping in Time of War*, New York: Brunner Mazel.

321 Toubiana, Y.H., Milgram, N.A. and Strich, Y. (1988) 'Crisis intervention in a school community disaster: principles and practices', *Journal of Community Psychology* 16: 228–240.

322 Trower, P., Casey, A. and Dryden, W. (1988) *Cognitive behavioural counselling in action*, London: Sage.

323 Tumelty, D. and Seed, M. (1990) *Social work in the wake of disaster*, London: Jessica Kingsley.

324 Turner, S.M. (1979) 'Systematic desensitisation of fears and anxiety in rape victims', Paper presented at a meeting of the Association for the Advancement of Behaviour Therapy, San Francisco, California.

325 Turner, S.W., Thompson, J.A. and Rosser, R.M. (1989) 'The King's Cross fire: planning a "phase two" psychosocial response', *Disaster Management* 2: 31–37.

326 Turner, S.W., Thompson, J. and Rosser, R.M. (1995) 'The King's Cross fire: psychological reactions', *Journal of Traumatic Stress* 8: 419–428.

327 Ursano, R.J., Ingraham, L.H., Wright, M., Bartone, P. and Cervantes, A. (1989) 'Coping with death and dead bodies', Paper presented at the 4th International Conference on Psychological Stress and Adjustment in Time of War and Peace, Tel-Aviv.

328 van der Kolk, B.A. (1994) 'The body keeps the score: memory and the evolving psychology of post-traumatic stress', *Harvard Review of Psychiatry* 1: 253–265.

329 van Der Kolk, B., Blitz, R., Burr, W., Shery, S. and Hartmann, E. (1984) 'Nightmares and trauma: a comparison of nightmares after combat with lifelong nightmares in veterans', *American Journal of Psychiatry* 141: 187–190.

330 van der Kolk, B.A., Roth, S., Pelcovitz, D. and Mandel, F.A. (1993) 'Complex post-traumatic stress disorder: results from the DSM-IV field trial of PTSD', Unpublished manuscript: Harvard Medical School.

331 van der Kolk, B.A., Dreyfuss, D., Michaels, M., Shera, S., Berkowitz, R., Fisler, R. and Saxe, G. (1994) 'Fluoxetine in post-traumatic stress disorder', *Journal of Clinical Psychiatry* 12: 517–522.

332 van Duin, M. and Pijnenburg, B. (1990) 'The Zeebrugge ferry disaster: elements of a communication and information processing scenario', Unpublished paper.

333 Vaughn, K. and Tarrier, N. (1992) 'The use of image habituation training with post-traumatic stress disorders', *British Journal of Psychiatry* 161: 658–664.

334 Vaughn, K., Armstrong, M.F., Gold, R., O'Connor, N., Jenneke, W. and Tarrier, N. (1994) 'A trial of eye movement desensitisation compared to image habituation training and applied muscle relaxation in post-traumatic stress disorder', *Journal of Behaviour Therapy and Experimental Psychiatry* 25: 283–291.

335 Veronen, L.J. and Kilpatrick, D.G. (1983) 'Stress management for rape victims', in D. Meichenbaum and M.E. Jaremko (eds) *Stress Reduction and Prevention*, New York: Plenum Press.

336 Volkan, V. (1972) 'The linking objects of pathological mourners', *Archives of General Psychiatry* 27: 215–221.

337 Weiseath, L. (1983) 'The study of a factory fire', Doctoral dissertation, University of Oslo.

338 Weisman, A.D. (1973) 'Coping with untimely death', *Psychiatry* 36: 366–378.

339 Weller, E.B., Weller, R.A., Fristad, M.A., Cain, S.E. and Bowes, J.M. (1988) 'Should children attend their parent's funeral?', *Journal of the American Academy of Child and Adolescent Psychiatry* 27: 559–562.

340 Wilkinson, C.B. (1983) 'Aftermath of a disaster: the collapse of the Hyatt Regency hotel skywalks', *American Journal of Psychiatry* 140: 1134–1139.

341 Williams, C.L., Solomon, S.D. and Bartone, P. (1988) 'Primary prevention in aircraft disasters', *American Psychologist,* September: 730–739.

342 Williams, R. (1989) 'Towards a cognitive-behavioural model for PTSD', Paper presented at EEC symposium on PTSD, London.

343 Williams, R. (1995) 'Attitudes to emotion, crisis support, and distress 30 months after the capsize of a passenger ferry disaster', *Crisis Intervention* 1: 209–214.

344 Wilson, J. (1988) *Trauma, transformation and healing*, New York: Brunner Mazel.

345 Wilson, J.P. and Lindy, J.D. (1994) 'Empathic strain and countertransference', in J.P. Wilson and J.D. Lindy (eds) *Countertransference in the Treatment of PTSD*, New York: Guilford Press.

346 Wilson, K. and Lebedun, M. (1983) 'Project resurgence', Unpublished paper, National Institute of Mental Health.

347 Wolf, M.E., Alavi, A. and Mosnaim, A.D. (1988) 'Post-traumatic stress disorder in Vietnam veterans: clinical and EEG findings. Possible therapeutic effects of carbemazepine', *Biological Psychiatry* 23: 642–644.

348 Wong, M.R. and Cook, D. (1992) 'Shame and its contribution to PTSD', *Journal of Traumatic Stress* 5: 557–562.

349 Worden, J.W. (1983) *Grief counselling and grief therapy*, London: Tavistock.

350 World Health Organisation (1992) *ICD 10 – International statistical classification of diseases and related health problems*, 10th revision, Geneva: WHO.

351 Wortman, C.B. and Silver, R.C. (1989) 'The myths of coping with loss', *Journal of Consulting and Clinical Psychology* 57: 349–357.

352 Wright, B. (1991) *Sudden Death*, Edinburgh: Churchill Livingstone.

353 Yehuda, R. and McFarlane, A.C. (1995) 'The conflict between current knowledge about PTSD and its original conceptual basis', *American Journal of Psychiatry* 152: 1705–1713.

354 Yule, W. and Gold, A. (1993) *Wise before the event*, London: Calouste Gulbenkian Foundation.

355 Yule, W. and Williams, R.M. (1990) 'Post-traumatic stress reactions in children', *Journal of Traumatic Stress* 3: 279–295.

INDEX

249